Studying Shakespeare's Contemporaries

D1663975

Studying Shakespeare's Contemporaries

Lars Engle and Eric Rasmussen

WILEY Blackwell

This edition first published 2014
© 2014 Lars Engle and Eric Rasmussen

Registered Office
John Wiley & Sons Ltd, The Atrium, Southern Gate, Chichester, West Sussex,
PO19 8SQ, UK

Editorial Offices
350 Main Street, Malden, MA 02148-5020, USA
9600 Garsington Road, Oxford, OX4 2DQ, UK
The Atrium, Southern Gate, Chichester, West Sussex, PO19 8SQ, UK

For details of our global editorial offices, for customer services, and for information
about how to apply for permission to reuse the copyright material in this book please
see our website at www.wiley.com/wiley-blackwell.

The right of Lars Engle and Eric Rasmussen to be identified as the authors of this work
has been asserted in accordance with the UK Copyright, Designs and Patents Act 1988.

All rights reserved. No part of this publication may be reproduced, stored in a retrieval
system, or transmitted, in any form or by any means, electronic, mechanical,
photocopying, recording or otherwise, except as permitted by the UK Copyright,
Designs and Patents Act 1988, without the prior permission of the publisher.

Wiley also publishes its books in a variety of electronic formats. Some content that
appears in print may not be available in electronic books.

Designations used by companies to distinguish their products are often claimed as
trademarks. All brand names and product names used in this book are trade names,
service marks, trademarks or registered trademarks of their respective owners. The
publisher is not associated with any product or vendor mentioned in this book.

Limit of Liability/Disclaimer of Warranty: While the publisher and authors have used
their best efforts in preparing this book, they make no representations or warranties
with respect to the accuracy or completeness of the contents of this book and specifically
disclaim any implied warranties of merchantability or fitness for a particular purpose. It
is sold on the understanding that the publisher is not engaged in rendering professional
services and neither the publisher nor the author shall be liable for damages arising
herefrom. If professional advice or other expert assistance is required, the services of a
competent professional should be sought.

Library of Congress Cataloging-in-Publication Data applied for
Hardback ISBN: 978-1-4051-3243-5
Paperback ISBN: 978-1-4051-3244-2

A catalogue record for this book is available from the British Library.

Cover image: Caravaggio, *The Cardsharps*, c.1594. © 2012 Kimbell Art Museum,
Fort Worth, Texas / Art Resource, NY/Scala, Florence
Cover design by www.simonlevyassociates.co.uk

Set in 10/12pt Sabon by Laserwords Private Limited, Chennai, India
Printed in Malaysia by Ho Printing (M) Sdn Bhd

1 2014

For Holly, Carl, and Sage
LDE
For Vicky, Tristan, and Arden
ECR

Contents

Acknowledgments

Parts of this book, in revised forms, have appeared as Lars Engle, "Watching Shakespeare Learn from Marlowe" in Peter Kanelos and Matt Kuzusko, eds., *Thunder at a Playhouse* (Susquehanna 2010), and as Lars Engle, "The Self," in Emily Bartels and Emma Smith, eds., *Marlowe in Context* (Cambridge 2013). Several pages from the book appeared in Lars Engle, "Oedipal Marlowe, Mimetic Middleton," *Modern Philology* 105:3. I am grateful for permission to reprint here. Parts have also been given as lectures or papers at MLA, SAA, OVSC, Texas A&M, and the University of Queensland, and have benefited from audience questions and comments. The entire text was carefully annotated by Mark Rideout, of the University of Tulsa, and James Mardock, of the University of Nevada, to its great benefit. Holly Laird has also read parts of the book and has encouraged its author. My work on the project was supported by a grant from the University of Tulsa's Research Office, for which my thanks.

This book is in many ways a companion to *English Renaissance Drama: A Norton Anthology*. I worked on that project with David Bevington and Katharine Eisaman Maus as well as my present coauthor, and I incurred many debts of gratitude and understanding to all three of them.

This book was first commissioned from Lars Engle by Emma Bennett, then of Blackwell, and Emma and Ben Thatcher, now at Wiley-Blackwell, have shown consistent interest, patience, and persistence in bringing it in to being. My thanks to them both and to all at Wiley Blackwell. I also wish to thank Eric Rasmussen for his characteristic generosity and energy in stepping in to coauthor this book and helping mightily to complete it. Collaboration can in fact be an extremely pleasant activity with the right coauthor, and for me, Eric has been that.

Lars Engle

For my part, I am enormously grateful to Mark Farnsworth, Jennifer Forsyth, and Dee Anna Phares for helping to draft several sections of the book, and to Sarah Stewart for compiling the stage history appendix. Allston James read an early draft of the manuscript and provided invaluable notes from his perspective as a theater practitioner. James Mardock read multiple versions of the manuscript, virtually every page of which has been improved by his trenchant readings. Ashley Marshall offered both insight and encouragement. To these friends and colleagues, I say thanks, and thanks, and thanks again.

Collaborating with Lars Engle has long been one of the great joys of my professional life. Work on this project, which was begun while sitting courtside at a Lakers versus Thunder basketball game, has been particularly joyous.

Eric Rasmussen

Preface: How to Use This Book

Shakespeare's preeminent importance has both sustained and deformed the study of the drama of the late sixteenth and early seventeenth centuries in England. As the title of this book suggests, the other playwrights who wrote at the same time and for the same players and public as Shakespeare are always in danger of being relegated to the background: treated as part of Shakespeare's context. There are of course worse things than being part of Shakespeare's background. Serious students of Shakespeare need to know the work of Kyd, Marlowe, Jonson, Webster, Middleton, and their many contemporaries and collaborators. In the process, they usually come to care deeply about these authors. In another way, however, Shakespeare is part of the background for study of other English Renaissance dramatists, as one almost invariably comes to their plays after having studied some of his. The expectations that Shakespeare's most-studied plays arouse – expectations about depth and complexity of characterization, about density of brilliant metaphor in language, about intellectual coherence and social insight – are sometimes fully gratified by the works of other dramatists (though not often all at once). Masterpieces like *The Duchess of Malfi*, *The Changeling*, *The Alchemist*, or *Doctor Faustus* resemble Shakespeare in a number of kinds of excellence. But English Renaissance drama is also full of plays that are wonderful in ways that are quite un-Shakespearean: for example, in the hilarious literary spoofing in *The Knight of the Burning Pestle*, or the savagely funny satire of *The Revenger's Tragedy*, or the unsentimental generosity about women's sexual lives in the city comedies of Middleton. *Studying Shakespeare's Contemporaries* works on the assumption that the privative term "non-Shakespearean" need not be a deterrent to pleasure or profit. We might wish to substitute the less negative "para-Shakespearean" in the minds of our readers. The book aims to accompany students who have embarked on first readings of major plays, illustrating the ways the plays take up issues that we care about, and opening them up as sites for pleasure in reading or performance as well as for reflection on important aspects of life.

The book proceeds by brief individual treatments of major non-Shakespearean Renaissance plays organized according to a movement outward from psychological interiority to large social and political structures. From the perspective of beginning students, there is nothing more frustrating than an argument that uses as evidence a series of brief references to plays they have never read. *Studying Shakespeare's Contemporaries* avoids this by handling each play in a discrete, independently readable section, under the assumption that some of its users may well open the book to the sections on the particular play they are reading. At the same time, it offers a developing overview of major issues in the field of study. Some of these issues are indicated by section topics and subtopics in the table of contents. The book also, in discussions of some of the most widely taught plays (e.g., *Doctor Faustus, The Changeling, The Duchess of Malfi*), describes the conditions under which plays were commissioned, written (often collaboratively), licensed, staged, and published. The final section offers brief descriptions of the careers of Shakespeare's most important contemporaries, discussing their lives in the theater alongside Shakespeare's. Throughout, the goal has been to provide a brisk, appreciative, and accessible guide to what keeps these plays alive for readers. Plays are quoted from *English Renaissance Drama: A Norton Anthology* unless otherwise noted.

Part 1

Inwardness

Twenty-first century readers are used to the idea that the cultivation and exploration of an inner self is both a predominant literary concern and one of the rewards of literary study. Their central experience of serious literature is usually the novel, which features narrative description of the contents of the minds of characters, or internal monologs in which those minds are revealed, or both. Their predominant experience of drama comes from television and film, which feature revelatory close-ups of expressive faces and occasional voice-overs of thought. As an assumption to bring to Early Modern drama, the idea that inner selves are being explored is both helpful and misleading. It is helpful in that theatre consists of unusually self-revealing action, and Renaissance theatre is no exception to this. But it is somewhat misleading in that Early Modern ideas about what selves consist of differ from twenty-first century ideas, often in significant ways. This part of *Studying Shakespeare's Contemporaries* will discuss personal inwardness as it is presented in the plays of Shakespeare's contemporaries, beginning with techniques for the dramatic representation of inner states and moving on to discuss key features of the inner self. As the preface suggested, Shakespeare excels in evoking human inwardness, so much so that he is sometimes credited with inventing it (see Fineman, Bloom) and with exercising a critical influence on later mapmakers of modern inwardness like Freud. In the following sections, we will discuss a play that influenced Shakespeare in his representation of inwardness, Christopher Marlowe's *The Jew of Malta*, and then a play that is influenced in turn by Shakespeare's representation of inward disturbance in *Macbeth* and *Othello*, Thomas Middleton and William Rowley's *The Changeling*.

Studying Shakespeare's Contemporaries, First Edition. Lars Engle and Eric Rasmussen.
© 2014 Lars Engle and Eric Rasmussen. Published 2014 by John Wiley & Sons, Ltd.

1.1   The Inward Self

What makes you think you have an inner life? What makes you believe that other people do? Surely, one major constituent of these linked beliefs is your own capacity to talk to yourself, to maintain a discursive existence when not directly prompted by others, and your experience (which may well be more literary than it is personal) of overhearing other people talking to themselves. Of course, most such discourse is private and never rises to the level of audible speech. Part of its interest, indeed, derives from its variance in tone and intention from public speech. Honesty and candor may keep this variance from reaching the level of complete contradiction; the vice of hypocrisy consists in allowing one's public discourse to overtly contradict one's private internal discourse, and may include taking private pleasure in that contradiction. But even in honest, candid people there is substantial variance between internal and external discourse, and relations with particular others will be as it were measured for intimacy by how great that variance is.

This raises a question. Is there internal discourse that is not, in some way, a response, perhaps even a reply, to an external prompt or gesture? Is internal life private in the sense that it is entirely separate from a social matrix, from the outer world of others speaking and writing and exerting authority that conditions all of the life most adults can remember (given that few can remember anything from before they were speakers and understanders)? Twentieth-century theorists have, on the whole, answered "no" to this question. To cite two famous examples among many that could be offered, Ludwig Wittgenstein denies that there could be such a thing as a private language, and Mikhail Bakhtin claims that every utterance is a reply, part of an always already ongoing dialogic exchange (Wittgenstein, 1974: 94–102, Schalkwyk, 2004: 120, Bakhtin, 1981: 276, Bakhtin, 1986: 121, Clark and Holquist, 1984: 348). Do such claims compromise the idea of inwardness? They certainly cast in question absolute claims about individual autonomy, and they point to the complexity surrounding the ideas of free choice and free will, but they do not in fact do much to undermine the less complex idea that human beings have inner lives that are in large part concealed from those around them, and that those inner lives are objects of the curiosity, and sometimes of the urgent or violent inquiries, of others. These observations, in their generality, do not seem located in any particular historical moment. They seem likely to be true of any culture that shares the moral vocabulary in which lying and hypocrisy are (at least officially) bad and honesty and candor, good. Although strong claims have been made in discussions of Renaissance culture about the emptiness or nullity of the inward self in the Renaissance (see e.g., Belsey, 1985: 48), these claims often seem based on twentieth-century thinking about the social and linguistic imbeddedness of inward mental life rather than directly on readings of Renaissance texts. As Katharine Eisaman Maus remarks of critics who deny interior life to Renaissance subjects, "such critics characteristically work from philosophical positions that reject as illusory the possibility of a subjectivity prior to or exempt from social determination. That is, they are making a claim not only about English Renaissance subjectivity, but about subjectivity *tout court*" (Maus, 1995: 26). She suggests that hostility to the idea of Renaissance inwardness may derive from "a false sense of what is necessitated by the premises of cultural-materialist and new-historicist criticism" (Maus, 1995: 26, see also 2–3 for a set of quotations of cultural materialist and new-historicist critics on interiority).

New historicism and cultural materialism are the names of related schools of historically oriented literary criticism that arose in the 1980s – the first on the whole in the United States and the second on the whole in Britain – and have deeply influenced the way literature is read in universities since. Both emphasize the ways works of literature are properly to be seen as documents in larger social processes involving conflict and domination. Not only literary works, but human lives, are elements in such processes, obviously, and both movements question the independence of the self at the same time that they dispute the autonomy of the literary work seen as a self-sufficient aesthetic whole. Thus these movements work against a cherished idea about literary reading that used to be central to the declared purposes of literary education – the idea of a modern self becoming "deeper" and "richer" by gaining a satisfactory experience of the rich self-sufficient wholeness of a literary masterpiece. Clearly, the issue of Renaissance inwardness has a number of contentious political dimensions, dimensions that may be an aspect of the difficulty of understanding works from a different historical period, or may be an aspect of the philosophical problem of other minds. These are hard and important issues, and it may be better to approach them more simply by asking yet another question. Do questions about inner selves arise differently in the Renaissance, or at any rate in Renaissance drama, from the way they do now? This is the question this part will attempt to answer, first by looking at the direct ways Renaissance dramatists represent human inwardness, then by moving on to discuss religious dimensions of English Renaissance inwardness, the treatment of psychological obsession in Renaissance drama, and, finally, inner strength and personal honor, inward characteristics that empower or condition the ways characters can act, or can feel obliged to act, on others. As is suggested by its part titles, this book as a whole moves outward from the psyche to the social and political order, so that by its later parts it will be promoting ways of looking at drama which differ from the intentionally individualistic focus of this part.

1.2   The Inward Self in Soliloquy: *The Jew of Malta*

Drama has two powerful techniques for making inward discourse directly available: the soliloquy, where a character speaks his or her thoughts alone on the stage, and the aside, where a character turns away from the action and speaks a thought that is unheard by some or all of the other onstage characters. By discussing soliloquy first in Marlowe's *The Jew of Malta*, this section approaches an inwardness technique in a play that is emphatically *not* prized for its successful evocation of stable, deep selfhood. Moreover, as Jews in sixteenth-century Europe and the Near East were people with limited political rights, tolerated in some Christian and Islamic states and officially expelled from others (from England in 1290, from Spain in 1492), they had fewer communal resources for self-stabilization than citizens or subjects whose religious and ethnic affiliations were those of the dominant culture. The Jews who appear on the Renaissance English stage are usually isolated. As we shall see in later parts, however, English Renaissance drama was profoundly interested in outsiders, and many sixteenth- and seventeenth-century Londoners were aliens, criminals, Catholics, or Puritans, and some were Jews, black Africans, transvestites, sodomites, or atheists. Any person in these categories could easily identify him or herself as a persecuted member of a disempowered group, and all except black Africans and Puritans might well be involved in forms of self-concealment that distorted firm, stable identity. Barabas, Marlowe's Maltese Jew, is at any rate no exemplar of consistency; as Emily Bartels points out, he "appears in so many postures that his character seems to consist more of what he is not than of what he is" (Bartels, 1993: 97). Close readings of a series of soliloquies might seem a more natural way to approach a play like *Hamlet*, preoccupied with the inadequacy of outer life to inward experience, than Marlowe's "farce of the … serious even savage comic humour" (Eliot, 1932: 16), which moves from rapid action at the start to frenzied action at the end. Nonetheless, as we shall see, Barabas's inward life is strongly represented.

Marlowe's *The Jew of Malta* begins with a prologue by "Machiavel" followed by a soliloquy by Barabas. One of the aspects of Machiavelli's 1513 book *The Prince* that made it notorious in sixteenth-century Europe was its recommendation that leaders be able to dissimulate their intentions, to lie, when it is expedient to do so. That is, Machiavelli disputes the idea that lying is in all circumstances bad and that honesty is invariably good. This strategic rationing of one's inward thought for purposes of control and safety was one of many ways in which Marlowe found Machiavelli provocative. As Maus remarks, "Marlowe … keeps returning to the implications of a personal inwardness withheld or withholdable from others" (Maus, 1995: 210). The Machiavel of Marlowe's prologue expects those who read him to dissimulate their indebtedness to his advice, "such as love me guard me from their tongues, / ... /Admired I am of those that hate me most" (Prologue 6–9). His comments prepare audiences for two important aspects of *The Jew of Malta*: deceptive self-presentation (set off by private self-revelation), and ambivalence toward a figure who presents a strong but amoral version of the reality of human economic and political life. The first is established early on by soliloquy and aside.

Barabas's first soliloquy, "*in his countinghouse, with heaps of gold before him*," as the stage direction has it, seems at the outset impersonal, the talking to himself of a merchant reckoning his accounts: "So that of thus much that return was made; / And of the third part of the Persian ships, / There was the venture summed and satisfied" (1.1.1–3). But the soliloquy soon becomes more expressive, although it remains focused on the wealth in front of him. He reveals impatience at having to account for small sums: "Fie, what a trouble 'tis to count this trash!", contrasting himself with "The needy groom that never fingered groat" who would wonder at "thus much coin" (1.1.7–14). As he proceeds to an approving account of the hoards of "the wealthy Moor" (1.1.21), he seems enthralled by the way objects of enormous economic value concentrate beauty and power in tangible form:

> Bags of fiery opals, sapphires, amethysts,
> Jacinths, hard topaz, grass-green emeralds,
> Beauteous rubies, sparkling diamonds,
> And seld-seen costly stones of so great price
> As one of them, indifferently rated
> And of a caret of this quantity,
> May serve, in peril of calamity,
> To ransom great kings from captivity.
> (1.1.25–32)

As an exposure of inwardness, this does not seem very inward. It represents Barabas's participation in the thrill of possessing what others desire, and an awareness that such objects also represent the resources others may desperately need. The neediness of those who do not have his resources – the groatless groom, the captive king – is a major component of the resources themselves, from Barabas's viewpoint. Although Barabas is talking in part about others, he is also placing himself among them, at the same time registering his own difference as a disenfranchised Jew who has no home ground from which wealth can be directly extracted. The "wealthy Moor" can, in Barabas's fantasy at least, simply "pick his riches up" from the "Eastern rocks" where precious stones abound, but Barabas's own more laborious work as a merchant achieves the same kind of concentrated potential by separation of wealth from the ordinary people who are enmeshed in a market-world they cannot control:

> This is the ware wherein consists my wealth;
> And thus, methinks, should men of judgment frame
> Their means of traffic from the vulgar trade,
> And, as their wealth increaseth, so enclose
> Infinite riches in a little room.
>
> (1.1.33–37)

"Judgment," for Barabas, consists of concentrating the world-spanning reach of human transactions in a private space: the "little room" of his countinghouse, or the privacy of his intentions, unavailable to the "vulgar." The idea that this is, potentially, a king's ransom suggests that it represents security and even power as well as accomplishment. Machiavel promises us "the tragedy of a Jew / Who smiles to see how full his bags are crammed" (Prologue 30–31), and Barabas's soliloquy demonstrates how much more interesting and complex the situation of such a Jew seems from inside his own consciousness than when looked on unsympathetically from the outside. At the same time, Machiavel's comment warns us that Barabas will not smile for long.

What, then, does this soliloquy accomplish in terms of the representation or evocation of inwardness? It establishes a kind of baseline for Barabas's later frenzy, in that his complacent account of his own success is shot through with expressions of impatience at the life he has led to achieve "thus much coin," "wearying his fingers' ends with telling it" (1.1.16). He clearly prefers to think of his achievement in terms of the solidity and brilliance of hidden gems, "seld-seen costly stones" (1.1.28), rather than as a pile of coins that have passed through many hands and may at any time return to promiscuous negotiation. Moreover, when the soliloquy resumes after an interruption in 1.1, it also sets the terms on which he finds his adversarial relation to the dominant Christians of Malta tolerable:

> Who hateth me but for my happiness?
> Or who is honored now but for his wealth?
> Rather had, I, a Jew, be hated thus
> Than pitied in a Christian poverty;
> For I can see no fruits in all their faith
> But malice, falsehood, and excessive pride,
> Which methinks fits not their profession.
>
> (1.1.111–118)

Barabas sees his relation to the Christians as a struggle lightly masked by hypocritical professions of charity on the Christian side and the systematic forgoing of political authority on the side of the Jews:

> They say we are a scattered nation;
> I cannot tell, but we have scambled up
> More wealth by far than those that brag of faith.
>
> …
>
> I must confess we come not to be kings.
> That's not our fault. Alas, our number's few,
> And crowns come either by succession
> Or urged by force; and nothing violent,
> Oft have I heard tell, can be permanent.
>   (1.1.120–132)

We moderns think of the inner self as prone to ambivalence and contra-diction. So far – and in this Marlowe typifies Renaissance norms – Barabas's soliloquy has been marked by a high level of rhetorical consistency and for-mality; except in its frankness, his speech to himself does not seem that different from a speech he might deliver to an assembly. Nonetheless, as suggested already by our account of Barabas's impatience discussed earlier, the "alas" and the "not our fault" register Barabas's distress at the denial of political power to match the economic accumulation the greatest Jews have achieved. Clearly, it is *faute de mieux*, suppressing his own distress, that Barabas concludes "Give us a peaceful rule; make Christians kings, / That thirst so much for principality" (1.1.133–34). His reference to Abi-gail, his "one sole daughter, whom I hold as dear / As Agamemnon did his Iphigen; / And all I have is hers" (1.1.136–8), both ominously foreshadows a sacrifice and suggests that Barabas is in his imagination a man who would be king. The punctuated soliloquy of 1.1, then, establishes both Barabas's precarious complacency and his awareness that it is endangered by the col-lective vulnerability of the Jews. Indeed, the soliloquy locates in Barabas's psyche the social thought-experiment that is at the center of the play: what are the consequences when economic power is concentrated in the hands of the politically powerless?

The first consequence is that when they really need it, the politically powerful will grab the money of the powerless rich. In 1.2 Barabas is, in rapid, plausible succession, summoned to the senate house, told by the Christian governor, Ferneze, that the Turks have demanded payment of 10-years' neglected Maltese tribute, and asked to contribute half his wealth on penalty of forced conversion to Christianity and total dispossession if he refuses. When Barabas declines to be christened and says (in an echo of his opening soliloquy) "Half of my substance is a city's wealth. / Governor, it was not got so easily; / Nor will I part so slightly therewithal" (1.2.86–8), he is held to have "denied the articles" and thus to forfeit all possessions to the state. When his fellow Jews (who have quickly submitted to the expropriation of half their goods, and have so escaped Barabas's total loss) attempt to console him, Barabas rejects their consolations in terms that remind us of the foregone aspirations to power in his first soliloquy. Here his lost money becomes a general's defeated army and reminds us of the way he likened himself earlier to Agamemnon (see Shepard, 1998: 119):

> You that
> Were ne'er possessed of wealth are pleased with want.
> But give him liberty at least to mourn
> That in a field amidst his enemies
> Doth see his soldiers slain, himself disarmed,
> And knows no means of his recovery.
>
> (1.2.201–6)

When they leave him alone, he springs up and in a wonderful brief soliloquy reveals his sense that he is harder and more resistant to dissolution than ordinary men:

> See the simplicity of these base slaves,
> Who, for the villains have no wit themselves,
> Think me to be a senseless lump of clay
> That will with every water wash to dirt!
>
> (1.2.216–19)

This resistance to the suddenly fluid nature of his experience carries on even after Barabas's daughter Abigail brings the distressing news that Barabas's emergency reserve of gold and jewels ("stones infinite" [1.2.247]) is inaccessible. Barabas's house has been turned into a convent, and Barabas as a male Jew is of course forbidden to enter it. Barabas briefly considers despair and suicide, representing them as an even more radical form of dissolution:

> What, will you thus oppose me, luckless stars,
> To make me desperate in my poverty,
> And, knowing me impatient in distress,
> Think me so mad as I will hang myself,
> That I may vanish o'er the earth in air
> And leave no memory that e'er I was?
>
> (1.2.260–265)

Rather than thus allow himself to dissipate, Barabas embraces uncertainty:

> No! I will live, nor loathe I this my life.
> And since you leave me in the ocean thus
> To sink or swim, and put me to my shifts,
> I'll rouse my senses and awake myself.
>
> (1.2.266–9)

Neither a stone to sink nor a clod to wash to dirt, Barabas will be a swimmer and a shape-shifter. Much of the inconsistency and manic variety of the rest of the play derives from this resolution, as once Barabas leaves the precarious truce with Christian power he articulates in his opening soliloquy, he never achieves a position of stability, and indeed he dies at the end trying to reestablish something approximating the accommodation he started with.

In his first "shift," he responds to his exile from his own house by asking his daughter Abigail to pretend conversion to Christianity so that she can enter the nunnery and recover Barabas's rainy-day fund. After some natural hesitation, Abigail, persuaded, turns to the Abbess who is proceeding conveniently across the stage to take up her new residence and begs admission as a novice. While apparently cursing Abigail for her apostasy, Barabas arranges, in a series of hilarious asides, to come early in the morning to the new convent to receive the restolen goods. But when he arrives "with a light" before his house, his confidence in the arrangement appears to have given way to vengeful self-pity. The soliloquy with which Barabas opens the second act differs markedly in tone from his first.

> Thus, like the sad presaging raven that tolls
> The sick man's passport in her hollow beak,
> And in the shadow of the silent night
> Doth shake contagion from her sable wings,
> Vexed and tormented runs poor Barabas
> With fatal curses towards these Christians.
> (2.1.1–6)

As in his earlier soliloquy, this one at first seems to show Barabas's mental life as quite instrumental, focusing on powerful rhetorical presentation of his activities and intentions. At the same time, it mixes a myth of doom for his enemies with a somewhat comic sense of his own movements: no fatal bird of the air but instead a distracted earthbound creature trying with difficulty to hurry in the dark. Night has brought torment and self-doubt, as is seen in the way the raven's flight immediately becomes the flight away from him of everything he has counted and counted on:

> The incertain pleasures of swift-footed time
> Have ta'en their flight and left me in despair;
> And of my former riches rests no more
> But bare remembrance, like a soldier's scar,
> That has no further comfort for his maim.
> (2.1.6–11)

No longer an angry general on the field of his defeat, Barabas is now a poor soldier with only his scars to show for his losses. Lines 9–11 gain some of their poetic power – which derives partly from the sequential off-rhymes "air," "or," "er," "ore," "are," "ar," "ur," and "er" and the intense alliteration of the initial consonants "m," "b," and "r", and partly also from the way the pause after "remembrance" breaks the iambic pattern so dominant in Marlowe's pentameter line – from a subdued pun on "member" in "remembrance": the mutilated soldier can "remember" what he had, but he cannot regain the member he has lost.

The outdoor public Renaissance theatres – *The Jew of Malta* played mainly at the Rose, Philip Henslowe's venue, in the 1590s (see Gurr, 1996: 69–77) – tended to feature a curtained recess at back center stage that probably was the site of Barabas's countinghouse in 1.1, and also had an upper playing space above that recess with a windowlike opening. In this upper stage, while Barabas paces back and forth on the bare main stage carrying his lantern, Abigail appears, unheard by her father and searching for his treasure. Their soliloquies cross each other in one of the more brilliant Marlovian scenes, and one that, as suggested earlier, Shakespeare took note of. Square brackets around stage directions (which are always in italics) indicate that the directions are supplied by a modern editor for the reader's convenience rather than appearing in the early printed text or texts on which the modern edition is based.

> ABIGAIL [*to herself*]   Now have I happily espied a time
> To search the plank my father did appoint.
> [*Finding riches*] And here, behold, unseen, where I have found
> The gold, the pearls, and jewels which he hid!
> BARABAS [*to himself*]   Now I remember those old women's words
> Who in my wealth would tell me winter's tales
> And speak of spirits and ghosts that glide by night
> About the place where treasure hath been hid
> And now methinks that I am one of those.
> For, whilst I live, here lives my soul's sole hope
> And when I die, here shall my spirit walk.
>
> (2.1.20–30)

Barabas's words are, as we say, overdetermined – they have more than one appropriate and indeed necessary meaning. His "soul's sole hope" is his treasure, and the lost house in which he originally amassed it, and the daughter who might be expected to carry his inheritance into the future. Barabas's memory now associates his treasure with the spiritual traces of others who lost it before he gained it (or hid it before he found it). In his extremity, he also begins populating his inner self with voices from the past, old women who told him stories that undermine the confident account of the meaning and origins of wealth he gave in his first soliloquy. After all, the "spirits and ghosts" haunting hoarded treasure stand for the restless need for vengeance of those from whom it has been taken, and more generally touch on the social resentment of poor Christians for rich Jews that has turned on and victimized Barabas as well as on Barabas's own anger at dispossession. And as Barabas thus voices this line of inner thought, he is unheard by one of the objects of that thought who is herself recovering another object of it – the double soliloquy thus has an uncanny connection to the winter's tale of disembodied connection to lost possessions that Barabas remembers. Abigail too feels a mixed sense of elation and loss:

> Now that my father's fortune were so good
> As but to be about this happy place!
> 'Tis not so happy; yet when we parted last,
> He said he would attend me in the morn.
> Then, gentle sleep, where'er his body rests,
> Give charge to Morpheus that he may dream
> A golden dream, and of the sudden wake,
> Come, and receive the treasure I have found.
>
> (2.1.31–38)

Barabas, the unhearing object of Abigail's spoken thought, has meanwhile given up: "As good go on as sit so sadly thus" (2.1.41). Then he suddenly spies his daughter above him: "But stay! What star shines yonder in the east? / The lodestar of my life, if Abigail!"(2.1.42–3). If the title of *The Winter's Tale* is not a sufficient indication that this scene stuck in Shakespeare's memory – *The Jew of Malta* was first performed in 1589 or 1590, just before or simultaneously with Shakespeare's first plays (Hunter, 1997: 554), and Marlowe was the dominant dramatist in London from *Tamburlaine* in 1587 until his death by stabbing in 1593, so his then-less-prominent contemporary Shakespeare surely saw and perhaps read or even acted in his work – the way this moment of recognition of Abigail on the upper stage is recast at a key moment in Shakespeare's *Romeo and Juliet* 4 to 6 years later surely clinches it. Romeo dismisses Benvolio with a line that reworks Barabas's comments on scars and maims and then paraphrases Barabas's line as he looks up and sees a candle in the upper playing space: "He jests at scars, that never felt a wound. / [*A light appears above, as at Juliet's window.*] But soft, what light through yonder window breaks? / It is the east, and Juliet is the sun" (2.2.1–3). I will return to the way the rest of this scene affected Shakespeare in the following. What follows, although no longer in the mode of simultaneous soliloquy, remains remarkable for intensity:

> BARABAS [*He calls*] Who's there?
> ABIGAIL Who's that?
> BARABAS Peace, Abigail. 'Tis I.
> ABIGAIL Then, father, here receive thy happiness.
> BARABAS Hast thou 't?
> ABIGAIL Here. (*Throws down bags.*) Hast thou 't?
>   There's more, and more, and more.

> BARABAS   O my girl
> My gold, my fortune, my felicity
> Strength to my soul, death to mine enemy!
> Welcome, the first beginner of my bliss!
> Oh, Abigail, Abigail, that I had thee here too!
> Then my desires were fully satisfied.
> But I will practice thy enlargement thence.
> Oh, girl, oh, gold, oh, beauty, oh, my bliss!
>
> *(Hugs his bags)*
>
> (2.1.44–53)

Again, readers of Shakespeare's *The Merchant of Venice*, Shakespeare's play about Jews and Christians from around 1596, will notice how closely several key moments in that play are modeled on this scene from Marlowe: Jessica throwing her father Shylock's bags of ducats out of his window to her lover Lorenzo in 2.6, and, more importantly, Solanio's description of Shylock's confused grief and rage after Jessica and Lorenzo have eloped: "My daughter! O, my ducats! O, my daughter! / Fled with a Christian! O, my Christian ducats! / Justice! The law! My ducats, and my daughter!" (2.8.15–18).

The influence of Marlowe on Shakespeare, despite the connection between Barabas's memory and the title of *The Winter's Tale* (1610–11), one of Shakespeare's last plays, is usually held to extend up to midcareer, to *Hamlet* (1599–1601) and basically no further. There are good reasons for this; blustering martial characters whose verse reminds us of Marlowe's heroes, especially of *Tamburlaine*, basically disappear from Shakespeare at the end of the 1590s, and the seventeenth-century Shakespeare seems to have moved beyond imitating Marlowe's style. Nonetheless, the combination of brilliant stage and psychological effects in this scene – most notably the two family members hearing things in the dark, operating on different stage levels as they try to reach each other, the way their interaction, here so collaborative, will shortly after be broken so that they will be mutually destructive, and the way the dark itself is rendered emblematic of oncoming death and destruction by Barabas's initial speech – serves as a model for one of Shakespeare's more remarkable scenes in *Macbeth* (1606). In Act 2 scene 2, Lady Macbeth is waiting by torchlight for Macbeth to return from the upstairs chamber where he has gone to murder Duncan.

> LADY MACBETH   Hark! Peace!
> It was the owl that shrieked, the fatal bellman
> Which gives the stern'st good-night. He is about it.
> ...
> MACBETH [*within*]   Who's there? What, ho!
> LADY MACBETH   Alack, I am afraid they have awaked
> And 'tis not done. Th' attempt and not the deed

> Confounds us. Hark! I laid their daggers ready
> He could not miss 'em. Had he not resembled
> My father as he slept, I had done't.
> *Enter Macbeth, [bearing bloody daggers]*
> My husband!
> MACBETH I have done the deed. Didst thou not hear a noise?
> LADY MACBETH I heard the owl scream and the crickets cry.
> Did not you speak?
> MACBETH When?
> LADY MACBETH Now.
> MACBETH As I descended?
> LADY MACBETH Ay.
> MACBETH Hark! Who lies i' the second chamber?
> LADY MACBETH Donalbain.
>
> (2.2.2–20)

There is clearly a further development of the uncanny in the scene from *Macbeth*, but it reworks elements of this scene in *The Jew of Malta* that we know from three other Shakespearean plays imprinted itself on Shakespeare's mind. The Marlovian scene shares the sense of family feeling struggling against aggressive violence that we get in Lady Macbeth's comment about Duncan's resemblance to her father: "Had he not resembled / My father as he slept, I had done 't"(2.2.12–13). It is, incidentally, interesting that all the Shakespearean scenes with apparent echoes of Marlowe from *Merchant*, *Romeo*, and *Macbeth* occur early in second acts, as does the source-scene in *The Jew of Malta*.

Barabas's reception of his bags, his recovery of his happiness, is both exultant and sinister – he identifies them as "Strength to my soul, death to mine enemy" (2.2.48), and Abigail sometimes seems central to his felicity, sometimes a secondary adjunct to his vengeance. Of course, from the very earliest literature, personal happiness has been seen in part as the unhappiness it brings to one's enemies. Odysseus, stormbeaten, naked, and salty, clad only with a branch he holds before his private parts, praises marriage to the picnicking princess Nausicaa in book six of *The Odyssey*, as

> The blessing of a harmonious life.
> For nothing is greater or finer than this,
> When a man and woman live together
> With one heart and mind, bringing joy
> To their friends and grief to their foes.
>
> (Homer 2000, 6:185–89)

But here Barabas's exclamatory rhapsody is chillingly consistent with the way Abigail was invoked at the end of his soliloquy in 1.1., where he expressed his willingness to remain under Christian control in Malta in terms of his relatively slender connections to the state:

> Give us a peaceful rule; make Christians kings,
> That thirst so much for principality.
> I have no charge, nor many children,
> But one sole daughter, whom I hold as dear
> As Agamemnon did his Iphigen;
> And all I have is hers.
>
> (1.1.133–8)

Agamemnon, of course, sacrificed Iphigenia for fair winds to blow the becalmed Greek host to Troy. Winds are both of real and metaphoric concern in the play: after celebrating "Infinite riches in a little room" Barabas asks "But now, how stands the wind?"(1.1.36–7). And the Turkish pasha Callapine, asked what brings him to Malta, replies with the frankness that characterizes Turks much more than Christians or Jews in this play: "The wind that bloweth all the world besides: / Desire of gold"(3.5.3–4).

Barabas will use this desire repeatedly to betray his opponents, but he also uses their other desires, including the desire of Ferneze's son Lodowick for Abigail. Abigail, like many beautiful Jewish daughters in medieval and Renaissance stories about Jews, has fallen in love with a Christian, Mathias. As James Shapiro points out, Jewish women in Renaissance drama and fiction "are always depicted as young and desirable," unlike Jewish men, and their plot role is frequently that of alliance with male Christians (Shapiro, 1996: 132). When Mathias tells Lodowick about how struck he is with Abigail's beauty, Lodowick begins to pursue her (nothing so quickly arouses desire for another person than seeing a rival desiring her or him), and Barabas promptly exploits this mimetic rivalry, urging Abigail to pretend love for Lodowick and thus tricking the two young men into killing each other in a duel. But when Abigail learns that her father has sacrificed her beloved in his vengeance against Christians, she converts in earnest with a soliloquy of her own:

> Hard-hearted father, unkind Barabas,
> Was this the pursuit of thy policy,
> To make me show them favor severally,
> That by my favor they should both be slain?
> Admit thou loved'st not Lodowick for his sire,
> Yet Don Mathias ne'er offended thee.
> But thou wert set upon extreme revenge.
>
> (3.3.39–47)

How extreme emerges when Barabas reacts to the news that Abigail has now entered the convent as a genuine convert. He enters *reading a letter* (3.4.0 s.d.):

> What, Abigail become a nun again?
> False and unkind! What, hast thou lost thy father,
> And, all unknown and unconstrained of me,
> Art thou again got to the nunnery?
>
> (3.4.1–4)

Abigail and Barabas call each other "unkind," and both mean more than the modern sense of "hurtful" or "cruel" by the word: they also mean "unnatural, false to one's own kind." But for Abigail, her "kind" does not oblige her to shun Christians – rather Barabas's family link to her should make him welcome her lover, whatever his religion or race. For Barabas, Abigail, by repudiating her father's faith and cutting herself off from all communication with him, has turned her back on her own "kind," her faith, and family. This leads him to yet more "extreme revenge"

> Now here she writes, and wills me to repent.
> Repentance? *Spurca!* What pretendeth this?
> I fear she knows – 'tis so! – of my device
> In Don Mathias' and Lodovico's deaths.
> If so, 'tis time that it be seen into,
> For she that varies from me in belief
> Gives great presumption that she loves me not,
> Or, loving, doth dislike of something done.
>
> (3.4.5–12)

Barabas "sees into" the matter by poisoning the whole convent of nuns, including his daughter. In part, this serves a gangster's logic of wiping out all who might be able to testify about one's past crimes. This logic will in fact govern a great deal of the action in the rest of the play, as Barabas energetically but unsuccessfully tries to contain the spread of information by murdering the friar to whom the dying Abigail confessed, the servant who helped him murder the friar, and the pimp and prostitute who seduced the servant, got him to talk, and attempted to blackmail Barabas – a containment strategy that seems to be working until the dying courtesan reveals Barabas's guilt to the Christian governor Ferneze. But Barabas's destruction of Abigail also underlines the point this section's exploration of his interiority as revealed in his soliloquies has made clear: Barabas's strong selfhood includes a repudiation of any ties that might impede his freedom of action. "*Ego mihimet sum semper proximus*" (1.1.188), "my own affairs are my chief concern," seems a relatively innocuous although not conspicuously moral principle when Barabas first enunciates it, but it becomes considerably more disturbing as it exfoliates.

One of our fears about the interiorities of others is that they will be filled with desires that make them dangerous to us: desires to dominate us, hurt us, or take what is ours. In Barabas, we get a tour of such an interior space that, in making it credible, also makes it temporarily attractive. The soliloquies of many villains – including Shakespearean villains like Richard III, Claudius, and Iago – serve a similar dramatic purpose: so, as we shall see later, do those of revengers about whom it is harder to form a terminal moral judgment, like Vindice in *The Revenger's Tragedy* or Bosola in *The Duchess of Malfi*. As a tool for the exploration of inwardness, it is clear, the soliloquy does not always aim at the illustration of a mysterious or unconscious set of motives. Barabas's motives are very present to him and are cogently expressed. At the same time, his soliloquies, as this analysis of them has shown, offer a complex insight into the psyche of an able, ambitious, successful, but categorically reviled and excluded other.

1.3   The Inward Self in Aside: *The Changeling*

What kinds of inner thought do you most routinely conceal or dissimulate? Whatever your response – and who are we to tell you about your own interiority? – it seems not unlikely that sexual impulses, fantasies, or memories feature on your list in a fairly prominent position. Thomas Middleton and William Rowley's *The Changeling* uses "asides" – moments when characters break the flow of conversation in order to express a private commentary on it, audible to the audience but not to the other person in the conversation – in order to expose the decorum of conversation for what it often is, a mask for unavowable intentions, in this play usually sexual or aggressive ones. The play's double plot, half of it concerned with a madhouse where the insane act and speak out their inner lives without decorum, the other half with the breakdown of decorum in the household of an honorable Spanish governor whose fifteen-year-old daughter is about to be married, preoccupies itself with boundary-crossing and the intensities it exposes. The most important and memorable characters, the daughter Beatrice-Joanna, and the governor's ugly servant, De Flores, are both people of strong sexual impulses and few moral scruples who model a kind of extremity that may lie just below the surface of apparently quite civilized people. Thus the play offers a demystifying realism about human motives that is also a scary reflection on the fragility of the social conventions that usually mask them. As William Empson comments, linking the madhouse plot to the main plot by way of the title, "the idea of the changeling...makes you feel that the shock of seeing into a mad mind is dangerous; it may snatch you to itself. This shock is in all the discoveries of the play" (Empson, 1974: 50). Asides open minds so that we can see into them.

Most asides are brief. A typical example from *The Jew of Malta* – typical also in that it reveals an essential aspect of the speaker's inner being – is just two words. Barabas is responding to the concern of his fellow Jews at their summons to the senate house:

> Why, then, let every man
> Provide him, and be there for fashion sake.
> If anything shall there concern our state,
> Assure yourselves I'll look *(aside)* unto myself.
>
> (1.1.169–172)

In *The Changeling*, by contrast, asides tend to be quite long. This section will first illustrate the way the technique introduces us to a discrepancy between inner thought and public expression, then move on to a close description of a scene in which that discrepancy disappears, with shattering results.

De Flores has just overheard Beatrice, engaged to Alonzo de Piracquo, setting up a meeting with Alsemero, the man she has abruptly fallen in love with. De Flores begins the play sexually obsessed by Beatrice, and she in turn hates him and wishes to avoid his presence without knowing exactly why. Beatrice has just realized that, in refusing to allow Alsemero to attempt to kill Alonzo in a duel, she might call on De Flores for help with this. De Flores, in turn, sees Beatrice's movement toward betrayal of Alonzo as an opportunity for himself. He is reflecting on this in an extended aside as Beatrice, in another extended aside, considers her strategy for dealing with him. De Flores has a disfiguring rash on his face that comes up in their exchange:

> BEATRICE [*aside*]   Why, put case I loathed him
>   As much as youth and beauty hates a sepulchre,
>   Must I needs show it? Cannot I keep that secret,
>   And serve my turn upon him? --See, he's here.
>   [*To him*] De Flores!
> DE FLORES [*aside*]   Ha, I shall run mad with joy!
>   She called me fairly by my name, De Flores,
>   And neither "rogue" nor "rascal."
> BEATRICE   What ha' you done
>   To your face alate? You've met with some good physician.
>   You've pruned yourself, methinks; you were not wont
>   To look so amorously.
> DE FLORES [*aside*]   Not I;
>   'Tis the same physnomy, to a hair and pimple,
>   Which she called scurvy scarce an hour ago.
>   How is this?
> BEATRICE   Come hither. Nearer, man.
> DE FLORES [*aside*]   I'm up to the chin in heaven.
>
> (2.2.66–79)

De Flores, unlike many, entertains no illusions about his own appearance. At the same time, as we know from previous asides, he does not let his ugliness deter him from hoping for sexual satisfaction with Beatrice: "I'll despair the less / Because there's daily precedents of bad faces / Beloved beyond all reason"(2.1.83–85). As he comments in soliloquy at the end of the scene,

> Hunger and pleasure, they'll commend sometimes
> Slovenly dishes, and feed heartily on 'em –
> Nay, which is stranger, refuse daintier for 'em.
> Some women are odd feeders.

> (2.2.154–57)

Yeats's comment on the mates Helen and Aphrodite chose (and, implicitly, on the men Maud Gonne preferred to Yeats) comes to mind: "It's certain that fine women eat / A crazy salad with their meat" (Yeats, 1921: ll. 30–31).

So far there's a kind of comedy in these asides; they often evoke nervous laughter in performance. But because of these asides, readers and audiences know that Beatrice plays with fire when she tries to flirt with De Flores to get him to do her will. Because of the differences in class and appearance and age between them, she does not recognize in him the sexual attraction to her that she is delighted to arouse in Alsemero. His speeches, rich in sexual double meanings, convey only eagerness for money to her, as her asides (themselves unintentionally sexy) make clear when she delivers her charge to De Flores. De Flores is kneeling before her. Note that De Flores consistently addresses Beatrice as "you," the singular second person pronoun used with social superiors; Beatrice "thous" De Flores. This Renaissance English pronoun, lost in Modern English, is equivalent to "tu" in modern French and "du" in modern German; it has a full range of pronoun forms: "thou" as grammatical subject, "thee" as direct or indirect object, "thy" or "thine" as possessive, and its own set of verb forms as well: "thou art" or "thou hast," for instance, are the "thou" forms of "you are" and "you have" in Renaissance English. The "thou" form is used to address social inferiors, children, and intimates.

> De Flores   If you knew
>   How sweet it were to me to be employed
>   In any act of yours, you would say then
>   I failed and used not reverence enough
>   When I receive the charge on't.
> Beatrice [*aside*]   This is much, methinks;
>   Belike his wants are greedy, and to such
>   Gold tastes like angels' food. [*To him*] Rise.
> De Flores   I'll have the work first.
> Beatrice [*aside*]   Possible his need
>   Is strong upon him. [*She gives him money.*] There's to encourage thee:
>   As thou art forward and thy service dangerous,
>   Thy reward shall be precious.

DE FLORES   That I have thought on.
  I have assured myself of that beforehand,
  And know it will be precious; the thought ravishes.
BEATRICE   Then take him to thy fury.
DE FLORES   I thirst for him.
BEATRICE   Alonzo de Piracquo.
DE FLORES   His end's upon him. He shall be seen no more.
BEATRICE   How lovely now dost thou appear to me!

                                                    (2.2.122–138)

When De Flores returns with Piracquo's severed finger as a token of his completion of the task, Beatrice, delighted at the disappearance of Piracquo but disgusted by the finger, tries to get rid of De Flores as quickly as she can: "Look you, sir, here's three thousand golden florins; / I have not meanly thought upon thy merit" (3.4.60–61). But the result is not what she expects:

DE FLORES   What, salary? Now you move me.
BEATRICE   How, De Flores?
  ...
DE FLORES   I could ha' hired
  A journeyman in murder at this rate,
  And mine own conscience might have slept at ease,
  And have had the work brought home.

                                                    (3.4.62–71)

This is, of course, what Beatrice believes that she has done, but the work is being brought home to her in another sense. Beatrice's asides now make clear her confusion, naivety, and unwillingness to recognize the desire De Flores has been rather clear about all along:

BEATRICE [*aside*]   I'm in a labyrinth.
  What will content him? I would fain be rid of him.
  [*To him*] I'll double the sum, sir.
DE FLORES   You take a course
  To double my vexation, that's the good you do.
BEATRICE [*aside*]   Bless me! I am now in worse plight than I was;
  I know not what will please him. [*To him*] For my fear's sake,
  I prithee make away with all speed possible.
  And if thou be'st so modest not to name
  The sum that will content thee, paper blushes not;
  Send thy demand in writing, it shall follow thee.
  But prithee take thy flight.

                                                    (3.4.71–80)

Along with her suggestion that De Flores is inhibited by modesty, Beatrice's "bless me!" is, in the circumstances, remarkable. In *Macbeth*, a play that, along with *Othello*, has a clear influence on *The Changeling*, "amen" sticks in Macbeth's throat when he hears Malcolm or Donalbain say

"God bless us" as he descends from the bedchamber carrying the bloody knives with which he murdered their father Duncan, his guest and king (2.2.30–33). Beatrice, however, has no difficulty asking for blessing in the presence of the severed finger holding the ring she first gave to her guest and fiancé Piracquo. She really believes that the deed belongs to De Flores, her "journeyman in murder," but he soon disabuses her of the idea: "Why, are not you as guilty, in (I'm sure) / As deep as I? And we should stick together"(3.4.83–84). "Stick together" is a wonderful expression, as it encompasses the shared blood guilt in which they are "deep" and the sexual intimacy De Flores intends and the mutual dependence in evading detection that gives him his primary hold on Beatrice, all in one down-to-earth phrase. As he attempts to kiss her, she urges him to remember his place, as, if he seems overly familiar with her, it will be a suspicious sign:

> BEATRICE: Take heed, De Flores, of forgetfulness
>   'Twill soon betray us.
> DE FLORES   Take you heed first.
>   Faith, you're grown much forgetful; you're to blame in't.
> BEATRICE [*aside*]   He's bold, and I am blamed for't!
>
> (3.4.94–97)

The asides are much briefer now, as De Flores grows more direct, and the masks that have been (barely) covering their intentions from each other are being pulled off. De Flores is still using double meanings, but even Beatrice can now only with enormous effort misunderstand them:

> DE FLORES   I have eased you
>   Of your trouble; think on't. I'm in pain,
>   And must be eased of you; 'tis a charity.
>   Justice invites your blood to understand me.
>
> (3.4.97–100)

The peculiar combination of moral force and transgressive sexual invitation is brought out by line 100. "Your blood" is both "your sexual being" and "the blood you are soaked in by our crime." Beatrice has been unjust, not only to Alonzo, whom she has murdered, but also to De Flores, whom she has tried to turn into a tool for the satisfaction of her desires. It is only just, he suggests, that she use him sexually as well as criminally, given that he has desires too. Beatrice, now at last understanding, needs to feel that understanding is impossible:

> DE FLORES   Justice invites your blood to understand me.
> BEATRICE   I dare not.
> DE FLORES   Quickly!

> BEATRICE Oh, I never shall!
> Speak it yet further off, that I may lose
> What has been spoken and no sound remain on't.
> I would not hear so much offense again
> For such another deed.
>
> (3.4.101–105)

Now De Flores can enjoy an open presentation of his own intentions and feelings, the sort of expression that before has only occurred in asides. This is partly because Beatrice still has not understood the "justice" of his position, but it is also because she has now begun to take his feelings and intentions seriously, although she manifests this by being appalled by them.

> DE FLORES Soft, lady, soft.
> The last is not yet paid for. Oh, this act
> Has put me into spirit! I was as greedy on't
> As the parched earth for moisture when the clouds weep.
> Did you not mark? I wrought myself into't,
> Nay, sued and kneeled for't. Why was all that pains took?
>
> (3.4.105–110)

Not for money, De Flores says, although he of course needs money and intends to have it, but for a sexual reward:

> For I place wealth after the heels of pleasure,
> And, were I not resolved in my belief
> That thy virginity were perfect in thee,
> I should but take my recompense with grudging,
> As if I had but half my hopes I agreed for.
>
> (3.4.115–119)

We may find De Flores' anticipation of sex with a virginal Beatrice as intensely pleasurable puzzling as a sensual calculation. But we gather that his "pleasure" here includes his mastery over someone who had assumed her own dominance over him. Moreover, in taking Beatrice's maidenhead, De Flores will be triumphing over a set of males who also have also assumed their dominance over him (notably Alsemero, and Beatrice's father Vermandero, but also perhaps the murdered Alonzo) by getting first to a place he was never supposed to get at all. Thus De Flores plans to experience a complex pleasure, partly vengeful and sadistic, but partly (insofar as he intends Beatrice to experience some sort of pleasure too, as he has repeatedly suggested earlier and will again at the end of the scene) the fulfillment of a sense of self-worth with respect to everyone else that De Flores has been manifesting in his asides throughout the play. In confirmation of this view, note the subtle shift in pronouns: for the first time in the play, De Flores here "thous" Beatrice citing his "belief / That *thy* virginity were perfect in thee" (3.4.113).

Beatrice, horrified, makes explicit two beliefs that have been central to her moral thinking all along: in general, her own privileged insulation from male crudity as a beautiful upper-class daughter of good family, and, in specific, the importance of her avoidance of premarital loss of virginity – a limited notion of the moral, but one that a preoccupation with female chastity perhaps still encourages in fifteen-year-old girls.

> BEATRICE   Why, 'tis impossible thou canst be so wicked,
> Or shelter such a cunning cruelty,
> To make his death the murderer of my honor!
> Thy language is so bold and vicious,
> I cannot see which way I can forgive it
> With any modesty.
>
> (3.4.120–125)

De Flores replies with a clear refutation of claims to honor or modesty: "Push, you forget yourself. / A woman dipped in blood, and talk of modesty?"(3.4.125–126). ("Push" is an exclamation of contemptuous dismissal, like "pish" or "pooh.") That is, Beatrice, not De Flores, is the one who does not know her place. But Beatrice, although becoming more aware of the true moral description De Flores is forcing on her, still reels from the shock of being talked to in this way:

> Oh, misery of sin! Would I had been bound
> Perpetually unto my living hate
> In that Piracquo than to hear these words.
> Think but upon the distance that creation
> Set 'twixt thy blood and mine, and keep thee there.
>
> (3.4.127–131)

De Flores replies in the most-quoted passage in this much-quoted play:

> Look but into your conscience; read me there;
> 'Tis a true book. You'll find me there your equal.
> Push, fly not to your birth, but settle you
> In what the act has made you; you're no more now.
> You must forget your parentage to me.
> You're the deed's creature; by that name
> You lost your first condition, and I challenge you,
> As peace and innocency has turned you out
> And made you one with me.
>
> (3.4.132–140)

"I challenge you" means "I claim you as my own."

This speech is both a climax in an intense conversation and a philosophical assertion about the conditions of inwardness and self-possession. Basically, it makes clear to Beatrice that her claims to possess her inward self rest on her avoidance of such acts as murder – as a killer, she has become "the deed's creature." Beatrice murdered to preserve herself from a life of "living hate" married to the wrong man; that is, she murdered to keep a kind of harmony between her inward, desiring, choosing self and her outward condition. But by breaking with the social order, she has become a possession of her partner in crime, De Flores, and her claims to be distinct from him by birth, or beauty, or decency fall away. "You're the deed's creature" registers a terrible loss in self-possession, and, for Beatrice, the loss is connected with the sexual demand that accompanies it. Of course, for a woman, loss of virginity is as it were the paradigm of such a life-changing "deed"; it opens interior space to another in physical terms, and in the inflexible moral terms of the time, sex without marriage turned a woman from maiden to whore in one bewildering and blood-stained minute, as sex within marriage was necessary to transform a woman from one man's daughter to another man's wife. The play is well aware of this both as something that is physically imminent for Beatrice as the consummating moment in the marriage she plans, and as something that is part of De Flores's plan for her. Alonzo's cut-off finger is a kind of symbol of it – a would-be bridegroom's bloody member – as is De Flores's name with its sense of defloration. The speech is a reminder of how dependent inward stability is on circumstances that permit more or less leisured reflection. Even the stoic interiority that preserves itself amid torture and degradation depends on the sense of having done right. Beatrice has done wrong, and what should be the prop of her inward moral life, her conscience, in fact undermines it.

Of course it is not only Beatrice's moral fall that puts her in De Flores's grasp. He now has a strategic hold on her, and when she responds to his assertion with an instinctive counter that there is still a huge difference between them, he holds out both stick and carrot. In De Flores's reply to her, "urge" means "provoke" or "dare."

> DE FLORES [P]eace and innocency has turned you out
>   And made you one with me.
> BEATRICE With thee, foul villain?
> DE FLORES Yes, my fair murd'ress. Do you urge me?
>   Though thou writ'st maid, thou whore in thy affection!
>   'Twas changed from thy first love, and that's a kind
>   Of whoredom in thy heart; and he's changed now,
>   To bring thy second on, thy Alsemero
>   Whom (by all sweets that ever darkness tasted),
>   If I enjoy thee not, thou ne'er enjoy'st.
>   I'll blast the hopes and joys of marriage.
>   I'll confess all; my life I rate at nothing.
>   (3.4.139–149)

Note how he now "thous" Beatrice in forcing her to acknowledge her degradation. He is demonstrating to her (as he did in giving her Alonzo's finger) that she has already passed over the line between innocence and guilt, and is already a "whore" by any true moral reckoning. His willingness to sacrifice his life to wreck hers astonishes Beatrice, as well it might. De Flores explains that he is enduring the pangs of disprized love and might as well be dead if he cannot have her, and he overbears her attempts to make him a final offer in his eagerness to state his lover's case, and express the plight he has been concealing from everyone:

> BEATRICE   De Flores!
> DE FLORES   I shall rest from all lovers' plagues then.
>   I live in pain now; that shooting eye
>   Will burn my heart to cinders.
> BEATRICE   Oh, sir, hear me!
> DE FLORES   She that in life and love refuses meIn death and shame my
>   partner she shall be.
>
>   (3.4.150–155)

Of course it is impossible, even in a boundary-breaking conversation like this one, to distinguish posturing from sincere self-expression with certainty. We could not do it with a living human being, and, of course, we cannot do it with a literary character. De Flores certainly works to dominate Beatrice, and it is vital to his intent that she believe him capable of choosing to be executed alongside her rather than allowing her to escape him. Renaissance drama has a number of male characters who kneel before women, present them with swords or daggers, and open their shirts, asking to be slain if they cannot be loved. Two notable examples are Shakespeare's Richard III and Giovanni in John Ford's *'Tis Pity She's a Whore*; in Richard's case at least we can be quite sure he has no intention of being killed. But De Flores has already taken a huge risk in murdering Alonzo to get into this situation, and he has been revealing a layer of ardent feeling and of passionate moral reflection in these speeches that is certainly a plausible exposure of interiority, even though (unlike asides or soliloquies) the speeches have a persuasive intent and thus a strategic aspect. At any rate, De Flores offers a very powerful expression of commitment in his answer to Beatrice's last appeal:

> BEATRICE   Stay, hear me once for all! I make thee master
>   Of all the wealth I have in gold and jewels;
>   Let me go poor unto my bed with honor,
>   And I am rich in all things.
> DE FLORES   Let this silence thee:
>   The wealth of all Valencia shall not buy
>   My pleasure from me.
>   Can you weep fate from its determined purpose?
>   So soon may you weep me.
>
>   (3.4.156–163)

At this Beatrice gives up. Accepting that she is the deed's creature, she accepts also that De Flores is her fate. Her next speech would, in other circumstances, be an aside: it is the sort of frank self-assessment that is not usually, in this play or in other circumstances, offered to another person, because it gives that person too much power and also offers too dark a view of the other person's actions. The rhymed couplets indicate that we are reaching the end of the scene, and indeed this could be its last speech.

> BEATRICE   Vengeance begins;
>   Murder, I see, is followed by more sins.
>   Was my creation in the womb so curst
>   It must engender with a viper first?
> $\qquad\qquad$ (3.4.163–166)

But note how De Flores's response to this not-uninsulting reflection shows his self-confident mastery, now that Beatrice is yielding to him. Having been domineering, morally imperious, and threatening, he is now comforting:

> Come, rise, and shroud your blushes in my bosom.
> Silence is one of pleasure's best receipts.
> Thy peace is wrought forever in this yielding.
> 'Las, how the turtle pants! Thou'lt love anon
> What thou so fear'st and faint'st to venture on.
> $\qquad\qquad$ (3.4.167–171)

While we noted earlier that De Flores's "pleasure" has a sadistic aspect, here (as in a number of general comments on sex earlier in the play) he promises to please her; having forced her to accept that she is on his level, he will now endeavor to make her enjoy it.

What, then, has a close reading of this climactic scene shown about inwardness and the aside?

The most important personal conversations people have involve the clarification (or sometimes the dramatic reversal) of other's knowledge of interior mental states. Declarations of love or hatred or indifference, disclosures of hidden truths or secret histories, revelations of vulnerability or resentment or dependence, all involve the opening of barriers that block access to inwardness. Such conversations are dramatic, and of course plays are full of them. Rarely do they achieve the level of intense mutual revelation and forced transformation that this one has. Middleton and Rowley's use of the aside to establish an unusually explicit and visible gulf between outer and inner mental life is a major contributor to the power of this scene.

1.4   A Digression: The Inner Life of Modernized Texts

Part of what we want to know about the inward life of other people is how they got the way they are. Large parts of interiority are personal history – a set of key experiences. "You can't understand X without knowing about that father s/he had" makes sense over a wide range of values of X, both fictive and real, from X equals Hamlet to X equals Alfred, Lord Tennyson or Lord Olivier or Jane Fonda; surely you can supply many examples of your own. How do the English Renaissance plays you read get to be the way they are? Being modernized and annotated in the process of being edited is the last step in the process, and it may be helpful to move backward from the text you see to a hypothetical point or period of genesis by focusing for a bit on what editors do and what materials they work on.

We have already mentioned that many stage directions are editorial, meaning that they have been inserted into the text by editors to make things clearer for readers. Most editions have some way of indicating whether a stage direction is editorial or whether it occurs in the early printed text on which the edition is based, known as the "*copy-text.*" In the Norton *English Renaissance Drama*, for instance, editorial stage directions are in square brackets (e.g., "[*aside*]"), while stage directions included in the copy-text are simply in italics if given in full between lines or marginally in the copy-text, or are placed in parentheses (rather than square brackets) if in the middle of a line. Frequently, modern stage directions combine editorial additions with copy-text, as in this example from *The Changeling*'s madhouse subplot: "*Enter Lollio above [unseen by Isabella and Antonio]*" (3.3.177.2). (The final "2" in that citation indicates that this is the second line of stage directions following line 177 of Act 3 scene 3.)

Many a reader's eye has doubtless glazed over in the course of the previous paragraph, brief as it is. Editors work to make life easier for readers, but for most readers details of editorial practice make life harder. Nietzsche prayed for bowels distant and regular, like millwheels in the night, and readers may have similar feelings about textual editing: a necessary but deeply unglamorous task that should go on reliably and unobtrusively. But for students who want to know a play well, understanding what editors have done to it is part of what is there to know. For general readers and theater-goers the process that lies behind the book they hold, or the script the actors memorized, is well worth knowing about.

Much of what editors do in standard twentieth or twenty-first century versions of Renaissance plays is to modernize spelling and punctuation, and to provide explanatory notes and glosses intended to make unfamiliar terms or phrases intelligible. This is not, of course, quite as innocuous an activity as it sounds. Modernization can render unfamiliar meanings of words invisible and give readers a false sense that they know exactly what a speech means, for example, De Flores's final line in the first scene of the earliest printed edition of *The Changeling*, "Though I get nothing elſe, Il'e have my will" (Middleton and Rowley, 1653: B4r; we will explain "B4r" later).

This is modernized in the Norton by the simple expedient of substituting "s" for "f" and spelling "Il'e" as "I'll" – that is, it hardly needs changing: "Though I get nothing else, I'll have my will"(1.1.246). But by being rendered entirely familiar, and thus reducing a modern reader's awareness of historical distance from the words involved, the line may become deceptive. A modern reader needs to know that "will" includes "sexual desire" in Renaissance English as a primary meaning, and that it would be misleading to read this as just "Though I achieve nothing else, I'll do what I want to do (by continuing to stalk Beatrice)," when it contains a more tangible sexual intention, "Though I achieve nothing else in life, I'll consummate my sexual desire for Beatrice." The line thus foreshadows De Flores's final speech, where he boasts that, although dying, he is satisfied because he has taken Beatrice's virginity. This problem with modernization is more acute when the Renaissance word sheds part of its Renaissance meaning while being modernized. The word "travaile" in Renaissance English meant both modern "travel" and modern "travail," that is, "woe" or "suffering." Most editions of Shakespeare, for instance the Riverside, the Bevington *Complete Works*, the Norton, and William Carroll's *Arden 3*, using the Folio as a copy-text, render the following line from the Folio *Two Gentlemen of Verona* "In hauing knowne no trauaile in his youth" as "In having known no travel in his youth" (1.3.16), thus eliminating a pun on the two senses of "travaile." We should stress that this is in no sense a mistake – the context shows that "travel" is clearly the main relevant meaning of the word. But modernization makes invisible a potentially important secondary meaning. Editorial punctuation can also limit meaning for contemporary readers by solidifying a grammatical relation between clauses that is fluid in the early printed text (see Fowler, 1998: 9–10 for examples from Milton's *Paradise Lost*). And a wrong-headed gloss can mislead readers thoroughly.

Editors do more than this, however. In verse dramas like *The Jew of Malta* or *The Changeling*, where most of the time the characters speak unrhymed iambic pentameter lines, the editor often needs to fiddle with lines that were typeset nonmetrically to make regular lines. Sometimes editors actually add or change words in obviously faulty passages, a process called "emendation."

What are editors working with as they do this? What is the hidden background of the text you see? In the case of famous Renaissance plays, there is usually an extensive series of previous editions, all of them ultimately based on early printed texts (we have very few plays that have survived as manuscripts, that is, plays in the handwriting of authors or scribes). So a good modern editor will be looking at, or at least constantly referring back to, an early printed text or a facsimile (a photographic or digital copy) of an early printed text. He or she will also look at what previous editors have done.

Because the surviving copies of early printed play-texts adorn the shelves of book collectors or rare-book libraries, editors usually work from facsimiles – a photographic copy of the original. Two new databases, LION (LIterature OnLine) and EEBO (Early English Books Online), both produced by Chadwick-Healey and subscribed to by many universities, make early texts a lot more available to beginning students than they used to be. LION provides digitized and thus searchable (although far from error-free) transcripts of early printed texts. EEBO, more relevantly in the immediate situation we are discussing, provides digitized facsimiles of books published in England between 1473 (the date of the first English press-run we have a product of) and 1700. By accessing EEBO, you can put on your screen a copy of the printed page your edition has modernized and transformed for you to read.

This gets you to what editors are working with. But is this "the original"? Obviously in some sense not. For one thing, most early modern printed plays exist in a number of copies, which tend to differ from each other slightly because, in early modern printing-houses, printers made corrections during print runs as they noticed errors. The most scholarly sorts of modern editions work with a collation – a word by word, comma by comma, comparison – of all printed texts, and judge among the small variants. Moreover, many plays exist in different printings, and sometimes these printings are in significant variance from one another. The quarto and folio versions of Shakespeare's *King Lear* may qualify as two different plays, although it took very energetic scholarly argument to persuade most Shakespeareans that this is so; the 1604 and 1616 quartos of Marlowe's (and unnamed collaborators') *Doctor Faustus* certainly do.

More importantly, plays were in most cases performed well before they were printed (the exceptions are so-called closet dramas that may have been written to be read and were never performed for money, like Elizabeth Cary's *Mariam*). Thus the printed version of a play comes well after it has reached its primary target public, which is a theater audience rather than a set of readers. In deciding what to do with an early printed version of a play, modern editors work with a set of assumptions about how plays got into print that helps them interpret puzzles in the early printed texts. These assumptions rely on several sources of information. There are records involving printing, often derived from the Stationers' Company, a London guild that regulated printing and selling of books and other print or paper products. There are records involving censorship and court performance (related because the censor was also the Master of the Revels, charged with providing entertainment for Queen Elizabeth, King James, or King Charles). Besides, there are records involving the theater companies themselves, sometimes in law court proceedings or parish registers, sometimes in other materials like the diary of theatrical entrepreneur Philip Henslowe. Finding and interpreting this information has been a major activity of scholars. Indeed, the field of English studies, as a standard part of university curricula and faculties, was born in large part out of the attempt to understand and edit Shakespeare and Shakespeare's contemporaries.

This effort has yielded a more or less agreed-upon idea of how Renaissance plays got into print. To state a complex and controversial issue very briefly, play-texts were written by the poet or poets ("poet," not "playwright," was the Renaissance term for a dramatic author), often on a commission from a company of players or an entrepreneur, sometimes with an agreed-on outline or plan. When the script was completed, the company or entrepreneur that bought the script seems to have, in most modern senses of the word, owned it. Companies preserved a set of playscripts for the plays they kept in repertory. These scripts were over time annotated and often much modified, serving as a company library that was also a form of intellectual capital (although here we need to be wary of transporting modern notions of intellectual property back to a time before the existence of, for instance, copyright). We used to think that the playing companies thus had a vested interest in *not* publishing play-texts to keep rival companies from performing them, and thus that play-texts got published only when (i) a "pirated" version of the text had been performed or published by another company or a rogue printer, or (ii) when the playing company was in acute financial need. Recent work, however, has suggested that the publication habits of playing companies do not fit this idea well, and that companies published plays to serve a smallish market for readers of printed plays, and not out of some imperative dictated by the large market for performed plays (see Blayney, 1997: 386). Indeed, they seem to have published texts of plays in order to whet public interest in seeing those plays in performance, as a kind of "advertising," as Peter Blayney puts it. Lukas Erne has argued that the published versions of Shakespeare's plays tended to be substantially too long for performance, so that publication marked Shakespeare's aspiration for literary notice, and possibly also for a fuller expression of his literary imagination than stage performance could provide (see Erne, 2003).

Most plays were published in small volumes – "quartos" – that cost about a shilling and could be collected cheaply by play-fanciers. A few poets had large collections of plays published together in a large-volume format, as a "folio" – that is, a book in which the printed sheet of paper was folded in 2; in a quarto it was folded in 4, in an octavo in 8, in a duodecimo in 12. When, as discussed earlier, we cited a line in *The Changeling* as "Middleton and Rowley, 1653: B4r," we were specifying a page by reference to the quarto printing system, in which a given printer's sheet of paper, full size about 18 by 14 inches, will have four pages printed on each side. Each page is about 7 by 9 inches, and one sheet makes eight pages. Each printed sheet will have a capital letter printed at the bottom of the first page on the front side (and sometimes the same capital with a 2 after on the first page of the back side, that is, the fifth page of the eight on the sheet). These letters order the gatherings of the text, the eight-page units that get sewn together in alphabetical sequence to make the physical book. Thus "B4r" means "the recto of the fourth page in gathering B," and "recto" means the right or front page, while "verso" means the back page. Thus we have specified the seventh page of the second gathering, or page 15 in the book. Quartos do not usually have page numbers.

Folio publication of plays was unusual. Ben Jonson published a folio of his "Works" in 1616; the famous folio edition of Shakespeare's plays was published in 1623, 7 years after Shakespeare's death, by members of his playing company, the King's Men. A second folio of Shakespeare appeared in 1632, a folio of Marston in 1633, a second folio of Jonson in 1640, and a folio of Beaumont and Fletcher followed in 1647. These were expensive books to make and to buy, and they thus represented a substantial investment on the part of whoever paid to publish them. Quartos were published in small editions of under 1000 and involved a smaller outlay for both publisher and purchaser. The mechanical work was done by a printer, and the individual workman who set the type by hand into the wooden forms that made up a page was a compositor. The edition was usually commissioned by a bookseller; some printers were also booksellers. Compositors worked either directly from a manuscript or from an earlier printed text; for this reason, modern editors of works that were popular enough to be published in multiple editions usually use the earliest in a series of semi-identical editions of a printed text (designated as Q1, Q2, Q3, etc.) unless it looks as though there was some authoritative intervention to correct a printed text between editions.

Actual theatrical manuscripts from the period are rare, but at a time before typewriters, all authors wrote by hand or dictated to someone who wrote by hand. So all the plays we edit went through manuscripts. The manuscripts fall into three general categories. There are authors' "foul papers," that is, the manuscript the author or authors composed in their own handwriting, often with corrections, and usually with inconsistency in speech prefixes and a good deal of vagueness about entrances, exits, and who will be present in crowd scenes There are theatre "playbooks," which until recently tended to be called by the name nineteenth-century scholars gave them, "promptbooks," the text held by the "book-holder" or prompter in the theater to make sure that everything went as it should. These texts have more consistent prefixes, stage directions that often anticipate stage action, and exact notations of who goes on stage when and who goes off. And there are scribal "fair copies," sometimes of foul papers, sometimes of playbooks, commissioned either to give to someone or, more relevantly here, to make a clearer setting-text for the print shop or to avoid having to remove the playbook from the theater's collection of texts. Theories about what has gone wrong when an early printed text seems to have something wrong with it often refer back to the setting-text and hypothesize some problem with it: perhaps an author's cancellation mark that was missed by a scribe or by the compositors (producing repetition or something unnecessary), perhaps an author's addition between lines that was not seen.

Take a moment in the key conversation between De Flores and Beatrice in *The Changeling* that we were discussing just before this digression began. Beatrice offers De Flores a large sum of money to go away and let her get on with her life plan, and he rejects her with a show of indignation:

> BEATRICE   I understand thee not.
> DE FLORES   I could ha' hired
>   A journeyman in murder at this rate,
>   And mine own conscience might have slept at ease,
>   And have had the work brought home.
>   (3.4.68–70)

So the passage appears in almost all modern editions. It is one of De Flores's characteristically brilliant and down to earth moral remarks. But if you look at the end of the play, under "Textual Notes," or at the bottom of the page in editions like the Revels Plays that have textual notes in small print there, you will find a notation something like "*slept at ease*: not in Q, editorial addition." The editor in question is Charles Wentworth Dilke (1789–1864), who felt there was something missing in the source text, "Q," an editorial shorthand for the quarto volume published in 1653, well after both Middleton and Rowley were dead. The Q text looks like this:

> BEA.   I underſtand thee not.
> DEF.   I could ha' hir'd a journey-man in murder at this rate,
>   And mine own conſcience might have,
>   And have had the work brought home.
> BEA.   I'me in a labyrinth;
>   What will content him ? I would fain be rid of him.
>   I'le double the ſum, ſir.
>   (Middleton and Rowley, 1653: E8r)

Apart from the substitution of the character "ſ" for "s" in four places, and the abbreviation of speech prefixes, this is not very difficult to read. The second line, however, is hypermetrical (too long); it goes on for 14 syllables and has seven beats. And the third line is too short, only seven or at most eight syllables – eight if "conscience" were pronounced "con-shi-entz." (An iambic pentameter line almost always has 9, 10, or 11 syllables, with five stresses falling more or less on every second syllable. Editors thus try to find ways of producing such lines when they do not appear in the copy-text, for example, "a JOURneyMAN in MURder AT this RATE.") To compound the problem posed by metrical irregularity, the third line does not make obvious immediate sense. With all of these issues converging on a particular passage, an editor is entitled to feel that something unusual needs to be done. The metrical issues can be reduced by some relineation. What David Bevington does in the Norton is to treat Beatrice's previous speech, which stands alone in Q, as a half-line, and have the beginning of De Flores's next line in Q fill it out to make a complete iambic pentameter line:

> BEATRICE   I understand thee not.
> DE FLORES   I could ha' hired
>   A journeyman in murder at this rate.
>   (3.4.69–70)

Note that Bevington modernizes the spelling of "hired" but preserves the Renaissance abbreviation "ha" (meaning "have") because that affects how the word sounds. Nonetheless, the way Bevington renders the passage as a whole still leaves us with two hypermetrical lines at the end.

> DE FLORES   And have had the work brought home.
> BEATRICE   I'm in a labyrinth.
>   What will content him? I would fain be rid of him.
>   (3.4.71–2)

Line 71 has 13 syllables and six stresses, line 72 has 12 syllables and either five or six stresses, although both lines can be helped in this regard by elision: pronouncing "And have had" as "And've had" and "I would" as "I'd." Nonetheless, a metrical irregularity remains.

Dilke, emboldened doubtless by the need to adjust meter, and feeling that the problem with both sense and line-length in "And mine own confcience might have" showed that something was missing, added "slept at ease" in his version of *The Changeling* in Volume IV of his 1815 *Old English Plays* (Bawcutt, 1973: 1).

Since editors normally are not in the business of adding their own words to plays, they need a strong reason to make such an addition. Dilke's emendation is more radical than a comparable standard example, the emendation in Shakespeare's *Henry V*, where, in Mistress Quickly's description of Sir John Falstaff's death in the 1623 Folio, we have the lines: "I knewe there was but one way: for his Nofe was as fharpe as a Pen, and a Table of greene fields" (Shakespeare, 1623: 429). No one could figure out what "a Table of greene fields" meant, although editors realized that it might be connected with the mysterious fact that Sir John's "nose was as sharp as a pen," as a "table" could mean a book to write in. The 1600 quarto of *Henry V* omits the phrase, possibly implying that the compositor could make no sense of it (although the passage differs in other ways too, being for one thing set as verse rather than prose):

> His noſe was as ſharpe as a pen:
> For when I ſaw him fumble with the ſheetes,
> And talk of Floures, and ſmile vpõ his fingers ends
> I knew there was no way but one.
>   (Shakespeare, 1600: B4v)

Puzzling over "a Table of greene fields," Lewis Theobald, an eighteenth-century editor, saw that "a Table" might be a compositor's error for "a babbled," where "a" is a contraction of "he," and that this connects with the "talk of Floures." This emendation, which, like Dilke's, shows brilliant poetic sensitivity, has been accepted by virtually all subsequent editions (see McDonald, 2001: 209), although not by the new *RSC Shakespeare*. But as it substitutes words that make beautiful sense for other words that could be confused versions of the substitutes, it is substantially less bold than Dilke's addition of three words to fill in what he saw as a blank.

The theory behind such an addition is that the compositor, or perhaps the scribe who copied the text sent to the compositor, left out a phrase, either through inattention or because the manuscript from which he was working was difficult to read. This does not seem to have happened often elsewhere in *The Changeling*, although there are other textual puzzles about it. As N. W. Bawcutt remarks in introducing the Scolar Press Facsimile of the 1653 quarto,

> A feature of the quarto is that a high proportion of the verse is not set out in its correct lineation. In many cases, however, two separate half-lines or a half-line and a complete line are printed together as a single line, and it looks as although the compositor tried to save paper (or perhaps to avoid too much white space) by compressing the text on to the page.
>
> The manuscript from which the quarto was set must have had a good and legible text, but its precise nature is not easy to determine. The quarto contains none of the features which often point to authorial foul-papers (such as inconsistent or muddled speech-prefixes) or alternatively to prompt-copy (such as anticipatory stage directions). Possibly Moseley had a fresh transcript of the play prepared before he sent it to the printer.   (Bawcutt, 1973: 2).

Amidst general uncertainty about the kind of manuscript the quarto was set from, we have this local textual crux. (A "crux" is a point of difficulty; a "textual crux" is usually a particular problem that may require emendation or an elaborate explanation of why not to emend.)

Suppose we wanted to make a case against Dilke's "slept at ease." We would start by saying the obvious: "slept at ease" has no positive textual authority whatsoever, originating as it does in an inspired guess. Could we construct an alternative emendation that would not insert the questionable easy-sleeping conscience, but would fix the meter? Although this has never been done, in fact we could, using the assumptions about dramatic verse and about manuscript-to-print transmission discussed earlier. One of the odd things about the lines "And mine own confcience might have, / And have had the work brought home" is the repetition of "might have / And have had." Dilke and all who follow him assume that the printer dropped something after "might have." But there is an alternative possibility. If "mine own conscience might have" itself was a late insertion to the manuscript by the author, it intervenes between two lines that make very good sense without any mention of conscience:

> I could ha' hir'd a journey-man in murder at this rate
> And have had the work brought home.

The conditional verb "could" governs both "ha' hir'd" and "have had the work brought home." If, then, we assume that the line about "conscience" is an afterthought on the part of Middleton (the author of this scene, it is generally agreed), the part line "And mine own conscience might have," has been put between these two lines. But if so, could it not be that the insertion was accompanied by a crossing out or bracketing for deletion of the words "And have had" in the next line – a deletion missed by the compositor? If this were the case, the author would have meant the passage to read as follows:

> I could ha' hir'd a journey-man in murder at this rate,
> And mine own confcience might have
> Had the work brought home.

Relineated, a modern edition of the passage would read as follows:

> BEATRICE   I understand thee not.
> DE FLORES   I could ha' hired
>   A journeyman in murder at this rate
>   And mine own conscience might have had the work
>   Brought home.
> BEATRICE [*aside*]   I'm in a labyrinth. What will
>   Content him? I would fain be rid of him.

By doing this, we have eliminated two hypermetrical lines that remain in Bevington's edition in the Norton (and in Bawcutt's Revels editions, Richard Dutton's Oxford Standard Authors edition, Bryan Loughrey and Neil Taylor's Penguin edition, Douglas Bruster's Oxford edition, Russell Fraser and Norman Rabkin's Macmillan anthology, Arthur Kinney's

Blackwell anthology, and Simon Barker and Hilary Hinds's Routledge anthology, to cite some other readily available texts), and we have eliminated a phrase that we know to have no demonstrable textual connection to Middleton and Rowley's authorship or to early performance.

Only two recent editions do not follow Dilke, and neither does what we have proposed here. A. H. Gomme preserves the original, giving De Flores the line "And mine own conscience might have, and have had / The work brought home." Joost Daalder's New Mermaid has the following:

> BEATRICE   I understand thee not.
> DE FLORES   I could ha' hired
>   A journeyman in murder at this rate,
>   And mine own conscience might have [had], and have had
>   The work brought home.
> BEATRICE [*Aside*]   I'm in a labyrinth;
>   What will content him? I would fain be rid of him.
>   (3.4.67–72)

This produces a line that does not make easy sense: "And mine own conscience might have [had], and have had" – moreover, it adds a word of its own, with the footnoted justification "my additional 'had' would help both sense and metre, and could easily have been omitted in transmission by anticipation of the second 'had'" (Middleton and Rowley, 1990: 65). In our view, the theory of error proposed earlier makes more sense than Daalder's, and the result is far more readable and attractive than either Gomme's or Daalder's. In what will surely be the most widely used edition of *The Changeling*, that in the Oxford *Collected Works* of Middleton, published in early 2008, the passage reads as follows:

> BEATRICE   I understand thee not.
> DE FLORES   I could ha' hired
>   A journeyman in murder at this rate,
>   And mine own conscience might have lain at ease,
>   And have had the work brought home.
> BEATRICE [*aside*]   I'm in a labyrinth!
>   What will content him? I would fain be rid of him.
>   (3.4.70–74)

Douglas Bruster, textual editor of the play, and perhaps Gary Taylor, a General Editor of the edition, have chosen to modify Dilke's emendation by substituting "lain" for "slept," but their substitution has no more authority than his, and all the arguments for the superiority of "And mine own conscience might have had the work / Brought home" still apply.

Does that mean it should or will be adopted in future editions? By the agreed-on rules of editing, yes; the emendation makes equally good sense of the text without doing anything but cutting two repetitive words, and it somewhat improves the meter. Our theory of what went wrong to produce the problem seems plausible.

On the other hand, the passage is less arresting without "slept at ease," which can be understood as De Flores's satirical version of the way Beatrice seems to think about the operations of conscience – an organ that sleeps until some immediate confrontation arouses it. He is, after all, awakening her conscience throughout the scene; given that intention on his part, Dilke's words are wonderfully relevant. So one can understand why future editors may not leap to adopt this textual reform.

The point of this excursion is not so much to change future texts of *The Changeling* as to suggest to new readers of English Renaissance drama that textual issues are interesting and important and not particularly difficult to gain access to. We should add that neither in this instance from *The Changeling* nor in the comments on "travel/travaile" in *Two Gentlemen of Verona* earlier do we suggest that modernizing or emending editors have made mistakes. They have made choices, and the choices they have made are subject to second-guessing. An ongoing process of mutual second-guessing is what makes editing fascinating, and it is also what makes "unediting," to borrow a term from Leah Marcus (Marcus, 1996), equally fascinating: going back to early printed texts partly in order to second-guess modernizing editors by looking for meanings their work has made it difficult to see.

"Unediting" is now possible for almost anyone with access to a networked university library. More and more libraries, including some public ones, have online access to facsimiles of the more than two hundred printed early modern plays, many of them almost entirely unread, and other early printed books. Not much work is required to become familiar with the conventions of Renaissance printing, and in future more and more students will gain that familiarity at the same time that they are studying modernized versions of standard plays and thus getting some familiarity with the literary conventions.

1.5   The Christian/Stoic Soul Under Duress: *The Duchess of Malfi*

One of the major constituents of human interiority in the Renaissance was the soul, seen as closed to other human beings but under the continual scrutiny of all-seeing God. In an era of religious wars and heresy trials, bringing forward the soul's true nature, under duress if necessary, was both a political objective and a natural aim of drama. Moreover, the heresy trial, as Katharine Eisaman Maus explains, exposed for examination not merely the alleged heretic, threatened with burning at the stake if he or she did not repent, but also the state religion in whose name this terrible exercise of force was undertaken. If the heretic did not repent and burned instead, the process demonstrated not only the overwhelming physical power of the state church but also the unrelenting spiritual strength of the martyr's faith: "the outcast's degradation and pain transform themselves into signs of the martyr's heavenly prestige" (Maus, 1995: 78). As an early preacher spreading the work of reformation put it in 1527 in London – after an official ban on Lutheranism, and well before Henry's break with Rome,

> If I should suffer persecution for preaching of the Gospel of God, yet there is seven thousand more that shall preach...therefore, good people, good people...think not you that if these tyrants and persecutors put a man to death...that he is an heretic therefore, but rather a martyr. (Brigden, 2000: 97)

Although in no sense controversially religious – English drama was forbidden overt commentary on religious matters in any case – John Webster's *The Duchess of Malfi* follows this pattern in its vindication of the interior strength of its heroine. It is one of the great plays of the English Renaissance, and we will consider it again. Here we focus on its treatment of the ways the power of interiority manifests itself in the soul's resistance to duress.

A beautiful, noble young widow, left at her husband's death to rule over Amalfi, the Duchess comes from a family that is hugely influential in the affairs of Italy. Her brother Ferdinand is "the great Calabrian duke" (1.1.86), and her other brother is a Cardinal who has come near to becoming Pope. Her brothers are deeply, in Ferdinand's case almost crazily, committed to keeping her a widow. Late in the play, Ferdinand reveals that they have a financial stake in her widowhood, and they may also have political reasons for their attempts to prevent her from remarrying. Ferdinand also finds the idea of her remarriage, and of any sexual activity on her part, emotionally disturbing. His jealousy of his family's honor verges on sexual obsession with his sister, although Ferdinand's quasi-incestuous preoccupation with the Duchess's physical being may be, as Frank Whigham has it, a "threatened aristocrat['s] ... desperate expression of the desire to evade degrading contamination by inferiors" (Whigham, 1996: 191) rather than sexual desire for her. In a process precisely designed to inflame Ferdinand's insecurities, the Duchess has fallen in love with her worthy, manly, honest, affectionate, but somewhat ineffectual steward, Antonio. A steward is an estate manager; given that the Duchess's estate is a small country, Antonio is a kind of secretary of the treasury. In a brilliant scene more relevant to intimacy than to interiority, the Duchess proposes to Antonio and marries him privately and secretly with only her maid as a witness.

Parts of this secret keep for a surprisingly long time. Ferdinand and the Cardinal have left a spy in the Duchess's household, however, the malcontent ex-convict Bosola. Nine months after the marriage, Bosola discerns that the

Duchess is pregnant, brings her into premature labor (perhaps inadvertently) by feeding her dung-ripened apricots that she greedily consumes (her craving itself being a clue to her pregnancy, as an overpowering desire for pickles or ice cream might be today). He reports back to his employers that the Duchess has given birth to a child, although he does not learn immediately who the father is. Ferdinand reacts hysterically to the letter bearing the news:

> FERDINAND Methinks I see her laughing,
>   Excellent hyena! Talk to me somewhat, quickly,
>   Or my imagination will carry me
>   To see her in the shameful act of sin.
> CARDINAL   With whom?
> FERDINAND Happily with some strong-thighed bargeman,
>   Or one o'th'woodyard, that can quoit the sledge
>   Or toss the bar, or else some lovely squire
>   That carries coals up to her privy lodgings.
> CARDINAL You fly beyond your reason.
> FERDINAND   Go to, mistress!
>   'Tis not your whore's milk that shall quench my wildfire,
>   But your whore's blood.
>
>   (2.5.38–49)

Given this brotherly resolution, it is not surprising that Ferdinand does his best, working through Bosola, to destroy his sister. Moreover, it is her private life, and thus in part her interiority, that he seeks first to know and then to injure. Several strange comments of Ferdinand's make it clear that the Duchess's combination of private selfhood and connection to him is what he finds unbearable. One comes immediately after the outburst above:

> CARDINAL   Come, put yourself
>   In tune.
> FERDINAND   So. I will only study to seem
>   The thing I am not. I could kill her now,
>   In you, or in myself, for I do think
>   It is some sin in us heaven doth revenge
>   By her.
> CARDINAL Are you stark mad?
>
>   (2.5.62–67)

That is, for Ferdinand the Duchess's act is partly his own and his brother's. Thus while its sexual pleasure excludes them, its moral and social taint is one they share.

The second comment, equally bizarre in the connection it proposes between the Duchess's affections and her brother's body, comes when the Duchess, mistakenly trusting Bosola after he praises Antonio, has disclosed that Antonio is her husband. The Cardinal moves swiftly to have the couple banished from Ancona, where they sought refuge in flight from Malfi. Under threat from Ferdinand, Antonio parts from the Duchess, taking their eldest son with him and leaving her with the two younger children. Bosola immediately enters with a troop of horsemen and takes her to a prison under Ferdinand's control. There Ferdinand visits her in pitch darkness – he vowed never to see her again when he discovered she was married – and pretends to give her his hand as a token of reconciliation:

> FERDINAND   I come to seal my peace with you.
>   Here's a hand,
> > *Gives her a dead man's hand.*
>   To which you vowed much love; the ring upon't
>   You gave.
> DUCHESS   I affectionately kiss it.
> FERDINAND   Pray do, and bury the print of it in your heart.
>   I will leave this ring with you for a love token,
>   And the hand, as sure as the ring; and do not doubt
>   But you shall have the heart too. When you need a friend,
>   Send it to him that owed it; you shall see
>   Whether he can aid you.
> DUCHESS   You are very cold.
>   I fear you are not well after your travel. –
>   Hah? Lights! Oh, horrible!
> FERDINAND   Let her have lights enough.
>
> > (4.1.43–53)

The hand, as Katherine Rowe argues, is the pledge of a contractual relation, and as such hand-giving has marked all the major transactions in the play. The giving of a severed dead hand here casts doubt on the validity of all such transactions by undermining the relation between interior will and the bodily agency that performs the willed act (Rowe, 1999: 89–110). What Ferdinand means to do is in one sense clear enough. He pretends to present her with his own hand in order to get her to accept a hand that (he pretends further through the line of sadistic double meanings) is the dead hand of her husband. It is a token of revenge against Antonio that he has, in fact, not succeeded yet in taking, but whose effect on his sister he wishes to experience. But by presenting her with a dead hand as if it were his own, he is symbolizing something else that is related to his earlier outburst to his brother: that in alienating himself from his sister, he has had to mutilate himself. Bosola will himself prove to be a kind of "dead hand" for Ferdinand, used to manipulate and finally to murder the Duchess. Ferdinand then casts Bosola off as a false instrument of Ferdinand's defective will. Before that happens, Bosola reproves his employer for excessive harshness (specifically, for the provision of waxwork bodies of Antonio and her children to follow up on the hand and persuade the Duchess that her family has been killed):

BOSOLA   Why do you do this?
FERDINAND   To bring her to despair.
BOSOLA   Faith, end here,
   And go no farther in your cruelty.
   Send her a penitential garment to put on
   Next to her delicate skin, and furnish her
   With beads and prayer books.
FERDINAND   Damn her! That body of hers,
   While that my blood ran pure in't, was more worth
   Than that which thou wouldst comfort, called a soul.
                   (4.1.117–125)

In this third outburst, Ferdinand in effect declares that the Duchess's soul, her essential individuality before God, her most privileged interiority, is less important than her physical relation to him. This is an aristocratic assertion (although a sacrilegious one), and it supports Whigham's claim that Ferdinand is above all committed to resisting contamination.

In response to this torment, the Duchess turns to a cultivation of a privileged interiority: that of the stoic whom the tyrant cannot break, or the saint whom the oppressor cannot bring to recantation. Looking at the dead hand and, as the stage direction has it, "*the artificial figures of Antonio and his children, appearing as if they were dead*"(4.1.55.1–3), she comments, "yond's an excellent property / For a tyrant"(4.1.65–66). Specifically recalling classical Roman stoic suicide, she summons one of its female exemplars, "Portia, I'll new-kindle thy coals again, / And revive the rare and almost dead example / Of a loving wife" (4.1.72–74). After Brutus's defeat by Marc Antony and Octavian, Brutus's wife Portia killed herself by putting live coals in her mouth. Brutus killed Julius Caesar because he believed Caesar was becoming a tyrant; thus by invoking Portia while accusing Ferdinand of tyranny, the Duchess reminds Ferdinand through Bosola that tyrants do not thrive and cannot triumph over the truly resolute. But as Bosola promptly points out, stoic suicide was for ancient pagan Romans, not Renaissance Catholic Italians: "Oh, fie! Despair? Remember / You are a Christian"(4.1.74–75). Although near despair, the Duchess does not succumb to it. She says to her maid Cariola in the following scene,

                           I'll tell thee a miracle:
I am not mad yet, to my cause of sorrow.
Th'heaven o'er my head seems made of molten brass,
The earth of flaming sulfur, yet I am not mad.
I am acquainted with sad misery
As the tanned galley-slave is with his oar;
Necessity makes me suffer constantly,
And custom makes it easy.
                   (4.2.23–30)

"Constantly" here means not only "all the time" but also 'with constancy," "exhibiting stoic virtue."

The Duchess moves, then, in the direction enjoined for Christians preserving an uncompromised interiority under oppression. She accepts the madmen her brother introduces to plague her with the comment to his servant, "Let them loose when you please, / For I am chained to endure all your tyranny" (4.2.59–60). Bosola comes to her in disguise as a bellman and introduces her executioners, with a coffin and the cords that will be used to strangle her, telling her that he carries "a present from your princely brothers" (4.2.161). In her reply, the Duchess continues to speak to her brothers through their agents: "Let me see it. / I have so much obedience in my blood, / I wish it in their veins to do them good" (4.2.163–5). She is both reminding them (especially Ferdinand) that they have not done away with blood connection by torturing her, and pointing out that she has a calm virtuous interior self-possession that she wishes they could share: "Tell my brothers / That I perceive death, now I am well awake, / Best gift is they can give or I can take" (4.2.220–23). And she dies explicitly likening herself to the martyr whose knowledge of interior truth has not been shaken by power imposed on her:

> EXECUTIONERS   We are ready. ... .
> DUCHESS   Pull, and pull strongly, for your able strength
>   Must pull down heaven upon me. –
>   Yet stay. Heaven gates are not so highly arched
>   As princes' palaces; they that enter there
>   Must go upon their knees. [*She kneels.*] Come, violent death
>   Serve for mandragora, to make me sleep! –
>   Go tell my brothers, when I am laid out,
>   They then may feed in quiet. *They strangle her.*
>   (4.2.224–234)

"Feed" in Renaissance English suggests animality, although less strongly than in Modern English (compare Hamlet's "What is a man, / If his chief good and market of his time / Be but to sleep and feed? A beast, no more" [4.4.34-6]). The Duchess's comment may be innocuous and self-denying, demonstrating her calm, generous spirit ("when I am dead, they may once again eat their meals in peace,"); it may be insulting ("when I am dead, they may go undisturbed to the trough"); it may be shocking ("when you have prepared my body, my brothers may come feed upon it in stealthy silence"). However one receives it, it is charged with a powerful reproach.

Thus the Duchess's death demonstrates the martyr's and stoic's logic by which a resolute inwardness defies and in the end demonstrates the failure of a tyrant. The Duchess herself is well aware of what she is doing. She says to Bosola of her brothers, "Let them, like tyrants, / Never be remembered but for the ill they have done!" (4.1.105-106). Bosola, having killed Ferdinand, says as he himself dies to the mortally wounded Cardinal,

> I hold my weary soul in my teeth;
> 'Tis ready to part from me. I do glory
> That thou, which stood'st like a huge pyramid
> Begun upon a large and ample base,
> Shalt end in a little point, a kind of nothing.
>
> (5.5.90–94)

And the Cardinal dies with a request to avoid the kind of memory the Duchess has willed upon him: "And now, I pray, let me / Be laid by and never thought of" (5.5.108–109). But the play makes sure that the "little point" in which the brothers end is our remembrance of their cruelty to their sister and her inward health and strength by contrast to their perversity.

1.6   How to Behave When You Have a Soul Always Already Damned: *Doctor Faustus*

We suggested at the beginning of this part that Renaissance ideas of the situation of the inward self differ in some ways from modern ones. *The Jew of Malta* creates a dangerous Jewish sensibility in violent resentment of Christian hypocrisy; *The Duchess of Malfi* demonstrates the resources of Christian consolation available to the Duchess, a strong-souled character largely immune to self-doubt. The title character of Marlowe's *Doctor Faustus* is both strong-minded and deeply self-doubting. In its presentation of his inward understanding of his spiritual situation, the play requires us to discuss in more detail aspects of Renaissance religious belief and unbelief. These are complex, because the Renaissance was a period of intense religious controversy. The Reformation – the birth of Protestant Christian churches opposing the Catholic Church of Rome, which had been the universal Christian church in Western Europe – was the chief political as well as theological influence on the sixteenth century in England. Henry VIII broke with Rome in the 1530s for dynastic reasons, when he could not get the Pope to agree to his desire for a divorce. In so doing, he established England as the first Protestant nation, although he did not substantially change doctrine aside from installing himself as Supreme Head of the English church. His son Edward VI instituted a Calvinist English church, exiling many committed Catholics and martyring some, after succeeding his father in 1547. Edward's half-sister Mary succeeded him in 1553 and restored Catholicism, burning resistant Protestants at the stake as heretics and earning the name

"Bloody Mary" as a result; Mary's half-sister Elizabeth succeeded her in 1558 and reestablished a Church of England that attempted by deliberate procedural vagueness about such contested matters as the substance of the wafer and wine at communion service to allow ceremonial participation by as many of her subjects as possible. Although it was sacramentally elastic, however, Elizabethan official religion was theologically Calvinist in that it held strongly to the doctrine that God predestines the elect for salvation and the reprobate for damnation. Here is the first paragraph of Article 17, "Of predestination and election," from a 1590 edition of the Thirty-Nine Articles that constituted the shared doctrines of the English church:

> Predestination to life, is the everlasting purpose of God, whereby (before the foundations of the worlde were layde) hee hath constantly decreed by his counsell secret to us, to deliver from curse and damnation, those whome he hath chosen in Christ out of mankinde, and to bring them by Christ to everlasting salvation, as vessels made to honour. Wherefore they which be indued with so excellent a benefit of God, be called according to Gods purpose by his spirite working in due season: they through grace obey the calling: they be justified freely: they be made formes of God by adoption: they bee made like the image of his onely begotten sonne Jesus Christ: they walke religiously in good workes, and at length by Gods mercy, they attaine to everlasting felicitie.   (Church of England, 1590: B1v)

Peter White notes that in the 1580s there were complaints from English Puritans that Article 17 "maketh no mention of reprobation" (White, 1992: 96). Nonetheless, as A. G. Dickens remarks in *The English Reformation*,

> article xvii cannot be glossed over by the phrase 'moderately Calvinistic'.... This is not the position of the moderate or 'sublapsarian' Calvinists, who at least conceded that the Fall was not predestined and that the election of the redeemed took place only thereafter. Article xvii still appears to contain the most rigorous 'supralapsarian' position – that the salvation of some men and (by implication) the damnation of others was from the first built into the very order of the universe.   (Dickens, 1964: 251–2)

And White sums up the church position on predestination by commenting that "however reluctant contemporaries were to admit it, the existence of doctrinal Puritanism can hardly be gainsaid" (White, 1992: 97). Dickens goes on to remark that, while the phrasing of article xvii is restrained and "urbane" (in that it omits to mention explicitly the prior ordination of the damnation of the reprobate), "the purely verbal nature of this restraint is stressed rather than concealed by the fact that article 17 hastens on to rather irrelevant considerations on the subject of human despair" (Dickens, 1964: 252). These "considerations" are, as we shall see, highly relevant to *Doctor Faustus,* however beside the theological point they may seem to Dickens:

> As the godly consideration of predestination and our election in Christ, is full of sweete, pleasant, and unspeakable comfort to godly persons, and such as feele in themselves the working of the spirit of Christ, mortifying the works of the flesh, and their earthly members, and drawing up their mind to high and heavenly things, ... : So, for curious and carnal persons, lacking the spirit of Christ, to have continually before their eyes the sentence of Gods predestination, is a most dangerous downefall, whereby the devill doth thrust them either into desperation, and into rechlesnesse of most uncleane living no lesse perilous then desperation.   (Church of England, 1590: B1v–B2r)

The Calvinist doctrine of the opening paragraph of article 17 (called *"double predestination"*) had harsh internal consequences for anyone who (i) accepted its truth and (ii) found him or herself to be prone to sin, recklessness, and unclean living. Moreover, a nation whose adults had been forced to change official faiths thrice in twenty years was naturally prone not only to religious schism but also to forms of doubt, and these persisted through Elizabeth's reign.

David Riggs's excellent biography of Marlowe focuses on the ways in which Marlowe's upbringing and education encouraged what would in his time have been called "atheism," although it differs in many ways from what we might mean by that term. Marlowe, a shoemaker's son, grew up in the cathedral town of Canterbury, attended the grammar school, and went to Cambridge on a scholarship; he was thus someone who owed his rise to prominence almost entirely to his intellectual abilities, nurtured on a humanist curriculum that emphasized pagan classics alongside Reformation theology. Riggs defines sixteenth-century "atheism" as the product of Calvinist doctrine, of political instability, and of literary and dialectical education:

> The Tudor programme of popular religious instruction created the agnostic reaction that it was meant to pre-empt. During the mid-1540s Sir John Cheke coined the word 'Atheists' to describe people who do not 'care whether there be a god or no, or whether ... he will recompense good Men with good things, and bad men with what is evil.' In 1549 Bishop Latimer notified the young King Edward VI 'that there be great many in England that say there is no soul, that think it is not eternal ... that think there is neither heaven nor hell.' ... Archbishop Cranmer drafted the first statute that distinguishes atheism from the older crime of heresy in 1553.   (Riggs, 2004: 29)

These "atheists," according to Riggs, were not in the position of modern atheists or agnostics who manage to live more or less tranquilly in a state of non-relation to religious discourse and to the idea of the divine.

Early modern unbelievers usually did not dispute the existence of God; they denied Gods capacity to intervene in their lives via the Son and the Holy Ghost. ... Within the world of post-Reformation Christianity, belief in God was inextricably linked to the fear of God. A deity who could not enforce his commandments – a God without sanctions – might as well not exist. Hence, anyone who rejected the immortality of the soul, the existence of heaven and hell (especially the latter) and the operations of Providence qualified as an atheist.   (Riggs, 2004: 29)

Such atheists were often the products of education in divinity, combined with the state's rapid alternation between Protestantism and Catholicism at mid-century. Riggs cites a humanist who commented that "men are nowadays glutted as it were with God's word, and therefore almost ready to vomit [it] up again," some by "turning to curious arts ... some Epicures, some Atheists" (Riggs, 2004: 30). Riggs also cites George Carleton, commenting that in 1572 "the realm is divided into three parties, the Papists, the Atheists and the Protestants" (Riggs, 2004: 30).

Moreover, the literary education sixteenth-century undergraduates received – especially their intensive study of Ovid – introduced them to a powerful counter-Christian understanding of creation: "Ovid's philosopher-hero Pythagoras ... in the last book of the *Metamorphoses* ... introduced Renaissance undergraduates to the ancient (un)belief system of Epicurus and his disciple Lucretius: hell is a fable, and belief in hell a craven superstition ... poets and rulers invented divine retribution to keep men in awe of authority" (Riggs, 2004: 88–89). Riggs sums up the presence of this material in Marlowe's work trenchantly:

> Tamburlaine invokes Ovid's creation myth to justify his winner-take-all ideology, and dies alluding to epicurean teachings on death. Small wonder that Marlowe's protagonist was soon dubbed 'that atheist Tamburlaine.' The epicurean Dr Faustus asserts that 'hell's a fable' (II.i.129). The Machiavellian Prologue to Marlowe's *Jew of Malta* boasts that: "I count religion but a childish toy, / And hold there is no sin but ignorance' (14–15). Atheism as such was not the issue in Marlowe's case. Renaissance academics and statesmen inherited the Roman view that philosophers and rulers were entitled to a sphere of private unbelief. Marlowe took the further, more provocative step of circulating epicurean ideas among the general public.   (Riggs, 2004: 89)

This view of Marlowe as the rash public representative of a large cohort of educated sixteenth-century skeptics allows us to reframe some basic questions raised by *Doctor Faustus*. In Marlowe's play, derived from a translation of a German account of the life of the historical Johannes Faust, a brilliant scholar is drawn to magic by the barrenness of the alternatives (philosophy, theology, and medicine). After consulting with magicians, he offers his soul to the devil for 24 years of life and the service of a demon, Mephistopheles. The contract, signed in his blood, is ratified, and the play takes Faustus through a series of rather trivial exercises of the power Mephistopheles has given him to the profound and powerful death scene in which the devils claim him. The play was published in two versions, the so-called A-text in 1604 and the longer B-text in 1616. The A-text was entered in the Stationer's Register in 1601 – that is, the intention to print and sell it was declared by a particular member of that guild, and rights over that play were thereby asserted by that publisher. In 1602, Philip Henslowe paid Samuel Rowley and William Birde four pounds "for ther adicyones in docter fostes" (Foakes, 2002: 206). We think at that point or just before it, Henslowe sent the now-superseded Marlovian A-text (itself a collaboration between Marlowe and someone else) to be printed, and that the longer B-text is a printed version that includes Rowley and Birde's "adicyones" (Marlowe, 1993: 71). Quotations in what follows are from the A-text, now held by most to be preferable as closer to what was performed in Marlowe's lifetime.

A question often encountered in teaching *Faustus* deals with an aspect of the hero's interior mental life. It is this: if Faustus is so smart, why does he often act so stupid? This question might be asked globally of Faustus's initial act of the play: why condemn yourself to eternal torture for temporal rewards, especially when it turns out that there is nothing very substantive that you want to accomplish in this world anyhow beyond impressing people? The question can also be asked (and I think is usually first asked) about particular moments early in the play. Most of the rest of this part will deal with such local moments. Critics have developed some fairly helpful answers to the global question – basically pointing out that almost everybody who lives a secular life at least risks eternal damnation by focusing on the temporal, and that Faustus thus is a super-Everyman, doing in a more egregious and self-conscious way what everyone else does without thinking it through.

Let us then look at some particular moments where Faustus seems stupid, where, as Riggs puts it, most interpreters conclude that he is "a bookish dunce,"(Riggs, 2004: 238). Such moments might include Faustus's response to Mephistopheles's rather magnificent evocation of hell (used later in its essentials by Milton's Satan):

> MEPHISTOPHELES: Hell hath no limits, nor is circumscribed
> In one self place, for where we are is hell,
> And where hell is must we ever be,
> And, to conclude, when all the world dissolves,
> And every creature shall be purified,
> All places shall be hell that is not heaven.
> FAUSTUS: Come, I think hell's a fable.

(2.1.122–8)

Faustus's reply is not only stupid in contradicting an eyewitness report from someone who would surely deny hell's reality if he could, it is also graceless, breaking the rhythm of Marlowe's mighty line. Why does Marlowe do it? Could the metrical anomaly be there to draw our attention to something that Faustus is up to?

Similarly, in Faustus's opening soliloquy, he is notoriously partial in his quotation from a Latin Bible that, as Riggs points out, turns out to be, in fact, Marlowe's or Faustus's translation back into Latin from English:

> When all is done, divinity is best.
> Jerome' Bible, Faustus, view it well.
> [*He reads.*] '*Stipendium peccati mors est*' Ha!
> '*Stipendium*,' etc.
> 'The reward of sin is death.' That's hard.
> [*He reads.*] '*Si pecasse negamus, fallimur,*
> *Et nulla est in nobis veritas.*'
> 'If we say that we have no sin,
> We deceive ourselves, and there's no truth in us.'
> Why then belike we must sin,
> And so consequently die.
> Ay, we must die an everlasting death.
> What doctrine call you this? *Che serà, serà?*
> 'What will be, shall be'? Divinity, adieu!
>   (1.1.37–50)

Note that once again Faustus's inadequate response breaks the rhythm of the line. Generations of professors have pointed out that Faustus leaves off the redemptive half of each of his scriptural verses. David Bevington's Norton introduction is representative:

> Any good Christian in Marlowe's audience would presumably know, however, that Faustus is quoting selectively and unfairly, playing games with the profundities of Christian faith that concede the inevitable sinfulness of humankind only to insist that God's great mercies are open to those who truly repent. From the start, Faustus betrays himself as a fool ...   (Bevington *et al.*, 2002: 246).

As Riggs points out, however, Faustus's misleading combination of half a line from Romans with half a line from the first epistle of John in fact distills the essence of Calvinist double-predestination from the point of view of a reprobate: the wages of reprobation is death; and if we deny our reprobation, there's no truth in us. Riggs comments,

> The so-called 'devil's syllogism' based on Romans 6:23 and 1 John 1:8 held a special fascination for Marlowe's contemporaries because it so closely resembled the Calvinist dogma adopted in England and Württemburg. Calvin too isolates the first half of Romans 6:23 and insists that 'all sin is mortal'. Article 15 of

the Church of England ended with the first half of 1 John 1:8 followed by a full stop. The Thirty-Nine Articles that constituted the Elizabethan Church nowhere suggest that all who confess their sins will be forgiven; on the contrary, God reserves the gift of grace only for the elect, who feel in themselves the working of the Spirit of Christ ...

So, for curious and carnal persons, lacking the Spirit of Christ, to have continually before their eyes the sentence of God's Predestination is a most dangerous downfall.

Critics rightly point out that Faustus is hideously mistaken about the Bible; but the Church he is rejecting has taught him to make precisely these mistakes. Marlowe, who had already been taxed with atheism, unveils in *Dr Faustus* the ecclesiastical basis of his own unbelief.   (Riggs, 2004: 240)

This suggests that the errors, and perhaps the stupidities, of Doctor Faustus may be part of an ironic strategy on Marlowe's part, and Riggs's way of resolving the problem they raise is to pose Doctor Faustus's own evident fictionality as the governing irony of the play:

Marlowe ... used the visual and auditory effects available in the playhouse to instill belief in hell and the devil. He used his poetic gift of irony, indirectness and erudite allusion to notify patient judges that Dr Faustus is a fictional being – a character in a book or an unwitting actor in the theatre of God's judgments. Marlowe's play appealed both to true believers and to freethinking skeptics.   (Riggs, 2004: 247)

This is a very fruitful suggestion. But we offer a somewhat different account of the way the play creates a double audience for itself or a double impression in individual readers and viewers.

It is possible to see Faustus as a more intelligible intellectual, rather than entirely as a transparent metafiction. Many of his apparently stupid replies to Mephistopheles are performative speech acts sketching an atheist stance. The key to this way of looking at Faustus, in our view, is a particularly puzzling, initially ludicrous exchange between Faustus and Mephistopheles. Mephistopheles gives his greatest speech, and Faustus gives one of his most bumptious and aesthetically unappreciative replies:

> MEPHISTOPHELES: Why, this is hell, nor am I out of it.
> Think'st thou that I, who saw the face of God
> And tasted the eternal joys of heaven,
> Am not tormented with ten thousand hells
> In being deprived of everlasting bliss?
> O Faustus, leave these frivolous demands,
> Which strike a terror to my fainting soul!

FAUSTUS: What, is great Mephistopheles so passionate
For being deprived of the joys of heaven?
Learn thou of Faustus manly fortitude,
And scorn those joys thou never shalt possess.
Go bear these tidings to great Lucifer:
Seeing Faustus hath incurred eternal death
By desp'rate thoughts against Jove's deity,
Say he surrenders up to him his soul…

(1.3.78–92)

"Learn thou of Faustus manly fortitude." What does this mean? Surely Faustus is not merely being arrogant and self-aggrandizing here. He is saying to Mephistopheles, "Stop being such a whinging devil and pay attention to how a resolute human being deals with the spiritual situation we share. Act like a Renaissance epicurean atheist (of the kind Riggs has so usefully described) and 'scorn those joys you never shall possess.'" Why never? To offer a tendentious paraphrase in the Empsonian manner, Faustus says to Mephistopheles, "Because we exemplars of manly fortitude know, as surely as you devils do too, that we are reprobates who have 'incurred eternal death' by the very way we think about God. But unlike you, we find something better to do than whine about it: we construct an alternative intellectual framework in which God's judgments do not matter."

Given this understanding of Faustus's attitude – an attitude Faustus here, consciously as it were, strikes at a moment where he must to some degree feel the overwhelming spiritual pathos of Mephistopheles's grief at being deprived of the divine presence – many of Faustus's odd remarks become understandable. Comments like "I think hell's a fable," spoken to a being who has just come from there, count as speech acts demonstrating the rhetorical possibility of defying God, exemplifications for Mephistopheles of "manly fortitude" vis-a-vis God and God's system. Remember that Richard Baines and Thomas Kyd – the first in a letter denouncing Marlowe to the Privy Council, the second in testimony under torture ordered by that Council, both accuse Marlowe of leading others to atheism (see Riggs, 2004: 328). In the Faustus–Mephistopheles relation we have a weird paradigm of intimate conversation between two men, both knowing themselves at odds with God, in which the bolder of the two tries to get the other to put a brave face on his irreversible deprivation.

Blaise Pascal, writing half a century after Marlowe's murder, famously proposed that however improbable the existence of God may be, the rewards of believing in God are so great that they justify belief in an improbability: God is a bet worth taking. This is known as "Pascal's wager." Faustus anticipates Pascal, but in reverse, and as Riggs has shown, he is exemplary in this of the sixteenth-century "atheists." Faustus, convinced that he is reprobate, undertakes a kind of inverted Pascalian wager in which he balances the hideous near-certainty of eternal torment against the difficulty of sustaining unbelief in a God-saturated world. If only he can *not* accept God's power, he can perhaps escape damnation, or at any rate lead a decent life while he has it. Faustus certifies that he is damned "by desp'rate thoughts against Jove's deity" (1.3.91), but as Riggs helps us see, in sixteenth-century England one could easily pass *from* the conviction that one was damned *to* thoughts against God's deity. And Faustus appeals in a variety of ways to Mephistopheles to recognize in Faustus a superior accommodation to the exiled state: he declares to the newly summoned Mephistopheles, speaking of himself in the third person like a major league baseball player, "This word 'damnation' terrifies not him, / For he confounds hell in Elysium. / His ghost be with the old philosophers!"(1.3.60–63).

Moreover, Faustus's description of himself as damned by desperate thoughts presumably applies to his internal state before he takes up magic seriously at the opening of the play. We can, in fact, see elements of partly suppressed anxiety about Faustus's relation to God's judgments and mercy in the apparently cavalier dismissals of nonmagical fields of study in his opening soliloquy. He dismisses medicine because it cannot "make man to live eternally" (1.1.24). He dismisses law after quoting part of a phrase in Latin, "*Exhaereditare filium non potest pater nisi – *"; this means "a father may not disinherit his son unless ... " Obviously, if Faustus is driven by a sense of being predestined to hell by God, he does not want to hear more about how a father can disinherit his sons. So he condemns law as "servile and illiberal" (1.1.36) – that is, consigning one to slavishness, and ungenerous in its basic terms – and turns to divinity. But, as we saw earlier, as soon as he thinks about theology he decides that he is disinherited: "'The reward of sin is death.' That's hard" (1.1.41). Faustus finally turns to magic as an affirmation of human mental strength, a strength that allows mental life to be a god unto itself: "his dominion that exceeds in this / Stretcheth as far as doth the mind of man. / A sound magician is a mighty god" (1.1.62–64). The opening soliloquy, then, illustrates what Maus means when she asserts that "the nature of theater in Marlowe's plays is refracted through what I would call a 'heretical conscience'" (Maus, 1996: 87). "Manly fortitude" of the sort Faustus claims to model for Mephistopheles consists in being a god for oneself.

So far this argument, although it differs from Riggs on what to make of Faustus's folly, is directly derived from his views about Marlowe and atheism. But what is one to make of the play's circumstantial refutation of the internalized and rejected Calvinism both Riggs and we see in Faustus?

The play's basic plot is, after all, inconsistent with double predestination. If Faustus were eternally destined to be damned by a God, however inscrutable that God's judgments, why should demonic agents strive so energetically to seduce or daunt him? They need not pretend to be active agents of God's will while awaiting his judgment, they already have it. If Faustus was predetermined to damnation since before time began, all they have to do is wait for him. If he is of the elect, nothing they can do could damn him. Obviously *they*, knowing themselves damned without reprieve, do *not* know this about Faustus. Nor do the Good Angel and the Old Man. Is it simply that Marlowe, despite his atheism, reworks a deeply Christian morality plot that originates in Catholic moral thinking, although, as David Bevington demonstrated in *From Mankind to Marlowe*, there is a long series of Protestant (and at least in intention Calvinist) moral drama between Marlowe and his Catholic precursors? Or is Marlowe actually thinking creatively within the ferment of late sixteenth-century Protestant doctrine about the issues of grace and predestination through this juxtaposition?

It is a coincidence, but we think a telling one, that in 1586, when Marlowe was coming down from Cambridge to London, Jacobus Arminius, a young Dutch theologian, returned from Geneva where he had studied with Calvin's chief disciple Theodore Beza to Leyden. In 1588, when Marlowe was, we think, beginning to write *Doctor Faustus*, Arminius undertook a defense of Calvin's doctrine of predestination against a Dutch theologian, a process that led him to his own reinterpretation of Romans, rejection of double predestination, and development of Arminian doctrines of the availability of grace even to the non-elect within a covenant involving election that became a key element in the development of Protestant doctrine. Similar views were developed independently in England in the 1580s and 1590s. Samuel Harsnett, later an archbishop himself, was censured by the Archbishop of Canterbury when he "attacked the harshness of the prevailing predestinarian doctrine in a famous sermon at Paul's Cross in 1584" (Woolrych, 2002: 36). That sermon aimed itself explicitly at the doctrine of double predestination, which Harsnett describes polemically as the belief that

> God should design many thousands of souls to Hell before they were, not in eye to their faults, but to his own absolute will and power, and to get him glory in their damnation. This opinion is grown huge and monstrous … and men do shake and tremble at it; yet never a man reaches David's sling to cast it down. (White, 1992: 99)

Harsnett ends by mapping what he sees as the quicksands of error surrounding the true path of the English church:

> To conclude, let us take heed and beware, that we neither (with the Papists) rely upon our free will; nor (with the Pelagian) upon our nature: nor (with the Puritan), *Curse God and die*, laying the burden of our sins on his shoulders, and the guilt of them at the everlasting doors: but let us fall down on our faces, give God the glory, and say, Unto Thee O Lord belong mercy and forgiveness. (White, 1992: 100, italics Harsnett's).

Marlowe doubtless knew about this sermon, given the controversy that followed it, and his Faustus exemplifies someone who is lost among these alternatives and who chooses, in effect, to make something creative and temporarily powerful out of the "curse God and die" option. Moreover, Marlowe could have heard similar argument at his university. Peter Baro and William Barrett preached and disputed against high Calvinism at Cambridge, and Baro at least did so during Marlowe's time there, although he was not officially censured by the Archbishop until 1595; he asserts the freedom of the will and God's interest in the contingency (as opposed to the necessity) of the sinner's sin and the good person's virtue in a disputation published in 1588 and delivered before Marlowe went down to London (see Baro, 1588: 515–20). These views that the Protestant way must include a less predetermined situation for sinners – views that well describe everything in *Doctor Faustus* except Doctor Faustus's own attitudes – got their most memorable summation in English poetry in the words of Milton's God in *Paradise Lost* (1667), describing a moral universe in which some are elect and some are not, but even those who are not should trust God to take an interest in their spiritual situation:

> Some have I chosen of peculiar grace
> Elect above the rest: so is my will.
> The rest shall hear me call, and oft be warned
> Their sinful state, and to appease betimes
> Th'incensed Deity, while offered grace
> Invites, for I will clear their senses dark
> What may suffice, and soften stony hearts
> To pray, repent, and bring obedience due.
> To prayer, repentance, and obedience due
> Although but endeavored with sincere intent
> Mine ear shall not be slow, mine eye not shut.
>   (Milton, 1998 3:183–192)

The spiritual power of Marlowe's play, its exposition of a profound crisis in the inward life of Marlowe and his generation, derives from its portrayal of a Calvinist atheist attempting to be a resolute Epicurean in a world frame that is Christian but not Calvinist. The play shows the brilliant, moving, but ultimately fairly hollow attempt at epicurean fortitude and self-consolation by a man convinced that the alternative is a passive conformist acquiescence in his own predestined damnation. But it sets the character exemplifying this attempt in a richly imagined spiritual universe that rejects predestined reprobation and damnation. Faustus may be a disappointing worldling who does not do much worthwhile with his hard-earned powers. But he is also multivalent figure for those who, raised in the wrong set of beliefs, misunderstand the possibilities of the world in which they cast off those wrong beliefs and thus lose the chance for the most meaningful kind of life. This kind of life story is not confined to those raised in Calvinist late-sixteenth-century England. People still map the developments in their inward lives according to their relations to the patterns of belief they have inherited. Many still try to get rid of aspects of inherited belief that they find stifling or unbelievable. When they attempt this, they still find that the alternatives they perceive as available are strongly conditioned by the belief systems they used to hold. For this reason, Faustus speaks profoundly for his age, and, by a set of analogies that will continue to hold as long as there are belief systems to cast off, for all time.

1.7   Obsession and Delusion: Comic Inwardness in *Every Man in His Humor*

The inwardness of tragedy is at least potentially our own; the inwardness of comedy is that of other people. Or, from another viewpoint, the interior life of the tragic hero is something we aspire to as well as fear; the interior life of the comic character is something we mock and feel superior to, even as we recognize it. The general idea that in comedy we look at people who are smaller and more limited than ourselves is as old as Aristotle's *Poetics*, but a particular connection between comedy and inwardness was established by George Chapman's highly successful new comedy of 1597, *A Humorous Day's Mirth*, and was extended in Ben Jonson's second surviving play, *Every Man in His Humor*, written and staged the following year. As the titles suggest, this was a comedy connected with the idea of the humors, the bodily fluids alleged in the ancient psychophysiology of Galen to govern each person's nature. We think of "humor" as that kind of activity that promotes laughter, and we think this largely because of the success of Renaissance comedy of humors combined with the failure and disappearance of Galenic humoral physiology. But in the Renaissance understanding of the body, a "humor" was one of four more or less fluid substances: blood, phlegm, choler or yellow bile, and melancholy or black bile. The prevailing relations among these in a particular person's body determined that person's temperament, and the temporary imbalance of one over another explained both moods and diseases (that is, both psychological and physiological states were understood in these terms). As Gail Kern Paster notes, in the English Renaissance "Every subject grew up with a common understanding of his or her body as a semipermeable, irrigated container in which humors moved sluggishly" (Paster, 1993: 8).

While we no longer believe in humoralism, and words like "black bile" and "choler" live on chiefly in footnotes in modern editions of old texts, the theory remains embedded in lots of living words and expressions. I have already mentioned "humor" and "temperament"; as Paster points out, "in English the symptomatological effects of the humors remain like archaic sediments in the ordinary language of the body: we catch 'cold,' are 'filled with' our emotions, are 'sanguine' or not about the weather (the stock market, the state of Western culture), are said to be in a good or bad humor" (Paster, 1993: 6).

Thus inwardness in Renaissance comedy and tragedy is related to humoralism: the material "inwardness" of characters and persons alike was conceived in terms of these dispositionally consequential balances. An oversupply of black bile made one melancholy – disposed, we would say, to depression, but also toward literature and philosophy; a lot of blood made one sanguine – disposed toward optimism, courage, love, and a life of action rather than contemplation; phlegmatic people are cautious and slow moving and often pale and heavy; choleric people are impetuous and quick to anger.

To make the humoral correspondences yet more suggestive, complex, and untestable, astrology, the theory that the situation of the stars and planets at the moment of one's birth had a determinative effect on one's life, was closely linked to the humoral understanding, in that the influence of the planets and stars manifested itself as humoral temperament. A person born when Jupiter was ascendant would tend to be sanguine, for instance, whereas Mars was a choleric influence and Saturn a melancholy one. Moreover, the humors had from classical times been linked to a theory that the four basic elements of the material world are earth (cold and dry), air (hot and wet), fire (hot and dry), and water (cold and wet); these are linked respectively to the humors, the planets, and the twelve houses of the zodiac, and as such live on in the sun-sign columns of daily newspapers.

A comedy of humors, then, has a significant physiology behind it, and lurking behind that a whole cosmology. But it is of course different from a medical or psychological treatise. By highlighting the idea of "humor" in his title and text, and by stressing that his comic characters think of themselves as having and indeed being swayed by "humors," Jonson emphasizes the way people's outward lives are often shaped by the desire to exhibit an interesting interior life, to develop a distinctive or fashionable temperament. Jonson does not in fact often suggest that outward behavior is in any way *determined* by an inward economy of sluggish fluids. But by running together a materialistic medical theory of mood and temperament with a satirical fascination with human susceptibility to fashions and to fantasies of self-construction, he explores a fascinating area of social feedback, in which our theories about the physical determination of patterns of social behavior in turn influence that behavior. (One might compare contemporary interest in the question of whether, and if so to what degree, sexual orientation inheres in one's genetic blueprint – or indeed, more generally, the contemporary belief in "genetic blueprints" for various temperamental factors. It may be simply true, for instance, that male homosexuality or heterosexuality is strongly shaped by physical differences in sexual response, but belief or disbelief in this theory will obviously influence both one's own behavior and one's attitudes toward the behavior of others.) Moreover, in Galenic theory (unlike modern genetics), the way one behaves can change the balance of one's humors, so the influences run both ways. That is, Galenic humoralism is thoroughly compatible with Aristotelian ideas about habituation: one can form one's humoral balance in desirable or undesirable ways by adhering to good or bad habits of behavior. At the same time, knowing one's own temperament will make it far easier to find the patterns of behavior that suit it. While, as Robert Watson puts it, Jonson's play treats a man in his humor as "in a melodramatic role that aggrandizes his true nature and his true role in the world" making him "monstrous" to others (Watson, 1987: 28), the play is also suffused with the possibility of a harmonious relation between humoral balance, self-understanding, and social role. This harmony, indeed, is what the play aims to encourage in its readers or spectators, although it does this largely by the provision of negative instances. Obvious examples of the ridiculous in the play would be Stephen's attempt to learn to be melancholy from Matthew and sanguine from Bobadill; but Wellbred and Edward's interest in the humors of others would count in the harmonious way, as a mode of self-cultivation. They are connoisseurs of folly who take full advantage of opportunities to enrich their internal lives with the spectacle around them. Both the connection to upper-class urban fashions and the multidirectional feedback involved in Jonson's "humor" is stressed when the educated servant Thomas Cash defines the term for the uneducated but lively minded water-carrier Cob:

> COB   Nay, I have my rheum, and I can be angry as well as another, sir.
> CASH   Thy rheum, Cob? Thy humor, thy humor! Thou mistak'st.
> COB   Humor? Mack, I think it be so, indeed; what is that humor? Some rare thing, I warrant.
> CASH   Marry, I'll tell thee, Cob: it is a gentleman-like monster, bred, in the special gallantry of our time, by affectation; and fed by folly.
> COB   How? Must it be fed?
> CASH   Oh, aye, humor is nothing if it be not fed. Did'st thou never hear that? It's a common phrase, 'Feed my humor.'
>
> (3.4.14–25)

Let us examine the plot of *Every Man in His Humor*. The play was first performed in 1598 in a version set in Florence. Jonson reset the play in contemporary London when he revised it before including it in his folio *Works* of 1616. Thus we have the play in two versions that differ somewhat in emphasis. Students usually read the English or Folio version, which many critics prefer (Watson, 1987: 235). But commentary refers often to the 1598 version, published as a quarto in 1601, which has Italian character names that often differ from the English ones in the Folio: Lorenzo Senior in the 1601 Quarto becomes Knowell in the Folio, his son Lorenzo Jr. becomes Edward Knowell; Thorello becomes Kitely, Prospero becomes Wellbred, Bobadillo becomes Bobadill, etc. We will reproduce both names the first time we refer to a character, then use the English names; citations refer to an edition of the Folio text with its English names and London settings (Jonson 1969; for a parallel-text edition see Jonson 1971).

The plot, like that of most comedies, is in part one of generational struggle, in which the old try to shape or repress the energies of the young and in the end fail to do so, but it is also (and this is more characteristically Jonsonian) a comedy in which the wiser delight in viewing and in exacerbating the folly of the foolish. Basically, the play is structured around three interlinked actions: (i) Prospero/Wellbred and Lorenzo Jr./Edward Knowell meeting in London in pursuit of entertaining folly (and, as it turns out, a wife for Edward); (ii) Lorenzo Sr./Knowell's pursuit of his son Edward into London in order to investigate and reprove his son's frivolity, assisted and then thwarted by his servant Musco/Brainworm; and (iii) Thorello/Kitely's attempts to get help from Giuliano/Downright to purge his household of Wellbred and Wellbred's associates, and get help from his servant Piso/Thomas Cash to assuage or confirm his jealousy of his new wife, Biancha/Dame Kitely. Entertaining folly turns out to be provided by practically everyone, but the characters singled out from the start as fools are Matheo/Matthew, the plagiarizing poet, Bobadillo/Bobadill the bragging theoretical soldier (discovered by Wellborn before the play begins, and offered to Edward Knowell as a reason to come to the city center), and Stepheno/Stephen, Edward's cousin, the country gull Edward brings along to entertain Wellborn. Cob and Doctor Clement/Justice Clement, at either end of the social spectrum, serve as observers and abettors of this action: collisions between plots occur preeminently at Cob's house (where Knowell goes to catch his son whoring; Kitely goes to catch his wife cuckolding him; and Dame Kitely goes to catch her husband committing adultery) and then at Clement's (where the final judgments on all are delivered).

All of these actions are bound up with the issues about self-conscious temperament we have been discussing under the heading of humors. At the beginning, after he intercepts Wellborn's letter, Knowell deplores the son's "humor" (1.1.16) for poetry and wit, just as he disapproves (more appropriately) of his idiotic nephew Stephen's addiction to new "gentlemanly" fashions, his tendency to spend his "coin on every bauble that you fancy, / Or every foolish brain that humors you" (1.1. 65–66). Even after learning that his father has intercepted and read the letter, Edward accepts the invitation and invites Stephen to accompany him (a third fool to go with the two Wellbred has promised), saying to himself that Stephen, who has just promised to be even "more proud, and melancholy, and gentleman-like" than he has been, "will do well for a suburb-humor; we may hap have a match with the city, and play him for forty pound" (1.3.110–115). Competition, even competition in serving up the most foolish companion, is at the heart of Jonsonian comedy.

Wellbred brings with him not only his pair of fools, Matthew and Bobadill (a part in which Charles Dickens would star in a famous nineteenth-century production of *Every Man In*), but also a second household with its own characteristic tensions, mostly between the older Kitely, a rich merchant whose humor is jealousy of his new younger wife (Wellbred's sister), and distrust and dismay at the liveliness Wellbred's young companions have brought to his staid household. Kitely asks his brother-in-law Downright, a choleric country squire in town for a visit, to chase away Wellbred's friends, confiding to Downright why he fears to confront Wellbred himself. We quote at some length, because the passage illustrates Jonson's treatment of "humor" as a concept and as a temperament, and also shows the wonderful vividness of his comic verse:

> Nay, more than this, brother, if I should speak,
> He would be ready from his heat of humor
> And overflowing of the vapor in him
> To blow the ears of his familiars
> With the false breath of telling what disgraces
> And low disparagements I had put upon him.
> Whilst they, sir, to relieve him in the fable,
> Make their loose comments upon every word,
> Gesture, or look I use; mock me all over,
> From my flat cap unto my shining shoes;
> And, out of their impetuous rioting fant'sies,
> Beget some slander that shall dwell with me.
> And what would that be, think you? Marry, this.
> They would give out (because my wife is fair,
> Myself but lately married, and my sister
> Here sojourning a virgin in my house)
> That I were jealous! Nay, as sure as death,
> That they would say. And how that I had quarreled
> My brother purposely, thereby to find
> An apt pretext to banish them my house.
> (2.1.93–112)

But of course, Kitely *is* jealous, although his jealousy may be part of a set of distrustful inner tendencies signaled by his offering, then withdrawing his key from his "trusted" servant Cash (2.1.3) and by his already noted suspicions that he is or will be mocked by the young. Their mockery is attributed to a combination of inner factors, "the heat of humor / And overflowing of the vapor in him" – hot humors worked on the brain by exuding "vapors" or "spirits" (see Paster, 1993: 73) – with external social facts like Kitely's "flat cap," which signals his status as a non-gentleman, and his "shining shoes," which may signal his intense desire to be unsustainably clean and respectable. Like the balcony scene in *The Jew of Malta*, Kitely's self-begotten jealousy seems to have made an impression on Jonson's contemporary Shakespeare, who, according to the Jonson Folio, acted in the 1598 first performances of the play, probably as Lorenzo Sr. Certainly the extended aside in the following text, in which Kitely lays out his jealousy of his affectionate and blameless wife and the social and personal insecurities connected with it, seems to have contributed to Shakespeare's unpacking of the jealous interiority of Othello in 1605 or so; Othello's name is of course a near anagram of "Thorello" (see Lever, 1971: xxiv–xxvi and McDonald, 1979: 56–7).

> Bane to my fortunes! What meant I to marry?
> I, that before was ranked in such content,
> My mind at rest, too, in so soft a peace,
> Being free master of mine own free thoughts –
> And now become a slave? What? Never sigh,
> Be of good cheer, man: for thou art a cuckold –
> 'Tis done, 'tis done! Nay, when such flowing store,
> Plenty itself, falls in my wives lap,
> The *cornu-copiae* will be mine, I know.
>   (3.6.14–22)

"*Cornu-copiae*," the mythical "horn of plenty," here refers to the invisible horns said to adorn the forehead of deceived husbands, called "cuckolds" in a word that derives from the practice of the cuckoo, a bird that lays its eggs in other birds' nests. There is a characteristically intense condensation of a variety of meanings: Kitely provides plenty of money and amusement for his young wife, who will give him horns of plenty in return; Kitely's rich nest houses the interlopers Wellborn and friends who will deposit their eggs; the "flows" of social and sexual life Kitely has set in motion by marrying are now overwhelming him and depriving him of the freedom and "free thoughts" he had before marriage; Kitely's social "rank" that used to bring him "such content" now becomes a source of his insecurity and torment. All of this is "humorous" partly because it is all Kitely's self-devised fiction – that is, it has no basis in Dame Kitely's behavior, and derives rather from the massive disruption of Kitely's humoral and social balance that has occurred with marriage. But it is also literary, that is, it is devised partly from Kitely's internalization of dramatic attitudes. When Justice Clement orders all the unbalanced characters to banish their dominant humors rather than feed them, Kitely renounces his jealousy (not entirely convincingly) by suggesting its point of origin:

> JUSTICE CLEMENT   Come, I conjure all the rest to put off all discontent. You,
>   Mr. Downright, your anger; you, Master Knowell, your cares; Master
>   Kitely and his wife, their jealousy.
>   For I must tell you both, while that is fed,
>   Horns i' the mind are worse than o' the head.
> KITELY   Sir, thus they go from me – [*He embraces his wife*] Kiss me,
>   sweetheart.
>   See, what a drive of horns fly in the air,
>   Winged with my cleansèd and my credulous breath.
>   Watch 'em, suspicious eyes, watch where they fall.
>   See, see! On heads that think th'have none at all!
>   Oh, what a plenteous world of this will come!
>   When air rains horns, all may be sure of some.
>   I ha' learned so much verse out of a jealous man's part in a play.
>   (5.5.64–78)

The "heads that think th'have none at all" are those of the men in the audience, who are invited by the speech to watch one another with "suspicious eyes." Kitely "cures" himself of jealousy by in effect universalizing it. As Othello says, "'Tis destiny unshunnable, like death" (3.3.291). Leontes, Shakespeare's jealous protagonist in *The Winter's Tale*, comments to the assembled company – again including the theatre audience –

> There have been,
> Or I am much deceived, cuckolds ere now;
> And many a man there is, even at this present,
> Now while I speak this, holds his wife by th' arm,
> And little thinks she has been sluiced in 's absence
> And his pond fished by his next neighbor, by
> Sir Smile, his neighbor.
>   (1.2.190–196)

"Many thousands on's / Have the disease and feel 't not" (1.2.206–207), Leontes adds.

These are, as Kitely puts it, jealous men's parts in a play, and *The Winter's Tale* at this point seeks, as *Every Man In* does, to spread the anxieties of the speaker to its audience, even though *The Winter's Tale* as a whole shows Leontes's jealousy to be perverse. Othello and Leontes echo Kitely's role rather than being the roles Kitely learned his attitudes and words from, however: Kitely's "humor" is evidently derived from the general popularity of comic plots in which an older merchant's wife is seduced by younger gallants. These plots are particularly common (indeed almost mandatory) in the Italian *commedia dell'arte* evoked in the original Italian setting of *Every Man In*.

Kitely's remark highlights the role of literature, read or viewed, in shaping the humors Jonson holds up for mockery. The irrepressible military boaster Bobadill has, as Jonas Barish points out, become able through "years of poring over books on the duello" to "mesmerize not only Matheo and Stephano but himself into a belief in his own valor" (Watson, 1987: 31). Although Bobadill gets beaten and shown to be a coward, he has bounced back from this by the ending, but the plagiarist Matthew has all his poems – stolen from Marlowe and Daniel and other popular poets – ceremonially burnt by Clement at the end of the play. As Anne Barton points out, in both the quarto and folio texts, "the subject of poetry remains deeply embedded, beyond the reach of revision, within the action of the play. Indeed, to a great extent, it can be seen to govern the real, as opposed to the superficial, plot of the comedy" (Barton, 1984: 54). That real plot, according to Barton, revolves around the kind of "poetry" involved in Brainworm's literary role-playing as he manipulates and exposes other characters, and the question of whether such actions reveal a worthwhile truth and thus exonerate Jonson himself from being the kind of manipulator Brainworm is. Robert Watson, reacting to some extent to Barton, emphasizes Clement's literary role-playing and his final actions, noted earlier, in liberating Kitely, Knowell, and Dame Kitely from the constricting roles they have fallen into: "the play about redeeming life from its bondage to theater and theater from its bondage to convention here weaves the two liberations into a unitary celebration" (Watson, 1987: 45). Both Barton and Watson see the play's Folio prologue as a vital clue to Jonson's intentions, and as in some ways a key to the purpose Jonson follows in much of his drama. Jonson placed *Every Man In* as the first play in the 1616 Folio, giving it the position *The Tempest* enjoys in Shakespeare's 1623 Folio, and of course his prologue stands at the opening of his play:

> Though need make many poets, and some such
> As art and nature have not bettered much,
> Yet ours for want hath not so loved the stage
> As he dare serve th'ill customs of the age
> Or purchase your delight at such a rate
> As, for it, he himself must justly hate.
>
> (Prologue 1–6)

"Ours," our poet, Jonson himself, leaves open the possibility that he turns to the stage out of "need," and acknowledges moreover that many who have written for money have been among the best. (The Jonson of the 1598 production was very needy indeed – bankrupt and recently convicted of felony manslaughter in the death of Gabriel Spencer; the Jonson of the 1616 folio in which this prologue appeared was at the height of an extremely successful career as public playwright, court entertainer, and arbiter of taste, and thus was far less needy.) But Jonson has not, he claims, been governed by his need to such an extent that he tries above all to please his audience by pandering to its weaknesses. Jonson thus proposes a fascinating relation between stage poets and their medium: one in which a responsible poet, not enslaved by his own need for money, must strive to maintain his self-respect against "th'ill customs of the age" and the tastes of the audience for shameful "delight." Catering to the audience's delight, however profitable it might be, would make him hate himself. Ill customs of the age may be literary, or they may be moral: for Jonson it is clear that bad literary taste is not a morally neutral phenomenon. Jonson goes on, however, to describe forms of popular drama that may involve absurdities of representation, but do not in any evident way deprave their audiences:

> Or purchase your delight at such a rate
> As, for it, he himself must justly hate:
> To make a child, now swaddled, to proceed
> Man, and then shoot up, in one beard and weed,
> Past threescore years; or, with three rusty swords,
> And help of some few foot-and-half-foot words,
> Fight over York and Lancaster's long jars,
> And in the tiring-house bring wounds to scars.
> (Prologue 5–12)

This echoes a famous complaint about the time-crunching plots of romantic dramas in Sir Philip Sidney's "Defense of Poesy" (1595): "ordinary it is, that two young Princes fall in love, after many traverses she is got with child, delivered of a fair boy: he is lost, groweth a man, falleth in love, and is ready to get another child, and all this in two hours space." Jonson's comment on how "three rusty swords" reenact the Wars of the Roses also echoes Sidney's mockery of the way history is portrayed in such plays: as Sidney puts it, "two armies fly in, represented with four swords and bucklers ... " (Jackson, 1969: 186). Again, though, we may ask, what is there about the provision of romantic drama to eager audiences that might make one hate oneself? Here is where the humoral physiology evoked in Jonson's title and unmentioned in his Prologue comes in. Bad unrealistic drama feeds absurd humors and thus abets ill customs. A humor is, as Cash puts it, a "monster, bred ... by affection, and fed by folly" (3.4.21–2). Good realistic drama, on the other hand, can help reattune its audiences to their actual lives:

> ... deeds and language such as men do use,
> And persons such as Comedy would choose
> When she would show an image of the times,
> And sport with human follies, not with crimes –
> Except we make 'em such by living still
> Our popular errors, when we know they'are ill.
> (Prologue 21–26)

Realistic comic drama, then, is offered as an antidote to habituation in folly, "popular errors," a habituation that Jonson explains partly physically, partly culturally, as "humorous." If literature is to be a moral agent, operating to alter the inward selves of his auditors and readers, their interiority needs to be, as Hamlet puts it to Gertrude, "made of penetrable stuff" (3.4.37). Humors, the prime candidates for being that "stuff," are subject in Jonson's comedy to a therapy that resembles modern biofeedback: they are excited and exercised in order to be rebalanced and rendered more harmonious. The therapy is administered by laughter, that complex mental–physical activity that, we can all testify, actually does seem to change our inner temper.

> I mean such errors as you'll all confess
> By laughing at them – they deserve no less;
> Which when you heartily do, there's hope left, then,
> You that have so graced monsters may like men.
> (Prologue 27–30)

The last line seems to mean "after showing favor to the monsters of other playwrights, and perhaps to the humoral monsters of my comedy, you'll be in a position to like me and each other" (Jackson, 1969: 38). Jonson's prologue emphasizes that laughing "heartily" is a process of making oneself *like* – both in the sense of affection and the sense of resemblance – what is good and attractive in other human beings.

Jonson was keenly aware and in some ways an imitator of the Latin comedies of Plautus and Terence, which were in turn modeled on the Greek "new comedy" of Menander. Northrop Frye summarizes the key characteristics of "new comedy":

> New Comedy unfolds from what may be described as a comic Oedipus situation. Its main theme is the successful effort of a young man to outwit an opponent and possess the girl of his choice. The opponent is usually the father (*senex*) ... The father frequently wants the same girl, and is cheated out of her by the son ... The girl is usually a slave or courtesan, and the plot turns on a *cognitio* or discovery of birth which makes her marriageable. Thus it turns out that she is not under an insuperable taboo after all but is an accessible object of desire, so that the plot follows the regular wish-fulfillment ... New Comedy is certainly concerned with the maneuvering of a young man toward a young woman, and marriage is the tonic chord on which it ends. The normal comic resolution is the surrender of the *senex* to the hero, never the reverse   (McDonald, 2004: 93)

Although Frye comments that "the conventions of New Comedy are the conventions of Jonson and Moliere," in fact Jonson's comedies are rarely driven by the sexual desire of the young in this clear way, and they do not often end in a marriage, although one is in the offing in *Every Man In*. Katharine

Eisaman Maus links this to Jonson's adoption of a Roman stoic attitude that sees passionate desire as something to be avoided rather than something to be fulfilled (see Maus, 1984: 80–82). This makes the sexual aspects of Jonsonian comedy peculiar among Renaissance plays, as most other Renaissance plays resemble most modern romantic fictions – novels, movies, plays, sex manuals – in regarding desire as something that ought to reach some sort of fulfillment. This also means that Jonsonian "inwardness" is liable to emphasize self-command and the imposition of self on an outer world as more significant than erotic imagination.

1.8   *Epicene*

These considerations bear strongly on Jonson's *Epicene*, old spelling *Epicœne*, also sometimes titled *The Silent Woman*, a comedy that everyone concedes is brilliant and entertaining but that few are sure how to evaluate in terms of the author's sympathies. "Inwardness" is not a word one associates easily with *Epicene*. Even the delusional and uncomfortable inner life of Kitely in *Every Man In* seems deep and cultivated by comparison with that of the characters in *Epicene*, who are conspicuously outward in their orientation, preoccupied with the performances they are giving or arranging for others. Although claims of learning are important status tokens in the play, we never see anyone reading anything, and Sir John Daw is mocked for owning books he never opens:

> CLERIMONT   They say he is a very good scholar.
> TRUEWIT   Aye, and he says it first. A pox on him! A fellow that pretends
> only to learning, buys titles, and nothing else of books in him.
> (1.2.74–77)

Clerimont, Truewit, and Dauphine, the three male friends at the play's center, are distinguished from all others in the play by their successful mastery of leisured urban culture. Young men about town who do not have any particular profession except to be young men about town, they are the models for the rakes and beaux of Restoration Comedy and more recent urbanites such as those in Oscar Wilde's *The Importance of Being Earnest* or the members of the Drones Club in the comic novels of P.G. Wodehouse (see Barton, 1984: 120 and Maus, 2002: 776). They have both class and street smarts, and they stand out as the genuine article amid the rest of the characters who aspire to have these things but do not prove able to cope. Nonetheless, given the morally strenuous nature of Jonson's imagination, *Epicene*'s protagonists do not so much float through intrigue (with unquenchable good cheer like Wodehouse's Bertie Wooster or unflappable nonchalance like Wilde's Algernon Moncrieff), but rather scheme and struggle, dominating the fools around them but competing with one another. Inward selfhood for them rests on a continually tested and necessarily rather fragile sense of superiority to most of the people they encounter.

There is one way, however, in which *Epicene* stands out as a study of inwardness: in its portrait of the obsessive and solitary Morose. Interiority is, after all, never more strongly and scarily manifested than in madness, where interior mental life carries people entirely out of normal conversational exchanges into a private world. Reclusive privacy and eccentricity, while distinct from madness, are like it in that they represent a high value placed on inner mental life and a resistance to conversation. Morose, the main "humor" character in *Epicene*, exemplifies this choice. The target of most of the plots in the play, Morose is a rich old man whose addiction to silence and his own company sorts oddly with his habitation in the heart of London. He is isolated from others by the strength and idiosyncrasy of his inward life. He claims to have abnormally sensitive ears, but his desire to live surrounded by mutes also derives from frank selfishness: as he comments, he only likes listening to himself – "all discourses but mine own afflict me; they seem harsh, impertinent, and irksome" (2.1.4–5). Given this, it is not surprising that he is a bachelor surrounded by deferential servants. Nonetheless, as the play begins, anger at his nephew Dauphine (who has obtained a knighthood, either by purchase or by the solicitation of noble friends, and thus gained social precedence over the uncle from whom he hopes to inherit) moves Morose to think about marriage. A complex intrigue follows, as Truewit attempts to dissuade Morose from marriage by impersonating a royal messenger and haranguing Morose brilliantly about the horrors of matrimony. This is a scene in which the one-sidedness of Morose's dialogues with his servants (in which they respond to his monologues with signs or whispers) is completely reversed, as Truewit bears down all Morose's objections and blows a trumpet to announce his arrival and departure. Truewit leaves behind the impression that he came at Dauphine's request, but Dauphine, without telling Truewit (although he does include Clerimont in part of the secret), has quietly arranged for Morose's barber Cutbeard to introduce a candidate wife to Morose: a young woman famous for silence and modesty. Morose interviews her:

> Very well done, Cutbeard. Give aside now a little, and leave me to examine her condition and aptitude to my affection. (*He goes about her and views her.*) She is exceeding fair and of a special good favor, a sweet composition or harmony of limbs; her temper of beauty has the true height of my blood. The knave hath exceedingly well fitted me without; I will now try her within. –Come near, fair gentlewoman. Let not my behavior seem rude, though unto you, being rare, it may haply appear strange. (*She curtsies.*) Nay, lady, you may speak though Cutbeard and my man might not, for of all sounds, only the sweet voice of a fair lady has the just length of mine ears. (2.5.14–25)

"Just length of mine ears," like "true height of my blood," is a materialistic way of saying "in measurable agreement with my physical needs," but it also unintentionally implies that Morose has long ears like an ass. Morose continues:

> I beseech you say, lady, out of the first fire of meeting eyes, they say, love is stricken: do you feel any such motion suddenly shot into you from any part you see in me? Ha, lady? (*Curtsy.*) (2.5.25–28)

This wonderfully direct and yet presumptuous question – presumptuous as it describes the lover's hope without any of the fear that would normally go with it – again receives only a sign in reply, and Morose again gives Epicene guarded encouragement to speak:

> Alas, lady, these answers by silent curtsies from you are too courtless and simple. I have ever had my breeding in court, and she that shall be my wife must be accomplished with courtly and audacious ornaments. Can you speak, lady? (2.5.28–32)

We do not know whether Morose's alleged courtliness is a pose he assumes to test whether Epicene will suddenly blossom into "audacious" loquacity, or whether it is part of his self-consequence to imagine himself in these terms (he has, after all, just been afflicted by Truewit posing as a court messenger). In any case, Epicene responds in just the way he would like, by deferring to his authority:

> EPICENE (*she speaks softly*) Judge you, forsooth.
> MOROSE What say you, lady? Speak out, I beseech you.
> EPICENE Judge you, forsooth.
> MOROSE O'my judgment, a divine softness! But can you naturally, lady, as
> I enjoin these by doctrine and industry, refer yourself to the search of my
> judgment, and – not taking pleasure in your tongue, which is a woman's
> chiefest pleasure – think it plausible to answer me by silent gestures so
> long as my speeches jump right with what you conceive?
> (*Curtsy.*) Excellent! Divine! (2.5.33–42)

Having found, he thinks, a silent woman he can live with, Morose resolves to marry her immediately, gloating at what this will mean for Dauphine. In assuming that Dauphine has acquired his knighthood specifically in order to domineer over his uncle, Morose reveals much of his own motivation for antisocial isolation:

> Oh, my felicity! How I shall be revenged on mine insolent kinsman and his plots to fright me from marrying! This night I will get an heir, and thrust him out of my blood like a stranger. He would be knighted, forsooth, and thought by that

means to reign over me; his title must do it. No, kinsman, I will now make you bring me the tenth lord's and the sixteenth lady's letter, kinsman; and it shall do you no good, kinsman. Your knighthood itself shall come on its knees and it shall be rejected; it shall be sued for its fees to execution and not be redeemed; it shall cheat at the twelvepenny ordinary, it knighthood, for its diet all the term-time, and tell tales of it in the vacation to the hostess; or it knighthood shall do worse, take sanctuary in Cole Harbor and fast. (2.5.96–108)

Jonson's unromantic attitude toward sexual feeling is at its clearest here, as Morose, planning his wedding night, thinks of his procreative act as aggression toward another man: he intends to "thrust [Dauphine] out" of his inheritance. Morose is not only fantasizing about revenge in this, he is also pointing to the insecure social position of young men like Dauphine, Truewit, and Clerimont who, without occupations, wait to inherit estates that will underwrite their social positions and habits. Should something go wrong with the inheritance, they will be unsupported urbanites, subject to debt and degradation. Morose, describing the descent of "it knighthood" in sarcastic baby talk, imagines a desperate Dauphine marrying a prostitute (rather than the heiress he presumably is waiting for) so that he will not starve: "the best and last fortune to it knighthood shall be to make Doll Tearsheet or Kate Common a lady, and so it knighthood may eat" (2.5.124–126).

Morose's interiority, then, is unattractive. It is not, however, unimpressive. At the end of the play, in a moment that, as numerous critics point out, turns audience sympathies somewhat toward Morose, he reveals that his isolation is the result of his construal of a paternal admonition. Morose at this point has been beaten down: his new wife has turned out to be garrulous, bossy, and sociable; his quiet house has been invaded by a raucous wedding party led by the Collegiate Ladies bent on inducting Epicene into their society of free conversation and sexual independence, and, in desperation, Morose seeks a divorce. He addresses two characters he believes to be a canon lawyer and a parson (they are in fact the barber Cutbeard and Tom Otter, husband of one of the Collegiate Ladies, in disguise):

Be swift in affording me my peace, if so I shall hope any. I love not your disputations or your court-tumults. ... My father, in my education, was wont to advise me that I should always collect and contain my mind, not suffering it to flow loosely; that I should look to what things were necessary to the carriage of my life and what not, embracing the one and eschewing the other. In short, that I should endear myself to rest and avoid turmoil, which now is grown to be another nature to me, so that I come not to your public pleadings or your places of noise. ... You do not know in what a misery I have been exercised this day, what a torrent of evil! My very house turns round with the tumult! (5.3.43–59)

Having been a blocking figure – that is, the older male relative who seeks to prevent the young hero or heroine from realizing his desires, a standard figure in classical New Comedy – Morose here becomes something of a locus for sympathy, although his willingness to declare himself impotent, stating publicly, to the assembled company, that he is "utterly unabled in nature, by reason of frigidity, to perform the duties or any the least office of a husband" (5.4.43-44), of course opens him to ridicule – he has been forced into a course of rhetorical self-degradation that parallels the economic one he intended for Dauphine. Even after this humiliating declaration – made so that the marriage can be annulled on grounds of nonconsummation – Morose is denied his divorce, because it seems unlikely that Epicene is an intact virgin. Sir John Daw and Sir Amorous La Foole, who have already boasted untruly of having had sexual relations with her, now testify again to this effect, and Epicene manifests shame and misery. Poor Morose is at a stand when Dauphine offers to come to his rescue:

> DAUPHINE I have been long your poor despised kinsman ... but now it shall
> appear if either I love you or your peace, and prefer them to all the world
> beside .... If I free you of this unhappy match absolutely and instantly after
> all this trouble, and almost in your despair now –
> MOROSE It cannot be.
> DAUPHINE Sir, that you be never troubled with a murmur of it more, what
> shall I hope for, or deserve of you?
> [...]
> MOROSE   ... Make thine own conditions. My whole estate is thine. Manage
> it; I will become thy ward.
> DAUPHINE Nay, sir, I will not be so unreasonable.
>
> (5.4.154–171)

All Dauphine asks is a signed contract to give him, of Morose's £1,500 a year, "five hundred during life, and assure the rest upon me after"(5.4.175–176). This done and signed, he pulls off Epicene's wig, and reveals that Morose's bride is a boy. He then dismisses Morose quite brutally:

> Now you may go in and rest, be as private as you will, sir. I'll not trouble
> you till you trouble me with your funeral, which I care not how soon it come.
> [*Exit Morose*]   (5.4.212–14)

The shock is felt by everyone else on stage as well as everyone in the audience. The Collegiate Ladies have initiated Epicene into their secrets, Sir Amorous La Foole and Sir John Daw have boasted of sexual relations with him, and Truewit and Clerimont have been parties to a plot of Dauphine's whose most audacious feature they knew nothing of. Truewit acknowledges rather resentfully that Dauphine has triumphed: "you have lurched your friends of the better half of the garland," he says, parodying a line from Shakespeare's *Coriolanus* that Jonson evidently thought ludicrous ("In the brunt of seventeen battles since / He lurched all swords of the garland"

[2.2.100–101]). "Lurched" means "cheated" or "robbed." But despite bowing to Dauphine in this way, Truewit also insists on using the revelation to dismiss La Foole and Daw in disgrace and dominate the stage for the final several speeches. While Morose's humor has been exposed and ridiculed, as have La Foole's and Daw's and, to a lesser extent, those of the Collegiate Ladies, Truewit's own carries on unchecked. It is a humor to dictate to others the meaning and value of their own experiences, and as such it might be thought to be close kin to Jonson's own dominant disposition as a writer. Although in fact, as Ian Donaldson points out, an eighteenth-century commentator suggested that Jonson both played Morose in *Epicene* and that Morose's character was "a picture ... which he drew from himself" (Donaldson, 2011: 261), and this implausible view of the sociable Jonson persisted into the twentieth century.

Most comedies end in marriage. *Epicene* ends in an annulment that reveals that the marriage (in seventeenth-century terms) was always already invalid: there was no real woman involved. In part, this seems related to the harsh representations of the "real" women in *Epicene*: the Collegiate Ladies, who attempt to set up a leisure class pursuit of autonomous satisfaction for women to parallel that undertaken by the young men about town. The play is quite hard on them, and David Riggs speculates that the satire on both real and apparent women is Jonson's reaction to having had to spend a lot of literary energy flattering the Queen and her ladies in his work for the court (see Riggs, 1989: 152–157). In part, however, the exposure of *Epicene* is also Jonson's reflection on the conditions of his theater. In the adult companies, young female parts were taken by boys whose voices had not yet broken; in the children's companies like the one for which *Epicene* was written, all the parts were taken by boys from choir schools. Such works, the product of male authors and male playing companies, will feature male–male competition and male representations of femaleness that may in reality just be maleness in disguise. Certainly Jonson's exploration of humorous inwardness in *Epicene*, as in *Every Man In His Humor*, focuses on the inwardness of males.

1.9   *Tamburlaine the Great 1 and 2*: Interior Strength, External Weakness

Christopher Marlowe's *Tamburlaine the Great* was a huge success when it opened in London in 1587. His first publicly performed play, it was quickly followed by a sequel by Marlowe and a string of imitations by other playwrights. From the start, the play seems aware that it offers something new. Marlowe's prologue to *1 Tamburlaine* stresses the play's dramatic and stylistic originality.

From jigging veins of rhyming mother wits,
And such conceits as clownage keeps in pay,
We'll lead you to the stately tent of war,
Where you shall hear the Scythian Tamburlaine
Threat'ning the world with high astounding terms
And scourging kingdoms with his conquering sword.
View but the picture in this tragic glass,
And then applaud his fortunes as you please.

(Prologue 1–8)

Marlowe, in part, here alerts us that we are, so to speak, moving from the comedy to the action aisle (his hero was enacted by Edward Alleyn, one of the two most charismatic actors of the late-sixteenth-century stage). But Marlowe also promises a degree of seriousness and largeness in his play and an amplitude of style to match that seriousness. As auditors, we will confront a kind of truth about war and will, at the same time, be astounded by eloquence. A theater of action and rhetoric does not sound like a theater of inwardness.

Nonetheless, part of the amazing and seductive force of these plays comes from their convincing portrait of an exceptional sensibility. I said earlier that we associate inwardness with shy and contemplative people. Another way of saying this would be that inwardness generates itself around sensibilities that hesitate with respect to action; this is a common, although somewhat misleading, way of talking about Shakespeare's *Hamlet*, often seen as the greatest single step forward in the literary representation of inwardness. In *Tamburlaine*, we have the very reverse of this. Tamburlaine acts without inhibition, he never second-guesses himself, and he remakes the political and social institutions of the world in accordance with his will. As the inwardness of most people might be said to coalesce around failure or limitation, Tamburlaine's forms itself around an unbroken series of successes. Thus the play demonstrates how mistaken we are if we think of inwardness as a special property of contemplative people. Men of action have interiority too. But their inward life is in a peculiarly close relation to the outer world and tends to bear real rather than imaginary fruits. Marlowe's Tamburlaine, reproached by the dying Cosroe (whom he has just turned on and defeated in battle, after helping him take the Persian crown from his incompetent brother) explains his temperament:

The thirst of reign and sweetness of a crown,
That caused the eldest son of heavenly Ops
To thrust his doting father from his chair
And place himself in the empyreal heaven,
Moved me to manage arms against thy state.
What better precedent than mighty Jove?

(2.7.12–17)

Tamburlaine models himself on a supreme god, Jove, whose dominance derives from a transgressive struggle, in this case against Jove's father Saturn (married to Ops). Tamburlaine from the start links power and self-achievement to both transgression and vulnerability (Jove himself can be thrust aside, as perhaps he has been for most Renaissance Europeans like Marlowe by Christ or for most late medieval Central Asians like Tamburlaine by Mohammed). But Tamburlaine has not only a history of the gods, but also a theory of human psychology, to justify his casting-off of loyalty to Cosroe:

> Nature, that framed us of four elements,
> Warring within our breasts for regiment,
> Doth teach us all to have aspiring minds.
> Our souls, whose faculties can comprehend
> The wondrous architecture of the world
> And measure every wand'ring planet's course,
> Still climbing after knowledge infinite,
> And always moving as the restless spheres,
> Wills us to wear ourselves and never rest
> Until we reach the ripest fruit of all:
> That perfect bliss and sole felicity,
> The sweet fruition of an earthly crown.
>
> (2.7.18–29)

Thus the natural content of the human mind, the consequence of the humoral system with its conflicting tendencies, is an interiority of boundless aspiration and energy that models itself after the most impressive possible achievements: the self-installation of the gods. But Marlowe (following Ovid, as discussed earlier with respect to *Doctor Faustus*) stresses how the Olympian gods model transgressiveness and will to power rather than transcendence of earthly struggle. Such an inner self may be energized by the dynamic nature of physical and physiological reality, "four elements, / Warring within our breast for regiment" (that is, striving for rule within us), but it finds its full expression in dominating rather than reacting to the outer world. Moreover, the outer world in *Tamburlaine* is relatively plastic or fluid. Persia, Turkey, and Egypt are, for Marlowe's English audiences, regions at the edges of maps (and the "Scythia" where Tamburlaine begins life as a shepherd is vaguer yet). The regimes Tamburlaine takes control of are similarly fragile, although this reflects European political understanding of what would later be called "Oriental despotism" – systems in which total allegiance of subjects to rulers means that no one except the person who bears "an earthly crown" can possess him or herself fully. Thus the world of the play is one in which there are no settled places, but rather struggling tendencies; a world dominated by upward mobility, in which fixed social structures are fragile. A play written on this principle opens up a startling set of possibilities for its audiences, possibilities underwritten by audience awareness that Marlowe's play is based on the history of a real conqueror, Timur the lame (1336–1405), who rose from Central Asian obscurity to rule a huge empire encompassing Mongolia, northern India, southern Russia, Asia Minor, and the Middle East, with Egypt and Byzantium as tributaries. Marlowe's play thus can present itself, as his prologue suggests, as a piece of sensational realism about politics, showing the influence of Machiavelli.

A Scythian shepherd by birth, Marlowe's hero has, at the beginning of *1 Tamburlaine*, become the leader of a band of thieves, sufficiently annoying to warrant the dispatch of a troop of cavalry to apprehend him. Mycetes, the king of Persia who sends General Theridamas to do this, is so weak and unsuccessful a monarch that his brother Cosroe has conspired with Persian noblemen to usurp his throne. Before Theridamas reaches Tamburlaine, Tamburlaine captures the caravan escorting Princess Zenocrate across Persia to return to her father, the sultan of Egypt. With engaging frankness, Zenocrate pleads with Tamburlaine for her release.

> Ah, shepherd, pity my distressèd plight,
> If, as thou seem'st, thou art so mean a man,
> And seek not to enrich thy followers
> By lawless rapine from a silly maid.
>
> (1.2.7–10)

Her follower Magnetes takes another tack, seeking to intimate that Tamburlaine and his followers are out of their depth. Magnetes mentions his safe passage from the Persian king: "We have His Highness' letters to command / Aid and assistance if we stand in need"(1.2.19–20). Tamburlaine's reply shows that he accepts neither Zenocrate's estimate of him, nor her estimate of herself, nor is he in the least intimidated by the names of potentates she and Magnetes have dropped.

> But now you see these letters and commands
> Are countermanded by a greater man,
> And through my provinces you must expect
> Letters of conduct from my mightiness
> If you intend to keep your treasure safe.

Tamburlaine's claims of "mightiness" are part of a strategy to achieve what he asserts, and he cheerfully treats his seizure of Zenocrate and her baggage in these terms:

> But since I love to live at liberty,
> As easily may you get the Sultan's crown
> As any prizes out of my precinct,
> For they are friends that help to wean my state
> Till men and kingdoms help to strengthen it,
> And must maintain my life exempt from servitude.
> But tell me, madam, is Your Grace betrothed?
>
>   (1.2.21–32)

Zenocrate rewards Tamburlaine's self-confidence with an immediate social promotion: "I am, my lord – for so you do import"(1.2.33). But Tamburlaine, although moved by her word "lord," has no interest in portraying himself as anything other than what he is.

> I am a lord, for so my deeds shall prove,
> And yet a shepherd by my parentage.
>
>   (1.2.34–5)

Still, Zenocrate's regard for him and her beauty move him to a new imagination of his future and a consequent reshaping of himself:

> But, lady, this fair face and heavenly hue
> Must grace his bed that conquers Asia
> And means to be a terror to the world,
> Measuring the limits of his empery
> By east and west, as Phoebus doth his course.
> Lie here, ye weeds that I disdain to wear;
>   *[He takes off his shepherd's garments.]*
> This complete armor and this curtal ax
> Are adjuncts more beseeming Tamburlaine.
>   *[He puts on armor.]*
> And, madam, whatsoever you esteem
> Of this success and loss unvaluèd,
> Both may invest you empress of the East,
> And these, that seem but silly country swains,
> May have the leading of so great an host
> As with their weight shall make the mountains quake.
> Even as when windy exhalations,
> Fighting for passage, tilt within the earth.   (1.2.36–51)

We have quoted at some length here in order to illustrate the way Tamburlaine characteristically works from inside to outside, forcing or persuading what is exterior to conform to his inner sense of self. The costume change that he performs during this speech, in which he takes off a brigand's rags and dons a lordly suit of armor that he has probably just appropriated from Zenocrate's baggage train, happens partly in response to Zenocrate's willingness to believe he is a lord.

Her belief in him and her unsullied status as a sultan's heir make her into an exceptionally important figure in both *Tamburlaine* plays. And Tamburlaine's promise to make her yet greater than she is, while conferring greatness on his followers Techelles and Usumcasane, who "seem but silly country swains" at the moment, are part of a claim that what is inside Tamburlaine is both more formidable and more promising and exciting than what is outside. Tamburlaine's success in sweeping Zenocrate off her feet not only enables his rise, in many ways Zenocrate herself seems to constitute Tamburlaine's good fortune, and Tamburlaine's decline into tyrannical eccentricity followed by illness in 2 *Tamburlaine* begins with her death, followed swiftly by his murder of their eldest son, his declaration of enmity to Mahomet, and his burning of the Koran (Engle, 1993: 201).

Stepping back from this to think about Tamburlaine's peculiar interiority, we might say that *Tamburlaine* illustrates a kind of vulnerability or interior weakness to the institutions and social patterns that bind and limit ordinary people. That is, the play shows its audience what they might do in the world, had they Tamburlaine's inner strength. Tamburlaine's unbroken string of successes, his imposition of his own will on two Persian kings, the emperor and empress of Turkey, the prince of Arabia, and the sultan of Egypt – to consider only 1 *Tamburlaine* – illustrates not just spectacular political and military success, but the fragility of human institutions.

Tamburlaine's impact on his followers includes their belief that he will enhance their lives. This is expressed fairly naively and straightforwardly by Usumcasane and Techelles when they meet Theridamas. They announce that following Tamburlaine will make them kings. Theridamas' impression that Tamburlaine's "looks do menace heaven and dare the gods" (1.2.157) shows the charismatic personal power that Tamburlaine wields as a self-confirming attribute of his being. That is, he is strong, purposeful, and successful, and his strong purposes succeed in part because other people believe this about him. Both Zenocrate and Theridamas, although at times dismayed by Tamburlaine's boldness or cruelty, find enhanced selfhood through associating with him.

Of course, Tamburlaine's opponents find destruction, not self-enhancement, in the same place. Although Marlowe does not emphasize this, it seems clear that Tamburlaine learns about the possibility of successful usurpation from Cosroe, and that he learns how to be a cruel victor from the elaborate threats he hears from the Turkish emperor Bajazeth, who promises before their battle that

> By the holy Alcoran, I swear
> He shall be made a chaste and lustless eunuch
> And in my sarell tend my concubines,
> And all his captains that thus stoutly stand
> Shall draw the chariot of my emperess.
>
> (3.3.76–80)

Prior to this, Tamburlaine has triumphed over his foes without any particular malice. But after defeating Bajazeth, he starves him in a cage, uses him as a footstool, and offers him broken meats on the point of his sword. In a famous moment in *2 Tamburlaine*, he enters in a chariot pulled by captured kings with bits in their mouths.

So Tamburlaine's cruelty, like his will to rule, is partly learned behavior. Nonetheless, neither Marlowe nor Tamburlaine emphasizes Tamburlaine's receptiveness, because awareness of his receptiveness detracts, or might detract, from the overwhelmingly masterful inner strength that all who encounter Tamburlaine find in him. The inner life of the tyrant, as W. H. Auden points out, tends to be externalized in the forced sensitivity of others to that inner life:

> When he laughed, respectable senators burst with laughter,
> And when he cried the little children died in the streets.
> (Auden 1966 127)

We see this particular aspect of the inner life of the masterful at the death of Zenocrate in *2 Tamburlaine*, when Tamburlaine burns the town near which she died "because this place bereft me of my love" (2.4.138) (Marlowe, 1973: 174).

Tamburlaine is perplexed by only two events in the course of two plays: Zenocrate's death in *2 Tamburlaine*, as we have seen, and her plea for the lives of her countrymen at the siege of Damascus in the first play. In each case, Tamburlaine responds with violent action. Tamburlaine has a three-color rule for cities he besieges: his white tents the first day indicate that if you surrender immediately he will show mercy to everyone; red tents the second show that if you surrender with only a day's delay he will only put combatants to death; black tents the third indicate death to all when he takes the town. Damascus's stubborn governor refuses to capitulate until the black tents are put up, and all Damascenes, including the innocent virgins sent to plead Damascus's case, are put to the sword.

We noted earlier that Tamburlaine models his trajectory, and his sense of how high-pressure interiority necessitates ceaseless struggle, on Jove, seen in Ovidian terms as a god who succeeds to power by violent disloyalty to a father and maintains power by threatening his sons and brothers. The main rival gods to Jove in *1 & 2 Tamburlaine* are, however, not Neptune and Pluto, but Christ and Mahomet. Although Christians and Muslims struggle violently, neither Christianity nor Islam provides the model for unapologetic self-assertion that Marlowe's version of Greek Paganism does. They are religions of transcendence and self-abnegation, and this was we think clear to Marlowe even though in the Renaissance Islam was often seen as a warrior's faith in contrast to Christianity. One of Marlowe's enduring interests as a dramatist, discussed indirectly earlier with respect to *The Jew of Malta* and *Doctor Faustus*, is the poor fit between human desires for dominance and the model provided by Christ, and the hypocrisy among Christians that results from it. As Una Ellis-Fermor comments, "it was the practice of Christianity he hated, not its original inspiration or the personality of its founder" (Ellis-Fermor, 1927: 143). In *1 & 2 Tamburlaine*, there is some evidence that Tamburlaine sees himself as a champion of Jove's doctrine of ceaseless struggle, setting himself against monotheistic transcendence. In *2 Tamburlaine*, Tamburlaine reiterates, as he kills his cowardly son Calyphas in front of captured Muslim kings, that his own violent essence is modeled on Jove's, but he also makes clear that this makes him an unreliable and dangerous follower of Jove:

> Here *Jove*, receive his fainting soule againe,
> A Forme not meet to give that subject essence,
> Whose matter is the flesh of *Tamburlain*,
> Wherein an incorporeall spirit mooves,
> Made of the mould whereof thy selfe consists,
> Which makes me valiant, proud, ambitious,
> Ready to levie power against thy throne,
> That I might moove the turning Spheares of heaven,
> For earth and al this aery region
> Cannot contain the state of *Tamburlaine*. [*Stabs Calyphas*]
> (*2 Tamburlaine* 4.1.111–120)

At this point, he vows vengeance on Jove for the cowardly nature of Calyphas in the name of "*Mahomet*, thy mighty friend" (4.1.121) implying both that all these gods are happy associates and that Tamburlaine can play them off against one another. Later in the same scene, Tamburlaine tells the captured Muslims that "I am made Arch-monark of the world, / Crown'd and invested by the hand of *Jove*," not for bounty or nobility, but to "exercise a greater name, / The Scourge of God and terror of the world" (4.1.150–154). Is Tamburlaine Jove's scourge or Jove's rival?

In *1 Tamburlaine*, Marlowe shows his audience the social order giving way to overwhelming strength and self-confidence in a low-born improviser. *2 Tamburlaine* continues a course of conquest that is to some degree reconquest – Bajazeth's son Callapine escapes Tamburlaine's control by offering his base-born jailor a kingdom, thus applying lessons learned from Tamburlaine's seduction of Theridamas in *1 Tamburlaine*, and Tamburlaine reconquers the alliance of monarchs that attempts to reestablish the Turkish Empire. This part of the second play seems rather repetitive, although it demonstrates that one who has established himself by conquest must, as Andrew Marvell puts it, "still keep [his] sword erect" (see Engle, 1993: 205–7) against legitimists – those who defend an old, established social order against insurgents. But the second play also has a philosophical dimension. In it, Tamburlaine moves on from mere human opponents to take aim at the roots of human self-limitation: time, mortality, and belief in the supremacy of gods who transcend human limits.

Some of his attempts to defeat time are quite normal, although he goes about them in typically radical fashion. Tamburlaine is preoccupied in the second play with passing on his own characteristics to his sons – he worries, for instance, that they physically resemble Zenocrate rather than him, and she reassures him that they have his nature: "My gratious lord, they have their mothers looks, / But when they list, their conquering fathers hart"(1.3.35–36). After Zenocrate's death, to exemplify battle strength for them, he wounds himself, something that no enemy has ever managed to do, and his two younger sons offer to follow him. Tamburlaine, interestingly, invites his sons to explore the gash he has given himself: "Come boyes and with your fingers search my wound, / And in my blood wash all your hands at once, / While I sit smiling to behold the sight"(3.2.126–128). There may be an echo here of John 20:27, where the risen Jesus invites doubting Thomas (in the words of the Geneva Bible, current in Marlowe's lifetime) "Put thy finger here, and see mine hands, & put forth thine hand, and put it into my side, and be not faithlesse, but faithfull." His long speech of military instruction to his sons just before this has included instruction in how to "dryfoot martch through lakes and pooles, / Deep rivers, havens, creekes, and litle seas," which again reminds one of Jesus's walking on the waters to the disciples, Peter's several steps on the surface of the water followed by his collapse through it, and Jesus's reminder that faith is needed to be his disciple at Matthew 14:25–31. Tamburlaine ends his discussion of how to "make a Fortress in the raging waves" with the comment that "when this is done, then are ye souldiers, / And worthy sonnes of *Tamburlain* the great"(3.2.88–92). Unfortunately Calyphas, the eldest, does not prove worthy. He dislikes the idea of learning war because "we may be slaine or wounded ere we learn"(3.2.94), he does not volunteer to have his arm sliced open after his father has wounded himself, commenting, "Me thinks tis a pitiful sight"(3.2.130), and he will not enter the battle against Callapine's alliance, refusing his younger brothers' exhortations on the rational grounds that "my father needs not me, / Nor you in faith"(4.1.15–16) and that if he enters the fray, "I might have harme, which all the good I have / Join'd with my fathers crowne would never cure"(4.1.57–58). After the battle, in which his other sons distinguish themselves, Tamburlaine kills Calyphas in front of the defeated Turks, ignoring appeals for clemency from his other sons and from his generals Theridamas, Techelles, and Usumcasane. As noted earlier, Tamburlaine presents his act as a challenge to the god he serves: "here *Jove*, receive that fainting soule againe, / A Forme not meet to give that subject essence, / Whose matter is the flesh of *Tamburlain*"(4.1.111–113).

The philosophical language of interiority here – Calyphas's soul is the principle of organization, the "form," for the physical matter that he derives from his bodily father – mixes with a rather breathtaking reversal of the metaphysics normal at executions, in which the temporal sovereign judges and condemns the body but leaves the judgment of the soul to God (consider the traditional conclusion to a death sentence: "and may God have mercy on your soul"). Karen Cunningham remarks that Marlowe "expose[s] the fraud at the core of public punishments" and "understood the unsettling duplicity of the drama of death" (Cunningham, 1990: 156). Here Tamburlaine, refusing the implicit alliance between judge and God that public trials and executions usually assert, says that he himself judges the soul unworthy, and returns it as defective to the God who provided it. You have, Tamburlaine, in effect, says to Jove, in this case failed to supply a spiritual essence worthy of what the best of us need and exemplify. As Cunningham suggests, Marlowe demonstrates here that our ideas of a god who judges and punishes may derive from the practices of human power rather than the other way around. Tamburlaine makes this visible with his usual effrontery. But the moment is also one in which we recognize that Tamburlaine has crossed another boundary. His care for his sons' education as conquerors is Tamburlaine's acknowledgment of his own mortality. He is preparing to pass on his empire, and he seeks to pass it on to sons who are similar to him in martial prowess, although by his existence, nature, and achievements Tamburlaine guarantees that they will not make themselves or be able to take personal credit for their greatness in the way he has (unless they were to rise up against him and overthrow him, which would be the truest form of succession but one he shows no signs of encouraging). Thus he begins their training while Zenocrate lives, and then weeds out the weak son when she has died. (Weak children are in danger when their mother dies; there is a famous example of this in *The Godfather II*.) In injuring his own body and killing part of his family, Tamburlaine breaks the charmed circle that enclosed him and his in *1 Tamburlaine*.

He has also repudiated Jove in the process, rather than simply challenging him. Neither alien human opponents nor pagan gods sufficiently challenge or define him. In *1 Tamburlaine*, Marlowe sets his transgressive hero in loose alliance with the pagan gods in a vaguely Ovidian challenge to Christianity ("A god is not so glorious as a king," Theridamas remarks at *1 Tamburlaine* 2.5.57); in *2 Tamburlaine* his hero challenges all gods much more directly, as though his entire career has been an attempt to prove that they are either human constructs (and thus fictive) or weak by comparison to human greatness. If human greatness manifests itself by refusing inherited limitations and breaking received boundaries, the repudiation of the gods is one of the highest manifestations of inner strength. Tamburlaine dies in this enterprise. But as he dies, he offers his sons his own spirit in a parody of the Christian Eucharist that Anthony Dawson calls "a daring move that seems both reverent and blasphemous" (Dawson and Yachnin, 2001: 12). Tamburlaine's son comments that Tamburlaine's soul has become part of his sons' bodies (what he calls, as Dawson points out, their "subjects" [Dawson and Yachnin, 2001: 11]). Tamburlaine replies with a reflection on how his own interior life has proven too great for even his own mighty and imposing body, and must live on, Christ-like, through participation in the bodies of others:

> But sons, this subject, not of force enough
> To hold the fiery spirit it contains,
> Must part, imparting his impressions
> By equal portions into both your breasts;
> My flesh divided in your precious shapes
> Shall still retain my spirit, though I die,
> And live in all your seeds immortally.
> (II.5.3.164–74, in Marlowe 1997b)

Thus Tamburlaine passes on his powerful interior life to others.

1.10   Disguise and Honor in *The Malcontent*

When Tamburlaine changes his appearance, it is in order to become more fully himself. This is in accord with a hidden moral principle of theater: that by taking on roles we can take steps toward self-realization that we have trouble making as ourselves. But we can also take on roles or disguises in order to deceive others, and this process taps into another kind of basic theatrical energy: the delight audiences take in watching characters make basic identity mistakes and the moral delight they take in watching would-be deceivers deceived. This theatrical process depends on a least common denominator of human inwardness, the fact that other people can conceal their intentions from one another.

John Marston's *The Malcontent*, written originally (like Jonson's *Epicene*) for the Children of the Queen's Revels, a boy company, was published in an augmented version that had been performed by Shakespeare's adult company, the King's Men, in 1604. The augmentations were partly by Marston himself and partly by John Webster. In a section on inwardness, what *The Malcontent* most tellingly contributes is a strong presentation of moral disguise, in which an ultimately well-intentioned deceiver is able to express fully both his disgust at and his desire for vengeance on a morally defective society that has mistreated him. The play's title figure, the malcontent Malevole (a name that means "ill will" or "an ill-wisher," similar to that of Malvolio,

the anti-festive steward in Shakespeare's *Twelfth Night*), disguises himself
as a cynical critic of court life. The Genoese court he criticizes and inhabits
is that from which, as the upright Duke Altofronto, he was banished in a
recent usurpation by Duke Pietro, himself about to be usurped by his wife's
Machiavellian lover Mendoza. We do not know terribly much about what
Altofronto was like before being banished, but the moral tone of his faithful
follower, Celso, is very high, and that of his wife Maria is lofty to the point of
stiltedness. Held prisoner by the usurper Mendoza, who seeks to marry her
in order to legitimize his usurpation, Maria responds to Mendoza's proposal
(conveyed by Malevole, whom she like everyone else cannot recognize):

> MARIA   O my dear'st Altofront, where'er thou breathe,
> Let my soul sink into the shades beneath
> Before I stain thine honor. This thou hast,
> And, long as I can die, I will live chaste.
> MALEVOLE   'Gainst him that can enforce, how vain is strife!
> MARIA   She that can be enforced has ne'er a knife.
> She that through force her limbs with lust enrolls
> Wants Cleopatra's asps and Portia's coals.
> God amend you.
>
> (5.3.24–32)

One can, in our view, safely conclude that not only is Altofronto's noble
identity concealed by Malevole's shabby exterior, but also his habitually
high-minded moral style is hidden by Malevole's aggressive cynicism. We get
a sample of this in the speech Altofronto/Malevole gives to Celso describing his own banishment, a speech that both describes Altofronto as above
Machiavellian manipulation and also suggests that Machiavellian prudence
and deceptiveness may be necessary for effective rule:

> Behold forever-banished Altofront,
> This Genoa's last year's duke. O truly noble!
> I wanted those old instruments of state,
> Dissemblance and suspect. I could not time it, Celso;
> My throne stood like a point in midst of a circle,
> To all of equal nearness, bore with none;
> Reigned all alike, so slept in fearless virtue,
> Suspectless, too suspectless; till the crowd
> (Still lickerous of untried novelties),
> Impatient with severer government,
> Made strong with Florence, banished Altofront.
>
> (1.4.7–17)

Malevole, then, both disguises himself as a railing malcontent and
expresses a new identity as a reformed idealist who is no longer "too

suspectless," that is, excessively unsuspicious, but in fact suspects everyone of base motives and is usually right. Inwardness in this play bears the imprint of recent personal history, and *The Malcontent* bears this out by being that rarity: a revenge drama in which no one actually gets killed, but the erring realize their bad ways and request forgiveness.

1.11   Conclusion: A Drama of Interiority?

Our discussion of techniques and issues of interiority in the plays treated in this bears witness to a well-known but easily forgotten paradox about the very idea of inwardness. Interiority only forms itself or matters because of invitations and constraints from what is outside the self. Thus any attempt to define or map interiority turns into a history of what is external but close or significant to the self. Inner resources develop, as for the Duchess of Malfi, when external supports and loved ones are removed. Sardonic consciousness emerges, as for Malevole, when an accustomed social role is stolen. The inner self bursts out in angry or lustful asides in constant counterpoint to the pressure of propriety for De Flores and Beatrice in *The Changeling*; on a larger scale, the interiority Barabas or Tamburlaine emerges in denial of external attempts to define, or limit, or proscribe desire. Jonson's characters preserve interiority in part out of a sense of superiority to their interlocutors, but their interior life is frequently expressed in discussion or appreciation of humoral theories that Jonson clearly knows to be at least as discursive as they are scientific; the other main zone of interiority in Jonsonian comedy is the arena of secretive plotting, concealed from those outside but directed at defeating or surpassing them. When Morose's feelings about Dauphine burst out in an extended fantasy about Dauphine's future disinherited poverty, the fantasy appears to be actuated by resentment of Dauphine's rank, although Morose's interiority also has a poignant relation to his own upbringing.

One can see from this summary why the form of interiority exhibited by Shakespeare's Prince Hamlet – to choose the most spectacular as well as the best-known example of Shakespearean inwardness – derives from the techniques and patterns of interior exploration made available by early modern drama but also does something quite special with them. Hamlet's inwardness emerges in soliloquies and asides, it derives in part from a collision between skeptical philosophy and Christian moral psychology; it is troubled by the struggle for sexual realism and self-acceptance that is exemplified attractively by the Duchess of Malfi and negatively by De Flores. But Hamlet has that within him that he himself cannot entirely understand, even though he is enormously articulate and insightful about how people's minds work and how the social order constrains them. One of the great pleasures of reading Shakespeare's contemporaries is finding them handling themes or patterns that we think Shakespearean, but handling them differently and with different forms of success. In the next part, we will discuss their representation and contextualization of friendship and love.

Part 2

Intimacy, Rivalry, Family

Imaginative literature offers itself as a primary resource both for understanding the intimate relations we have and for learning how to have new or different intimate relations. Moreover, imaginative literature asserts the central importance of intimate relations. So as we move outward from the discussion of interiority in the previous part, Renaissance drama's representation of intimacy is a natural next step. Obviously, discussions of intimacy are also very often discussions of sexual relations and of gender relations, and, at various points in this part we will digress to discuss how conditions of the Renaissance London public theater – in this case, pre-performance censorship and all-male acting companies – appear to have shaped staged representations of sexual passion, both heterosexual and homoerotic.

Our discussion of inwardness naturally involved significant surrounds of selfhood: another person loved or hated, another person seen as a competitor, family members who share blood, upbringing, and projects. Inwardness always already involves such constitutive contexts, and the sort of linguistic inwardness registered in play scripts could not exist without the preexisting language communities that transmit speech. Nonetheless, as we have seen, certain dramatic techniques – notably the aside and the soliloquy – emphasize interior thought that goes on without immediate expression to another person. Imaginative literature offers itself as a primary resource both for understanding the intimate relations we have and for learning how to have new or different intimate relations.

Traumas of intimacy – prominently what Hamlet calls "the pangs of disprized love" (3.1.73) – offer many people their first strong intimation of tragic feeling. And it is a tragic feeling growing out of interior experience: there is considerable continuity between this part and the previous one. While many know heartbreak, each of us experiences it with respect to

Studying Shakespeare's Contemporaries, First Edition. Lars Engle and Eric Rasmussen.
© 2014 Lars Engle and Eric Rasmussen. Published 2014 by John Wiley & Sons, Ltd.

objects and situations that at least feel unique and that have to do with the vicissitudes of inner selfhood – its expansion in love, its violent contraction upon erotic rejection, and its gradual responsive transformations in extended intimacies. That said, however, we must also pay attention to the ways that representations of intimacy, like those of interiority, are shaped by the conventions and structures of Renaissance drama. While these plays represent a great deal of subtle interpersonal interaction, the conditions of visibility and audibility of a naturally lighted stage in an open-air theater seating as many as three thousand customers did not lend themselves to the flickers of intimate emotion that can be shown on faces in movies or on television. Renaissance drama is a wordy medium, and words need to be uttered quite forcibly to be heard on the public stages. Love is usually declared in speeches, not passionate glances or sighs.

Furthermore, Renaissance drama's treatment of intimacy does not emphasize private life in quite the way modern representations of intimacy usually do. The traditions of courtly love in which Renaissance love poetry developed tend to be aristocratic, and aristocrats are involved in power relations. Given that one of the major dramatic genres treating intimacy is tragedy, and that tragedy deals with the sufferings of the great, love on stage tends to be enmeshed with politics.

This is particularly true of plays depicting royal courts. Since public performance by the theater companies of Renaissance London was in theory permitted as a form of rehearsal for court performances, and since court performance provided an important part of the companies' revenue, players and theater poets were closely attuned to court audiences. Both Queen Elizabeth and King James (although in different ways) freely eroticized their political relationships. In Elizabeth's court, a political failure for a Leicester, Sidney, Raleigh, or Essex was also a kind of broken-off love relationship. Elizabeth's courtiers lived in an increasingly weird state of declared never-to-be-consummated passion for their aging queen; this meant also that they lived in a field of rivalry for her all-important and rapidly shifting attention and affection. This figuring of political maneuvering as romantic intrigue was also a key feature of life in James's court and in the various courts represented in plays we treat in this part.

Rivalry, according to René Girard, is not only a feature of attention seeking in a crowded field (the form in which schoolroom or athletic rivalry most obviously presents itself). It is also, Girard claims, a mechanism for the generation of personal desire, the kind of feeling Girard names "*mimetic desire*" and sees as a basic human attribute. We initially look at people as erotic objects because we see someone else look at them; we desire them because we see that someone finds them desirable. The instantaneous generation of such feelings from a social situation (rather than some deep interior recognition of affinity for the beloved) is a scandalous truth about human relations that, Girard claims, deep-self accounts of love consistently attempt to deny. We will discuss mimetic desire as a feature of love in several of the plays we discuss in this part.

2.1   Rivalry and Intimacy in *A Trick to Catch the Old One*

In Thomas Middleton's *A Trick to Catch the Old One* (1606), most of Middleton's dramatic energy goes into an often hilarious exposure of mimetic rivalry at work. The play shapes itself around a young bankrupt country gentleman, Theodorus Witgood, whose lands have been lost to his London uncle, the usurer Pecunius Lucre. He and his cast-off mistress, the Courtesan (aka Jane), join forces in an attempt to regain his lands and help him marry the niece of another rich usurer, his uncle Lucre's chief enemy, Walkadine Hoard. The Hoard/Lucre relation is entirely governed by Girardian mimetic desire: each takes the other's rivalrous malice as the spur to all action, and each acts so as to thwart the other. Moreover, each assumes a world in which such a motive trumps all others (as it has trumped familial loyalty in Lucre's repossession of Witgood's lands). This competitive dynamic shapes their professional activity as usurers: they often seem to regard usury as a competition between one another to acquire and pluck victims, rather than as a contractual arrangement between borrower and lender. Thus Lucre indignantly repudiates Hoard's claim of an original grievance against him over a business transaction (the fleecing of a promising prodigal):

> I got the purchase, true. Was't not any man's case? Yes. Will a wiseman stand as a bawd, whilst another wipes his nose of the bargain? No, I answer, no in that case. (1.3.12–15 in Taylor and Lavagnino, 2007a: 373–413)

Hoard's indignant reply associates rapacious rivalry with the ethos of Jews and, given its suggestions about back doors, sodomites. It also suggests that there are normal "friendly" business practices that Lucre has violated.

> Was it the part of a friend? No, rather of a Jew. Mark what I say. When I had beaten the bush to the last bird, or as I may term it, the price to a pound, then, like a cunning usurer, to come in the evening of the bargain and glean all my hopes in a minute! To enter as it were at the back door of the purchase, for thou ne'er cam'st the right way by it. (1.3.17–23)

Despite Hoard's evocation of friendship, throughout *A Trick*, rivalrous competition and habitual mutual betrayal enter into all transactions in the city. Witgood's successful scheme to recover his lands and stave off his London creditors depends upon it. He introduces the Widow – his past mistress the Courtesan in disguise, with papers and rumors attesting to her possession of 400 pounds a year in land – as a new possible wife for himself and thus causes his creditors to compete with one another in offering him gifts in earnest of new lines of credit:

> FIRST CREDITOR   [*aside to Witgood*] Pray, let my money be accepted before a stranger's. Here's 40 pounds I received as I came to you ... Let none of them see it, I beseech you ... .
> I hope I shall be first in your remembrance
> After the marriage rites ... .
> [*to Creditors 2 and 3*] What, do you walk, sirs?
> SECOND CREDITOR   I go. [*Aside to Witgood*] Take no care, sir, for money to furnish you. Within this hour, I'll send you sufficient. [*To Third Creditor*] Come, Master Cockpit, we both stay for you.
> THIRD CREDITOR   I ha' lost a ring, 'faith. I'll follow you presently. [*Exeunt First and Second Creditors*] But you shall find it, sir. I know your youth and expenses have disfurnished you of all jewels. There's a ruby of 20-pound price, sir: bestow it upon your widow. – What, man, 'twill call up her blood to you. Besides, if I might so much work with you, I would not have you beholden to those bloodsuckers for any money.
>
> (3.1.35–59)

From the first, Witgood's scheme has depended upon imitative desire. He correctly expects his uncle Lucre to catch his own desire for the Widow and her 400 pounds a year. Witgood aims to get his uncle to return his mortgage or at least lend him money: "he cannot otherwise choose (though it be but in hopes to cozen me again)" (1.1.86–87). But due to the omnipresence of Girardian rivalry, his plan works even better than he expects. Arriving in London, the Widow herself enters into yet another field of mimetic desire. Mrs Lucre, catching the desire to pursue the Widow by proxy from Lucre's endorsement of his nephew's suit, sends her simple son Sam (by a previous marriage) into the fray with golden gifts for the Widow. Hoard learns that Moneylove, a minor usurer, wishes no longer to pursue Joyce Hoard but rather to turn his pursuit to "the happy rumour of a rich country widow ... Four hundred a year,\ landed" (2.2.13–16). Moneylove gives Hoard two hundred angels to speak ill to her of "young, riotous Witgood, nephew to your mortal adversary"(2.2.26–7). Hoard accepts, but as soon as Moneylove leaves, comments,

> Fool, thou hast left thy treasure with a thief,
> To trust a widower with a suit in love!
> Happy revenge, I hug thee. I have not only the means laid before me extremely to cross my adversary and confound the last hopes of his nephew, but thereby to enrich my state, augment my revenues, and build mine own fortunes greater. Ha, ha!
>
> (2.2.42–48)

So Hoard begins his suit imitating Moneylove's desire for the unseen Widow (known only to Moneylove as the rumored object of Witgood's desire) and plumes himself on the suit because it will further his rivalry with Lucre. And Lucre himself sees the competing suits very much in terms of his personal rivalry with Hoard, even though Lucre does not seek the Widow's hand for himself. Lucre makes this clear after the aged Hoard and his friends have carried off the Widow more or less by force to marry her in a suburb of London:

> VINTNER   The widow's borne away, sir .... .
> LUCRE   Who durst attempt it?
> WITGOOD   Who but old Hoard, my uncle's adversary? ...
> LUCRE   Hoard, my deadly enemy! Gentlemen, stand to me.
>   I will not bear it. 'Tis in hate of me.
>   That villain seeks my shame, nay thirsts my blood.
>   He owes me mortal malice.
>   I'll spend my wealth on this despiteful plot
>   Ere he shall cross me and my nephew thus.
>
> (3.3.100 ... 112)

Indeed, when Hoard appears to have thwarted him, Lucre returns Witgood's mortgage (as he has told the Widow he would) in an attempt to outbid Hoard and fund a marriage between the Widow and Witgood:

> WITGOOD   Nothing afflicts me so much
>   But that it is your adversary, uncle,
>   And merely plotted in despite of you.
> LUCRE   Ay, that's it mads me, spites me! I'll spend my wealth ere he shall
>   carry her so, because I know 'tis only to spite me. Ay, this is it. Here,
>   nephew. [*Offering him a paper*] Before these kind gentlemen I deliver in
>   your mortgage, my promise to the widow.
>
> (4.2.29–36)

So far mimetic desire, for the most part explicitly attested, drives all important action in the play, and by its logic, Middleton illuminates the ways in which agents acquire purposes and also the general system by which their agency is diminished or enhanced. One might cite the foregoing as evidence for a strong general claim about this playwright's treatment of desire, and dub him "mimetic Middleton." It will not entirely do, however. Something more than Girard's version of mimetic desire is needed to deal with the remarkable ending of *A Trick*.

In it, the Courtesan – almost pure object for the projected desires of others (mostly males) through the heart of the play, but an articulate subject in the

opening scene with Witgood and again as the plot nears its completion –
manages her own redescription and revaluation from Courtesan to Wife.[1]
That is, she achieves the formal goal of male–female intimacy plots by understanding mimetic desire but by, to some degree, standing outside its field of
force. Indeed, by being truthful in explicit statements to Hoard and Lucre
("I promise you, I ha' nothing, sir" [3.1.204]), she adheres to a standard
of honest speech that no other character except the barely visible Joyce
Hoard maintains. The Courtesan describes her own dilemma in an aside
shortly after her marriage to Hoard, as she helps persuade Hoard to pay off
Witgood's discounted debts in exchange for Witgood's release of any claim
on her – a speech Shakespeare may adapt and adorn for Caliban:

> I'm yet like those whose riches lie in dreams.
> If I be waked, they're false. Such is my fate,
> Who ventures deeper than the desperate state.
> Though I have sinned, yet could I become new,
> For where I once vow, I am ever true.
>
> (4.4.148–52)

She recognizes here that she and Witgood are people venturing more than
they have. Yet she also recognizes that she might have the value she ventures,
if only she "could … become new." To do this, however, she must acquire
value *as a subject* in Hoard's eyes rather than as an object of mimetic rivalry
as pseudo-widow or, as whore, as an object of mere male exchange.

As whore, she would be an available triumph for Lucre (his rival "Hoard"
becoming someone whose name means "Whored"), although some shame
might stick on Lucre through Witgood – we see this in the odd exchange
after the revelation at the wedding feast:

> Kix   Marry a strumpet!
> Hoard   Gentlemen!
> Oesiphorus   And Witgood's quean! …
> Hoard [*to Jane*]   Speak!
> Jane   Alas, you know at first, sir
>   I told you I had nothing … .

---

[1]   Valerie Wayne discards the source text's "Courtesan" and renames the character "Jane" in
an editorial attempt to assert her agency as a female subject: (see Wayne, 2007: 375): "the speech
heading 'courtesan' fixes her in ways that make it difficult for readers to observe these shifts
in identity and grounds a misconception of the character's sexual inconstancy, constructing for
the contemporary reader a woman who makes her living by sexual commerce and is generally
available to men." While we agree with Wayne that Middleton intends us to see these shifts of
identity and value, we have not followed Wayne consistently in the name change because we
think the ambiguity of the term "Courtesan," and the character's status as an ambiguous object
of male rivalry and projection who becomes an articulate subject, help us see these shifts. We
do use "Jane" when quoting Wayne's text and stage directions.

LUCRE   Why, nephew, shall I trace thee still a liar?
   Wilt make me mad? Is not yon thing the widow?
WITGOOD   Why, la! You are so hard o' belief, uncle.
   By my troth, she's a whore.
LUCRE   Then thou'rt a knave.
WITGOOD   *Negatur argumentum*, uncle.
LUCRE   *Probo tibi*, nephew. He that knows a woman to be a
   quean must needs be a knave.

(5.2.97–114)

This demonstrates that there is not much positive profit for anyone in
asserting the new Mrs. Hoard's whoredom (although Witgood invokes the
double standard to defend himself against knavery, and Lucre does manage
a triumphant "ha, ha, ha!" at Hoard's expense [5.2.123]). In response, the
Courtesan's defense begins.

Witgood notes that she has not been "a common strumpet," adding
"I durst depose for her / She ne'er had common use, nor common thought"
(5.2.127–28) – probably an assertion that she was his mistress alone,
although also hinting that she is mentally and erotically out of the ordinary.
And she speaks for herself to her baffled new husband,

Despise me, publish me: I am your wife.
What shame can I have now but you'll have part?
If in disgrace you share, I sought not you.
You pursued me, nay, forced me.
Had I friends would follow it,
Less than your action has been proved a rape ....
Nor did I ever boast of lands unto you,
Money or goods. I took a plainer course,
And told you true I'd nothing.
If error were committed, 'twas by you.
Thank your own folly. Nor has my sin been
So odious but worse has been forgiven.
Nor am I so deformed but I may challenge
The utmost power of any old man's love.
She that tastes not sin before twenty,
Twenty to one but she'll taste it after.
Most of you old men are content to marry
Young virgins and take that which follows,
Where marrying one of us, you both save
A sinner, and are quit from a cuckold forever.
'And more, in brief, let this your best thoughts win:
She that knows sin, knows best how to hate sin.'

(5.2.129–151)

The Courtesan here for the first time in the play brings marital intimacy
out of a field of mimetic rivalry and asks that marriage be considered as

a contract between two persons, whose happiness or unhappiness will not entirely depend on how it plays to a group of rivalrous males. She suggests a more corporate view of success, and in so doing she transforms the play's treatment of agency. Since virtually the entire collection of rivals or potential rivals has assembled at the marriage feast, her assertions here are an attempt to persuade not only her husband, but also those who might use her to increase their being at his expense, that she should be thought of otherwise than as a token of one male's triumph over another.

Hoard's reply shows that his wife has reached him, but that he still has thought for one rival. I take "malice" and "spite" here (as in the preceding lines) to be terms for mimetic envy:

> HOARD   Cursed be all malice! Black are the fruits of spite,
> And poison first their owners. O my friends,
> I must embrace shame, to be rid of shame.
> Concealed disgrace prevents a public name.
> Ah Witgood! Ah Theodorus!
> WITGOOD   Alas, sir, I was pricked in conscience to see her well
> bestowed, and where could I bestow her better than upon your
> pitiful worship? Excepting but myself, I dare swear she's a virgin.
> And now by marrying your niece, I have banished myself forever
> from her.
>
> (5.2.152–161)

So a play devoted to exposing mimetic rivalry ends with a local, partial, and doubtless temporary escape from its dominance. Thus the play offers its audience a demystified view of marriage in terms of markets and mimetic rivalry, but also suggests that enhanced agency in marriage through a newly corporate view of social behavior may emerge from the demystification.

2.2   *The Tragedy of Mariam*: Intimacy, Tyranny, and Ambivalence

What is it like to be loved by a tyrant?

The question sounds like a lead-in to a study of domestic violence, marital inequality, and the dark side of patriarchy, of – to borrow a phrase from the title of a 1607 play by George Wilkins – the miseries of enforced marriage. Elizabeth Cary's *The Tragedy of Mariam*, written 1604–08 and published 1613, is about a miserable marriage, between the beautiful royal Jew Mariam and the Edomite Herod, but it is also a study of female exceptionality. As a Renaissance play authored by a woman, it is also an example of female exceptionality, a fact emblazoned on its title page:

THE

TRAGEDIE

OF MARIAM,

THE FAIRE

Queene of Iewry

Written by that learned,

vertuous, and truly noble Ladie,

E. C.

Like E.C., Mariam is learned, virtuous, and truly noble, and the play takes those qualities very seriously even as it focuses on the power of Mariam's extraordinary beauty and her vulnerability in marriage to a dangerous tyrant. Mariam psychologically is no victim, and indeed none of the women in the play shows any sign of depression or inhibition or self-limitation: the play is full of magnificent female expressiveness, much of it angry. While angry expressiveness is typical of tragedy, *Mariam* is unusual among English plays in treating Jewish characters as royal figures without overt reference to the relation of Jews to Christianity; it is also somewhat unusual in being thoroughly modeled on the Latin tragedies of Seneca. Moreover, it is, of course, of interest in being the first original play by a woman published in the English Renaissance (on this, see Part 4). As a Senecan drama intended mostly for reading, *Mariam* features lengthy formal declarations of feeling that often yield basic information about plot and motive slowly or in learned paraphrase; nonetheless, the feelings it treats are often unconventional and are almost always strong and plausible.

The play is neatly constructed with opposed panels around a central hinge: the revelation at 3.2. (the play's midpoint) that King Herod of Judaea, whom everyone believes to have been executed in Rome by Octavius Caesar for siding with Marc Antony, has in fact returned to Palestine with enhanced power. This return is a disaster for all those who have been in effect singing "Ding-dong, the witch is dead" for the first two-and-a-half acts: a group that includes Herod's brother Pheroras, who wants to marry the beautiful but low-born Graphina instead of the royal daughter Herod intends for him; Herod's brother-in-law Constabarus, who has been hiding the righteous sons of Babas from Herod's wrath; Queen Mariam's mother Alexandra, who hates Herod for killing her father and her son and for substituting his Edomite line for the true line of David; and to some degree Mariam herself.

In its representation of intimacy, the play emphasizes ambivalence. Mariam both respects her royal husband's love for her and resents his tyrannical oppression of her and of her family (before the play opens, he has murdered her gorgeous brother Aristobolus in a contrived swimming accident and executed her royal grandfather Hyrcanus on a trumped-up treason charge). Mariam is undaunted by this, and she is angry rather than frightened by the knowledge that Herod leaves behind instructions with trusted servants to kill her should he fail to return from trips to explain himself to his Roman overlords. At the play's opening, thinking Herod dead, Mariam comments self-correctingly that she should be at least somewhat unhappy about the loss of her husband:

> And more I owe him for his love to me,
> The deepest love that ever yet was seen ...
> It was for naught but love he wished his end
> Might to my death but the vaunt-courier prove;
> But I had rather still be foe than friend
> To him that saves for hate and kills for love.
> Hard-hearted Mariam! At thy discontent
> What floods of tears have drenched his manly face!
> How canst thou then so faintly now lament
> Thy truest lover's death ... ?
>
> (1.1.55–66)

Thus Mariam talks herself into tears of grief for Herod, only to attempt to conceal them when her scheming mother Alexandra, eager to take full political advantage of Herod's death, enters. Mariam here raises two important questions that the play treats as related throughout. What feelings are appropriate between husbands and wives? How should wives respond to the power to hurt them that law and custom give husbands?

These issues are not confined to the central character. Over and over in *Mariam*, passionate articulate women chafe in various ways at the restrictions imposed on them by men – not only the men who discard them for others, but also the men who love them too much or in the wrong way, or the men they used to love but love no longer. Doris, Herod's discarded first wife, resents Herod's male right to divorce her and curses Mariam for displacing her. Salome, Herod's sister, resents even more forcibly her own female lack of access to the right of Jewish men to divorce inconvenient spouses like Doris. She had to arrange the execution of her first virtuous husband, Josephus, to marry her current virtuous husband, Constabarus, and she and the Arabian Prince Silleus have now fallen in love, so she must somehow get rid of Constabarus. To do so, she intends to establish new laws equalizing male and female access to divorce:

> [Silleus] loves, I love; what then can be the cause
> Keeps me from being the Arabian's wife?
> It is the principles of Moses' laws
> For Constabarus still remains in life.
>
> (1.4.37–40)

If Constabarus only felt about Salome as Salome does about Constabarus, there would be no problem, as Jewish men can file bills of divorce on grounds of irreconcilable dislike: "If he to me did bear as earnest hate / As I to him, for him there were an ease; / A separating bill might free his fate" (1.4.41–43). Salome sees this as deeply unfair, and she clearly believes that God does not favor men over women:

> Why should such privilege to man be given?
> Or, given to them, why barred from women then?
> Are men than we in greater grace with heaven?
> Or cannot women hate as well as men?
>
> (1.4.45–48)

Were Herod alive, Salome comments, she could simply accuse Constabarus to her brother and thus do away with him, but in Herod's absence, she will have to be more innovative: "I'll be the custom-breaker, and begin / To show my sex the way to freedom's door" (1.4.49–50). She plans to do this by initiating a bill of divorce against Constabarus, and, it seems, then using class and wealth to buy off priestly objections: "with an off'ring will I purge my sin; / The law was made for none but who are poor" (1.4.51–52). When Constabarus reacts to this plan with conservative horror, suggesting that Salome's divorcing him will invert the order of nature and turn men into women or slaves, Salome replies presciently, "Though I be first that to this course do bend, / I shall not be the last, full well I know" (1.6.61–62).

This makes Salome sound like a feminist heroine and *Mariam* like a feminist play. But Salome declares herself a villain as she narrates how she arranged Josephus's death out of desire for Constabarus, summarizing her own lack of moral inhibitions: "Shame is gone, and honor wiped away, / And Impudency on my forehead sits. / She bids me work my will without delay" (1.4.33–35). By the play's end, Salome has worked her will by contriving the deaths of Constabarus, the sons of Babas, Sohemus, and Mariam, all by manipulating Herod through third parties. So she is hardly an exemplar. Moreover, feminine outspokenness in *Mariam*, although very pervasive and usually attractive, is often described as a fault or, at any rate, a tragic flaw. The play exemplifies free female speech without endorsing it. Mariam's compulsive honesty and directness make it impossible for her to conceal her dismay at Herod's return. Like Coriolanus, Mariam is both candid and easily made angry, so that she cannot survive a crisis that necessitates tactful reticence. Salome's comment "Now stirs the tongue that is so quickly moved" describes Mariam throughout (1.3.21), and Sohemus, worried about how Mariam will receive Herod, prophesies that "Unbridled speech is Mariam's worst disgrace, / And will endanger her without desart" (3.3.65–6). The Chorus offers a summation that suggests that Mariam's outspokenness is a kind of pride that pushes her to exceed the proper wifely bounds of private speech to her husband:

> Then she usurps upon another's right
> That seeks to be by public language graced;
> And, though her thoughts reflect with purest light,
> Her mind, if not peculiar, is not chaste…
> And every mind, though free from thought of ill,
> That out of glory seeks a worth to show,
> When any's ears but one therewith they fill,
> Doth in a sort her pureness overthrow.
>
> (3 Chorus 25–34)

In the crisis of her first meeting with the returned Herod, Mariam's candor turns out to be her downfall. Like Cordelia, Mariam is too honest to pass a vital love test:

> HEROD   Yet smile, my dearest Mariam, do but smile,
>   And I will all unkind conceits exile.
> MARIAM   I cannot frame disguise, nor never taught
>   My face a look dissenting from my thought.
>
> (4.3.57–60)

Like Desdemona, Mariam is too innocent effectively to refute contrived evidence of her infidelity when the Butler, suborned by Salome, brings a poisoned drink to the already furious Herod and claims that "The Queen desired me to deliver it" (4.4.2). "Did I?" asks Mariam, rather than strongly denying it. Her inarticulacy at this point doubtless derives from her incapacity to deny that she was pleased at the false news of Herod's death, once she had learned from Sohemus that Herod had once again left orders that she be killed. Moreover, although she never loved Sohemus, Sohemus clearly in a chaste way loves Mariam: "if I die, it shall my soul content, / My breath in Mariam's service shall be spent" (3.3.95–96).

We have commented that *Mariam* is unusual in that it ignores Christianity in treating Jewish history as part of the larger narrative of the ancient Roman world, a world that in political greatness and in various kinds of freedom of action exceeded Renaissance Europe. Like *Antony and Cleopatra*, however, *Mariam* does hint from time to time at the incipient gospel narratives in which a next-generation Herod and a next generation Salome play major parts. Mariam is beheaded off-stage at the end of Act 4. When the Nuntio describes Mariam's death to the already miserable Herod in Act 5, he reports her as predicting Herod's remorse:

> NUNTIO   'Tell thou my lord thou saw'st me lose my breath.'
> HEROD   Oh, that I could that sentence now control!
> NUNTIO   'If guiltily, eternal be my death' –
> HEROD   I hold her chaste ev'n in my inmost soul.
> NUNTIO   'By three days hence, if wishes could revive,
>   I know himself would make me oft alive.'
>
> (5.1.73–78)

A few lines further on, the Nuntio reports that he met the Butler who falsely accused Mariam and that he was in the act of hanging himself. The rope around his neck, he tells the Nuntio to tell Herod "Go tell the King he trusted ere he tried; / I am the cause that Mariam causeless died" (5.1.109–10). The three-day wished-for resurrection, and the suicide by hanging of the betrayer, liken Mariam to Christ (see Matthew 27:3–8, where after the crucifixion Judas says "I have sinned in that I have betrayed the innocent blood," and then hangs himself).

In *Mariam*, many of the good people are destroyed attempting to protect other good people from a tyrant's will. Josephus and Sohemus die for attempting to protect Mariam; Constabarus for attempting to protect the sons of Babas. Others, like the Butler, die of shame because they have served the tyrant's will in destroying the innocent and beautiful. The play gets much of its power by likening gender relations to tyrannical political relations. At the same time, as we have seen, the play moralizes itself in terms of restraint, moderation, and (for women) chaste modesty. The final chorus remarks that one day has seen an astonishing set of reversals, and that if Herod had shown more caution, he would not be miserable, and earlier choruses urged Mariam to curb her tongue. So the play does not imagine a brave new world in which neither tyranny nor male dominance will exist. Indeed, Cary is perhaps drawn to her unusual subject matter because she could allow female characters in a story out of Jewish history freer speech than she and her contemporaries enjoyed. At the same time, she has picked a story where the vicissitudes of marriage are all linked to the impossibility of good life under a tyrant's rule.

2.3   Domestic Tragedy and Moral Commentary: *Arden of Faversham*

During its heyday, the venerable police/legal procedural *Law and Order* was known for its topical storylines "ripped from the headlines." Although we tend to think that the age of the twenty-four-hour news cycle spawned our fascination with the "now," with whatever current grisly crime is garnering media attention, that fascination is early modern as well as modern.

The anonymously authored *Arden of Faversham* (1592) has a great deal in common with *Law and Order* and other televisual presentations of domestic murder. Like them, *Arden* takes as its subject a real-life slaying motivated by avarice, lechery, and a desire for power: the murder of Thomas Arden (Ardern). In 1551, just as now, murder was far from rare, but this case drew attention for two important reasons: class and conspiracy. Alice Arden's desire to do away with her spouse became newsworthy because she preferred the lowborn Mosby to her higher status husband, and because she suborned a hit squad from the lower orders to murder Arden for personal gain or revenge. What is remarkable about the play itself is its effort to both exhibit and examine a shocking example of contemporary criminality. Rather than presenting a simple morality tale that highlights the consequences of transgressing moral, ideological, and legal codes of conduct, *Arden of Faversham* reveals a world populated by characters of ambiguous virtue, but obvious vice; it complicates and humanizes both the victim and the perpetrators, looking beyond the notion of unequivocal guilt or innocence.

In the opening moment, the titular character – who should be cheerful because of the continuing improvement of his fortunes – can talk of little more than "how odious were this life" (1.10). While his friend Franklin reminds him, "My gracious lord, the Duke of Somerset, / Hath freely given to thee and to thy heirs, / By letters patents from His Majesty, / All the lands of the Abbey of Faversham," Arden cannot "leave this melancholy mood," rooted in fear of his wife's inconstancy (1.2–8). His anxiety over Alice's apparent dalliance with another man seems only partially motivated by the horror of so intimate a betrayal – such as giving Mosby her wedding ring as a love token. His principal complaint is that he has been thrown over for someone with less social cachet. Arden does not dispute Franklin's observation that wives may stray because "women will be false and wavering," but instead points out, "Ay, but to dote on such a one as he / Is monstrous, Franklin, and intolerable" (1.21–23). The objections are to Mosby's status not his treachery.

Yet, Arden continually referring to Mosby's training as a tailor or "botcher" – a man who labors with his hands – only hints at the source of the greatest disquiet: social mobility (1.25, 316). Mosby may have begun life as a "botcher," but through hard work, preferment, and, if Arden is to be believed, "servile flattery and fawning," Mosby is able to rise through the ranks to become the steward of Lord Clifford's house (1.28). Although Arden is one of the landed gentry, "by birth a gentleman of blood," his own fortunes have improved through his marriage to Alice, who is "descended of a noble house," and through his unsavory business practices (1. 36, 203). Arden, perhaps rightfully, fears that Mosby will take his place, first taking his ring, then his bed, and ultimately all his money, lands, and his status as "Master." When Arden confronts Mosby, verbally lowering his status as he declares that Alice is "no companion for so base a groom," Mosby responds by asking his rival to "Measure me what I am, not what I was" (1.306, 322). But the past is the source of Arden's self-worth and the only thing that distinguishes him from upward striving men like Mosby – which may be the reason why Arden ignores the claims that other men, including Mosby, Richard Greene, and Dick Reede have on the lands near Faversham Abbey; allowing them access to the land would bring them one step closer to being landed gentry.

Mosby, for his part, does hope to supplant Arden – and his motivations for the affair and the murder plot are ambiguous. Even Alice claims to have heard rumors that Mosby wants her for her money and the prestige associated with her "parentage," and, when he imagines his future, Mosby thinks killing Alice will provide him with peace of mind (1.492). He may have to be seduced to murder by Alice, much as Macbeth is tempted to kill by a persuasive Lady Macbeth, but Mosby (like Macbeth) falls out of love with his paramour but retains his fondness for wealth and power.

Alice Arden, for all of her fiendish *femme fatale* qualities, is remarkably consistent in one area: her love for Mosby. Although she periodically berates him and, like her husband, harps upon his lowly origins by calling him "Base peasant," Alice risks her reputation and her very life for Mosby (1. 199). Although their scheme to slay Arden is constantly thwarted by the incompetent assassins, Black Will and Shakebag, by happenstance, and even the weather, Alice is constant in her desire to dispatch the man who "usurps" her heart (1.99). And after Arden wounds Mosby in a fight, Alice is so enraged by the maiming that she nearly kills Arden herself:

> For when I saw thee hurt,
> I could have took the weapon thou let'st fall
> And run at Arden, for I have sworn
> That these mine eyes, offended with his sight,
> Shall never close till Arden's be shut up.
> This night I rose and walked about the chamber,
> And twice or thrice I thought to have murdered him.
> (14.82–88)

Although it seems ironic that Alice should refer to her oaths when in the first scene, she tells Mosby that "oaths are words, and words is wind, / And wind is mutable," she is remarkably *im*mutable in regard to her promises to Mosby – marking her as a paragon of inconstancy to one man and constancy to the other (1.437–438). And she does follow through with her pledge to slaughter her husband – which ultimately leads to her public execution: the real and fictional Alice are burned at the stake in Canterbury.

Alice gains nothing from the relationship with Mosby except Mosby, suggesting that affection, in the end, trumps wealth and rank. She is willing to gamble with her security for the promise of love, so it comes as no surprise that wagering or hazarding is a central part of the narrative. In the first scene, Alice sends Mosby a pair of silver dice "With which we played for kisses many a time, / And when I lost, I won, and so did he" (1. 124–25). This moment points to the ways that their fortunes are intertwined and how winning and losing are often indistinguishable. It is fitting then that when Arden's murder is finally carried out, he is playing a "game at tables," or backgammon, with Mosby (14.23). When Arden asks, "Come, Master Mosby, what shall we play for?" he does not know that he is hazarding his life (14.224). Engaged in the game, Arden does not see Black Will and Shakebag come up behind him and pull him to the ground so that all of the plotters – Will, Shakebag, Mosby, and Alice – can take part in the murder. Although their stratagems had been repeatedly thwarted throughout the play, when Arden himself assents to hazard by sitting at the table, he is finally bested. Ironically, the conspirators find themselves unwittingly participating in another game: hide-and-seek.

After leaving the corpse in a field, the murderers disperse, but their snowy footprints reveal both the body and the path the killers took. The bloody hand-towel and knife that were used in the murder also contrive to give them away, but it is Arden's carcass whose "blood condemns [Alice] and, in gushing forth, / Speaks as it falls" (16.5–6). All of them hazard and lose: Alice is burned; Mosby, his sister Susan, and Greene are hanged; the servant Michael is put to death; and those who appear to escape, Black Will and Shakebag, still meet ugly ends – the former burned at Flushing and the latter murdered in Southwark. Having multiple players simply leads to multiple losers.

The play, then, would seem to suggest that risking for potential reward is potentially fatal, that dreaming of a better life – whether in material or psychological terms – is futile. But, dreams play a significant role in *Arden of Faversham* – operating as both portents of things to come and as windows into the souls of the dreamers: Alice dreams of Mosby, alerting her husband to her infidelity; Michael cries out in his sleep because he regrets his assent to assist in the murder of his master; Arden dreams that he is caught in a hunter's net; and Mosby's sleep is invaded by fear of discovery of his part in the slaying. Throughout the play, dreams reveal the truth, just as Arden's bleeding corpse exposes his murderers.

While we might associate dreaming with aspiration and ambition, in *Faversham*, these are part of the waking world and the cause for sleeplessness. Dreams, then, provide revelation rather than inspiration, serving as warnings – although they always go unheeded. In each instance, the dreamers are presented with an opportunity for appreciating the truth about the waking world and making a conscious choice to see the world and themselves for what they are. However, all of the dreamers fail to choose correctly, which leads to their demise. The murderers and the murdered see what they want to see because to do otherwise would mean the abandonment of that dream.

The contemporary appeal of Thomas Arden's murder may have stemmed from the knowledge that the evil was discovered and that the malefactors were punished, but it may also have grown from the vicarious thrill of seeing people transgress, strive for something better – to dream and to hazard all to attain that dream. *Arden of Faversham*'s endurance is tied to these same ideas and to the anxiety about the security of our personal and financial states. Intimate rivals threaten our own dreams and make us pawns in their concealed games.

2.4   The Battle of the Sexes: *The Woman's Prize*

In John Fletcher's sequel to Shakespeare's *The Taming of the Shrew*, alternatively titled *The Woman's Prize, or, The Tamer Tamed*, the conflict between the freshly married Petruchio and Maria seems on the surface a farcical battle of the sexes. Like Shakespeare's highly popular comedy, *The Woman's Prize* draws on the evergreen comic resource of a power struggle within a marriage. At a more fundamental level, however, Fletcher's play questions traditional views regarding marriage, individuals, and communities, and even the representation of characters in comedies. The connection between Petruchio and Maria celebrates a view of romantic attachment in which flawed and inconsistent characters nonetheless love each other for their individuality. The romance between Maria's sister, Livia, and Roland provides a playful and ultimately unflattering view of more traditional romantic characters and comic tropes.

In the opening of Fletcher's play, the characters are celebrating the marriage of Petruchio, whose first wife, Kate, has died, to Maria. Petruchio believes Maria to be docile, in welcome contrast to his first wife. Although at the end of *The Taming of the Shrew*, Kate's shrewish nature appeared to have been "tamed," whether her personality had actually been altered or whether she simply had learned that feigning obedience would be more to her advantage, it soon becomes evident in *The Woman's Prize* that Petruchio and Kate's marriage was a struggle for dominance. Tranio (not a servant as in *Shrew* but a friend of Petruchio's) reports that "the bare remembrance of his first wife / … / Will make him start in's sleep, and very often / Cry out for cudgels, cowlstaffs, anything, / Hiding his breeches out of fear her ghost / Should walk and wear 'em yet" (1.1.31–36). In fact, Tranio suggests that, far from Petruchio having tamed a shrew, living with one had turned Petruchio into an oppressed shrew himself.

As Petruchio's friends discuss the new match, it becomes clear that they are concerned for Maria's welfare; Sophocles offers the bet that Petruchio "will bury her … within these three weeks" (1.1.47–78), and Tranio admits that if he were in Maria's position, he would "learn to eat coals with an angry cat, / And spit fire at him" (1.1.25–26) for his own safety. Hearing public judgment, even by Petruchio's friends, that Maria's father Petronius "has dealt harshly with her, / Exceeding harshly, and not like a father, / To match her to this dragon" (1.1.5–7), the audience is primed for Maria's manifestly justified rebellion. It is also reminded that in the early modern period, a married couple's life was under constant public scrutiny, and that the community could punish behavior deemed inappropriate. As we see here, the family plays a strong role in arranging the marriage. *The Woman's Prize* demonstrates the continued presence of parental mate selection, although the commentary of other characters indicates an uneasy acknowledgment that parents can make bad choices for their children. Besides marrying Maria to the choleric Petruchio, Petronius is also arranging a marriage for his younger daughter to the elderly but wealthy Moroso despite the fact that she wishes to marry Roland.

Once married, the spouses fulfill their socially gendered roles under community oversight. Other characters continually involve themselves when troubles arise. In the initial confrontation between Petruchio and Maria, what may seem to be a personal disagreement quickly escalates into a *Lysistrata*-style sex strike on Maria's part to preempt any attempts at wife-taming by Petruchio and establish gentle compliance as a new norm for husbands: Maria vows not to "give way unto my married husband's will, / Or be a wife in anything but hopes" (1.2.111–112) until she has "made him easy as a child / And tame as fear" (1.2.113–114). Supported by a veritable army of women, Maria barricades herself in the upper rooms of her house, while the male characters of the play present a smaller and less unified force in qualified support of Petruchio, first besieging and then negotiating with the women. These additional participants continually interject: for instance, Petronius joins in on Petruchio's side, urging his daughter to be obedient; Bianca, Maria's cousin – who seems to have instigated the rebellion in the first place although she denies it – encourages Maria and retorts directly to the men; and Petruchio's friends Sophocles and Tranio also comment on the action. It reflects the more open nature of household life in early modern society that servants and other citizens and countryfolk all eventually adopt positions in this matter that, from our modern perspective, would be thought personal and kept private. In early modern communities, a couple's relationship is essentially community property, and the community must be prepared to intervene if necessary in order to ensure behavior that it considers appropriate. This concept of the public marriage is vividly exemplified when Jaques recommends that it would be better "when she rails, / To have a drum beaten o'th' top o'th' house / To give the neighbors warning of her 'larm, / As I do when my wife rebels" (4.5.22–25), suggesting such community shaming rituals as the charivari, or skimmington, in which communities paraded effigies or actual offenders through town.

At the same time, while the audience follows the battle between the sexes, it is constantly reminded that, from the perspectives of the individuals involved, the stake for which they play is not primarily the good opinion of their family, friends, or neighbors but their love for each other. Whereas any affection or love between Kate and Petruchio in Shakespeare's *Shrew* is a matter of inference, Fletcher continually reinforces Maria's and Petruchio's affectionate attachment despite their differences. At the beginning of Maria's rebellion, Petruchio notes, "You were not forced to marry; your consent / Went equally with mine, if not before it" (1.3.144–145); Maria agrees, saying, "were I yet unmarried, free to choose / Through all the tribes of man, I'd take Petruchio / In's shirt, with one ten groats to pay the priest, / Before the best man living" (1.3.161–164). She, too, emphasizes her attachment to Petruchio (although she also seems to exaggerate for comic effect), describing herself as "His wife that, though she was a little foolish, / Loved him – Oh, heaven forgive her for't! – nay, doted, / Nay, had run mad had she not married him" (4.2.41–43).

Later, after further provocation (even though Petruchio has granted her conditions, Maria locks Petruchio in his house and removes all of the valuables on the pretext that he is deathly ill and must be quarantined, infuriating him to the point of venting misogynistic diatribes), when he sees Maria approach, Petruchio admires her, predicting, "I shall forgive her yet, and find a something / Certain I married her for: her wit" (4.2.25–27). Being privy to Petruchio's emotional state and witnessing his ability to admire Maria's cleverness in the midst of their quarrel helps convey the increasing importance of representing interior life not just in the tragedies but increasingly in other genres as well, and highlights the premium Fletcher places on the idea that each individual is constituted of a unique complex of views, attitudes, behaviors, and emotions. Maria and Petruchio appear to love each other as unique individuals, and to accept that a beloved individual will mix flaws with virtues.

Ironically, even Maria's apparently serious threat to leave Petruchio adds to the illusion of greater emotional realism. The brokenness of her speech as she responds to Petruchio's threat of violence further indicates the complex and inconsistent nature of emotional states. She is brave and resolute, referring both to her love for him and his for her, but nevertheless adamant in her refusal to tolerate such behavior: "I defy you! / And my last loving tears, farewell! The first stroke, / The very first you give me, if you dare strike, / Try me, and you shall find it so, forever / Never to be recalled. I know you love me, / Mad till you have enjoyed me. I do turn / Utterly from you" (4.2.142–148).

The insistence on their love despite their conflict continues. After Maria pretends to be insane and Petruchio tests her by insulting her and repenting of having chosen her to her face, she refers explicitly to her love for him five more times in that scene alone (4.5.130, 145, 152, 182, 202), notwithstanding the fact that she simultaneously encourages him to follow his stated plan of going abroad. Finally, after their ultimate reconciliation, the epilogue explains that the purpose of the play is "To teach both sexes due equality, / And, as they stand bound, to love mutually" (Epilogue 7–8). Because their love, although developed through farcical passages, draws upon techniques being used increasingly in tragedy to create the fiction of a real human consciousness, the play ends with a strong sense that, whatever diablerie they might get up to during the course of the play, these lovers genuinely belong together.

In contrast to the emotional connectedness of Maria and Petruchio, the relationship between Livia and Roland seems much more traditional and superficial, and their characters are less fully realized. The durability of Roland's attachment to Livia compares unfavorably to Petruchio's for Maria. Roland objectifies Livia, treating her as a prize to be won by his love or Moroso's wealth rather than as a human with a mind of her own, and he insists from the beginning on sexual pleasure when Livia refuses to run away with him instead of finding a way to sanctify their wedding socially. Initially, Roland presents Livia with the false dichotomy of running away together immediately so that they could consummate their love or admitting that she was lying about loving him, and asks, "What hope's left else / But flying, to enjoy ye?" (1.2.11–12). Instead, she plans a way to gain her father's agreement to a beneficial marriage contract, but when she says, "Ere I am three nights older, I am for thee. / You shall hear what I do" (1.2.50–51), Roland remains focused on the physical: "I had rather feel it" (1.251). When Roland forms jealous suspicions of Livia and determines to no longer love her, Tranio bets Roland 100 pounds that he'll take Livia back if she gives him the chance. In a plot reminiscent of Roman comic traditions, Livia then tricks Petronius and Moroso into signing a contract for her marriage with Roland.

Fundamentally, by offering the more humanized relationship between Maria and Petruchio, in stark contrast to the immature and shallow relationship between Livia and Roland, Fletcher's play marks a significant point in the transition from hierarchical to companionate marriage and from the exteriority of earlier comedies to the more psychologically nuanced depiction of characters and their emotions.

2.5   Intimacy, Rivalry, Family: *Women Beware Women*

Thomas Middleton's *Women Beware Women* is almost always (and rightly) understood as a very dark tragedy. Until Act Four scene one, however, the play seems more like a very cynical comedy about sex, marriage, and power where the intimate satisfaction of desire comes at a price, but everything is for sale if the price is right. For the first four acts, social conventions seem so malleable that a sufficiently subtle and solvent manipulator can get around even the most intransigent moral obstacles. As the play's title suggests, the subtlest manipulators are women.

The opening transgression is a very mild one: a triumph of natural affection over customary restraint. A sincere young Florentine commercial traveller, Leantio, tells us complacently how delighted he is to have eloped with a beautiful well-bred young Venetian gentlewoman, Bianca. He brings her home to Mother and plans the humble joys of urban matrimony: conceiving and raising children in contentment and thrift. His speeches about how hard it is to tear himself away from home to go to the warehouse in the morning, and Bianca's flirtatious urging that he take a day off and stay with her, suggest a happy honeymoon. Nonetheless, he has to leave town on his master's business, engaging both Bianca and his Mother to keep her presence secret – mostly for fear of her Venetian relatives, but also out of general treasure-hiding prudence. Leantio seems a bit fatuous in his uxorious self-congratulation, but not culpable: Bianca and the Mother seem surprisingly happy with one another for cohabiting in-laws abruptly introduced after the marriage. No sooner has Leantio left the stage, however, than the Duke of Florence proceeds down the street in an annual parade, and Bianca and the Mother hurry to an upstairs window to view him. Bianca thinks he is good-looking. The Duke in turn sees Bianca and is immediately smitten.

The play has a complex double plot. While the Duke solicits his courtiers for access to Bianca, Lady Livia's unpleasant brother Fabritio arranges with her unscrupulous courtier friend Guardiano to marry Guardiano's rich but mentally deficient Ward to Fabritio's lovely cultured daughter, Isabella. Isabella owes a good deal of her culture to her closeness to Hippolito, Livia and Fabritio's brother, who is his teenaged niece Isabella's inseparable companion. Livia tells Fabritio that he may command Isabella to marry the Ward but exceeds paternal authority when he insists that Isabella should love him. Hippolito, immensely distressed at the thought of Isabella's marriage to this idiot, makes a long-withheld confession to his niece:

> HIPPOLITO   Know the worst
> ISABELLA   Why so you ever said, and I believed it.
> HIPPOLITO [*aside*]   So simple is the goodness of her thoughts,
>   They understand not yet th'unhallowed language of a near sinner!
>   I must yet be forced (though blushes be my venture) to come nearer.
>   [*To her*] As a man loves his wife so love I thee.
> ISABELLA   What's that? ...
>   I'll learn to live without ye, for your dangers
>   Are greater than your comforts. What's become
>   Of truth in love, if such we cannot trust –
>   When blood that should be love is mixed with lust?
>
> (1.2.218–236)

Hippolito exits disconsolate and resolved on death after this properly moral rebuke to incestuous passion. But before finding some way to die of grief, he confides in his sister Livia, who urges him to "take courage, man," because of her own expertise in sexual arrangements: "Sir, I could give as shrewd a lift to chastity / As any she that wears a tongue in Florence" (2.1.40, 36–37). Livia believes that she can shake any chaste wife or maiden out of the saddle, and takes on this particular challenge because of fondness for her brother: "I am pitiful / To thy afflictions, and will venture hard – / I will not name for what, 'tis not handsome" (2.1.41–43). Even Livia, it seems, does not like the word "incest," but she assures her brother it is not the worst thing going on in Florence: "You are not the first, brother, has attempted / Things more forbidden than this seems to be" (2.1.46–47). In other words, Livia sees a sexual relation between her brother and her niece in the same light as the theft of Bianca without her parents' permission by Leantio: the overcoming of a social convention in order to satisfy a human desire and foster (or in this case, deepen) an attractive intimacy.

Livia's cynical realism here also manifests her sisterly affection for Hippolito, and moral evaluation of her decision to help Hippolito is framed by our awareness that an entirely legal and sinless transaction between two old men has consigned Isabella to an outrageous marriage. If we had at this point to pick the bad brother, it might well be Fabritio rather than Hippolito.

We learn immediately how very skillful Livia is at undermining chaste female resolve. Niece Isabella is announced; Livia dismisses Hippolito, comments in soliloquy on how there are "few sisters / That love their brothers' ease 'bove their own honesties" but that she is one such, and then greets the distraught Isabella, who complains not only of a secret grief she cannot disclose, but also of her marriage to the Ward: "I loathe him more than beauty can hate death / Or age, her spiteful neighbor" (2.1.84–85). Isabella cannot disobey her father, however, so she is bound to this marriage.

Now women's resourcefulness exhibits itself. Livia, sighing, reveals to Isabella that in fact Livia is not really Isabella's aunt, nor is Fabritio her real father, so Isabella may, in fact, disobey Fabritio without sin. Isabella's mother on her deathbed confided to Livia that Isabella was in fact the child of a great Spanish soldier, the Marquis of Coria, a secret Livia has told to no one before this.

This brilliant lie does four things at once. As a response to Isabella's complaint, it absolves Isabella of obedience to Fabritio (by fulfilling the unhappy child's common fantasy that a parent doing something unpleasant cannot be one's *real* parent). It gives Isabella a maternal example of, and thus parental permission for, adultery. It shows that adultery can remain successfully secret until long after the death of the adulteress. And, finally, it removes Hippolito from forbidden affinity so that adultery with him will not be incest. Livia's lie is much more convincing in dissolving the last three moral obstacles because it appears to be aimed only at the first, Isabella's obligation to daughterly obedience. Delighted, Isabella quickly sees her course: she will marry the Ward and use this marriage as a shield for a love affair with Hippolito. So we have a deeply unconventional but possibly stable resolution to the erotic crisis of the subplot.

Back in the main plot, Guardiano informs Livia that the Duke must have the young woman he spied in the Mother's window, and that preferment will follow to anyone who can bring her to him. The Mother, conveniently, turns out also to be, from Livia and Guardiano's perspective, the old widow whom they regularly invite to minor social events as a charity: "Our Sunday-dinner woman?" / "And Thursday supper-woman" (2.2.3–4). Livia again accepts the challenge to arrange the Duke's meeting with Bianca: "If I do't not, / ... / I'll quite give o'er, and shut up shop in cunning" (2.2.23–27). Livia invites the Mother for the afternoon, effortlessly playing the grande dame in need of an older woman's company. She presses the Mother to stay for the evening, extracts from her the news that she has a guest at home, and invites the guest as well. Since Livia is a great noblewoman and her house a luxurious palace, the Mother is delighted to visit and Bianca, when she arrives, enticed, is perhaps reminded of some luxuries she left behind in Venice. Old Guardiano offers her a tour of Livia's pictures and statues, including a special "monument," while Livia and the Mother play chess on the main stage. Chatting about art, Guardiano brings Bianca to the upper stage, where he disappears and is replaced by the Duke, who grasps the astonished Bianca in his arms. While Livia and the Mother talk about the chess game, in which Livia's rook or "duke" is wreaking havoc with the white pieces, the Duke makes it clear that if Bianca will not submit to his rank, his seductive appeals, and his promises of reward, he will rape her:

> I affect
> A passionate pleading 'bove an easy yielding,
> But never pitied any – they deserve none –
> That will not pity me. I can command;
> Think upon that.
>
> (2.2.363–366)

But he goes on to point out that Bianca can obtain permanent prosperity by yielding to him, and he seems well aware of her relative poverty in marriage to Leantio:

> Can you be so much your beauty's enemy
> To kiss away a month or two in wedlock,
> And weep whole years in wants for ever after?
> Come, play the wise wench, and provide for ever …
>
> (2.2.382–385)

They exit together to have sex, and downstairs, Livia announces checkmate.

While modern audiences can be depended upon to disapprove of rape, in the play's terms it is not immediately clear that Bianca's forced liaison is tragic, because her own attitude toward it is hard to be sure of. Having sex with the Duke outside wedlock of course changes her instantly: as she reemerges on to the main stage, she says in a threatening aside to Guardiano, "I'm made bold now; / I thank thy treachery, sin and I'm acquainted; / No couple greater … / I hate thee, slave" (2.2.442–6). But her threat shows that she believes she now outranks Guardiano. And as she greets the chess players her new style of speech, apparently upbeat in tone, includes a set of double entendres worthy of Livia herself:

> MOTHER   Are you so soon returned?
> LIVIA [*aside*]   So lively and so cheerful! A good sign, that.
> MOTHER   You have not seen all since, sure?
> BIANCA   That have I, mother,
>   The monument and all. I'm so beholding
>   To this kind, honest, courteous gentleman,
>   You'd little think, mother, showed me all,
>   Had me from place to place, so fashionably –
>   The kindness of some people, how't exceeds!
>   Faith, I have seen that I little thought to see
>   I'th'morning when I rose.
>
> (2.2.451–460)

Once again, a moral obstacle to intimacy has been swept away, although this time it is swept away in the name of the Duke's superior social power.

As might be expected, her encounter with the Duke also changes Bianca's relation to Leantio, the Mother, and their humble house, where we soon encounter Bianca bickering with her mother-in-law about the absence of luxury goods immediately prior to Leantio's return from his business trip. His attempt to determine why the atmosphere at home has changed is interrupted by a messenger from the Duke inviting Bianca Capella to a dinner at Lady Livia's. Poor Leantio tells the messenger there's no such person at his house and attempts to hide Bianca in a priest hole, but when he tells Bianca and the Mother about the invitation, Bianca immediately berates him for declining, the Mother tucks away a spare handkerchief to steal sweetmeats in, and they exit for Livia's forthwith. Leantio is left onstage to bewail the terms of marriage, but then the messenger comes to summon him to dinner as well.

At this dinner, the two plots join, as Fabritio, Isabella, the Ward, and Hippolito are present as well as all the principals of the main plot. The Duke in effect announces Bianca as his mistress, ordering all Florence to drink to her superior beauty. He appoints Leantio to the command of a fortress in distant Rouen, and to his own mind has evidently taken care of everything. Isabella and Hippolito celebrate their new sexual relationship by dancing together when the incompetent Ward declares himself too shy to lead the dancing with his fiancée Isabella: "Look, there's her uncle ... I'll have him do't before me ... then I may learn the better" (3.3.185–88). The dance is admired by all: indeed, it constitutes a visual enactment of the idea that the play celebrates the evasion of constraining moral conventions in the promotion of valuable unconventional intimacies. Gary Taylor and Andrew Sabol comment on the complexity of the moment:

> Hippolito is already Isabella's lover, though the Ward is her fiancé. The Ward's clowning probably endears him to at least a significant portion of the audience, which can also be expected to disapprove, morally, of the incestuous extramarital relationship between Isabella and Hippolito. Nevertheless, these allegiances must compete with our actual experience of the dancing.
>
> *Music. [Hippolito and Isabella] dance, making honours to the Duke and curtsey to themselves both before and after* (3.2.201.1–3)
>
> The perfect symmetrical formality of the etiquette here points to what must be the most noticeable effect of the dance: Hippolito and Isabella dance beautifully together. ... We know this, despite the absence of a choreography or report of their dance, because the surrounding dramatic script tells us a great deal ... both characters are young and beautiful; both are trained dancers who have been praised before they begin for their ability; their long friendship, followed by their more recent experience as lovers, makes them sensitive and responsive to each other's movements .... No one speaks during their dance; they have the undivided attention of the audience, on stage and off, and their performance is immediately followed by the Duke's praise. The aesthetic and emotional effect of this dance – the most perfect romantic couples dance in Middleton, or indeed anywhere in the drama of his time – is at least as powerful as the ironic discourse that surrounds it. (Taylor and Sabol, 2007: 132)

So this dance could be seen as a demonstration and celebration of Livia's success in creating a beautiful unconventional intimacy out of the conventional squalor of Isabella's forced marriage to the Ward.

Before the dance, Leantio accepts his military appointment with forced gratitude, calling it in an aside "a fine bit / To stay a cuckold's stomach" (3.3.50–51). But Livia's reaction reminds us of something that Leantio's new cuckold status may have made us neglect – he must be an extremely attractive young man to have induced the beautiful Bianca to elope with him in the first place. The thirty-nine-year-old Livia feels this strongly, saying in an aside that she never "truly felt the power of love / And pity to a man, till now I knew him!" (3.3.65–66). She immediately goes after him to "give your grief good counsel" (3.3.281), and counsels him to forget the "strumpet" Bianca and remedy the mistake he made in marrying "only for beauty"; such a marriage "brings on want, and want's the key of whoredom" (3.3.284, 291, 294–295). Livia's concise, cynical, and not entirely inaccurate analysis grounds her proposal to Leantio:

> Could'st thou love such a one, that, blow all fortunes,
> Would never see thee want?
> Nay, more, maintain thee to thine enemies' envy?
> And shalt not spend a care for't, stir a thought,
> Nor break a sleep; unless love's music waked thee,
> No storm of fortune should.
>
> (3.3.310–15)

This is, of course, very similar to the Duke's appeal to Bianca, "Come, play the wise wench, and provide forever." At first, Leantio declines, still sighing for and seething at Bianca. Livia exits in self-reproach for letting her desire overcome her timing: "Where's my discretion now, my skill, my judgment? / I'm cunning in all arts but mine own love" (3.3.320–21). Leantio, however, reconsiders his situation in a soliloquy in which he decides to hate Bianca and make the best of everything else. He reflects that the Rouen captaincy, while honorable, is not lucrative enough to live on. Thus he has entered a more receptive frame of mind when Livia returns to renew her suit. They kiss, and seal their deal in a double couplet:

> LIVIA   Only, sir, wear your heart of constant stuff.
>   Do you but love enough, I'll give enough.
> LEANTIO   Troth, then, I'll love enough, and take enough.
> LIVIA   Then we are both pleased enough.
>
> (3.3.382–85)

We seem at an equilibrium point. Everyone is getting something – even the Mother gets the extra sweets she carries home in her spare handkerchief.

The Ward gets a better wife than he deserves, while his wife gets a lover who has always cared for her and with whom she can make beautiful music. While Leantio has been horribly humiliated by Bianca, the Duke rather than Bianca has determined his situation (although he does not entirely know this), and he, like she, seems to have accepted the attractiveness of lucrative patronage from an aging noble in exchange for sexual favors. Bianca, indeed, is able at the beginning of Act 4 to reflect rather philosophically on how she (and perhaps her audience) might contextualize this marketing of unconventional intimacy as part of a coming-of-age process. She soliloquizes in her fashionable new apartment:

> How strangely woman's fortune comes about!
> This was the farthest way to come to me,
> All would have judged, that knew me born in Venice,
> And there with many jealous eyes brought up,
> That never thought they had me sure enough
> But when they were upon me. Yet my hap
> To meet it here, so far off from my birthplace,
> My friends, or kindred. 'Tis not good, in sadness,
> To keep a maid so strict in her young days;
> Restraint breeds wand'ring thoughts, as many fasting days
> A great desire to see flesh stirring again.
>
> (4.1.23–33)

Bianca concisely expresses what Michel Foucault calls the repressive hypothesis, and goes on to prescribe permissive parenting in the manner of Dr Spock: "I'll ne'er use any girl of mine so strictly" (4.1.34, see Engle, 2008: 421, 431).

We might, at this point in the play, feel we are at the dawn of a peculiarly secular age of open social and sexual relations, not necessarily entirely attractive, but permitting everyone to have the "enough" that Leantio and Livia have promised one another. But it is not to be. After Bianca's soliloquy, Leantio enters, decked out sumptuously by Livia, and the two have a conversation in which, with an edge, but not necessarily a mortally bitter edge, they take note of each other's dress, culminating in a tentative suggestion from Bianca that this may all be a good thing:

> LEANTIO You're very stately here.
> BIANCA Faith, something proud, sir.
> LEANTIO Stay, stay, let's see your cloth-of-silver slippers.
> BIANCA Who's your shoemaker? He's made you a neat boot.
> LEANTIO Will you have a pair? The Duke will lend you spurs.
> BIANCA Yes, when I ride.

> LEANTIO   'Tis a brave life you lead.
> BIANCA   I could ne'er see you in such good clothes
>   In my time.
> LEANTIO   In your time?
> BIANCA   Sure I think, sir,
>   We both thrive best asunder.
>
>   (4.1.53–62)

She seems to be saying, well, here we are, and we're clearly well-provided-for: let's accept it. At this, Leantio's bitterness breaks out: "You're a whore … [a]n impudent, spiteful strumpet"(4.1.62–63). Bianca reminds him of what her whoredom has earned him: "Oh sir, you give me thanks for your captainship; / I thought you had forgot all your good manners" (4.1.63–64). Again, she stresses that everyone is getting something. At this, Leantio shows her a love letter from Livia and carries on to threaten her with both hell after death and his own "revenge and anger" in the future when the Duke's flagging affections give Leantio opportunity to exercise them.

Leantio, in other words, has not signed on to the new community of amoral unconventional prosperous intimacies, and he repudiates Bianca's repeated attempts to get him to do so. Instead, he terrifies her with religion, and she runs to the Duke in tears describing what Leantio has said.

The Duke responds instantly, reassuring Bianca, then calling in Hippolito to inform him privately that a socially unworthy lover, "an impudent boaster," has bragged of sexual conquest of Hippolito's sister Livia, thus dissuading the Duke from arranging a great marriage for her (4.1.150). Hippolito may be morally flexible about incest, but he is punctilious about other forms of family honor, and he rushes off to challenge Leantio and wipe out the soiling of his sister in blood.

At this point, it turns out that the Duke has a touchy inflexible family of his own to worry about. His brother and heir the Lord Cardinal (a new character, hitherto unmentioned) enters with torchbearers in daylight to reprove him in the name of God and morality for the darkness of keeping Bianca. The Cardinal gives a terrifying speech about the proximity of death and thus hell for sinners. If a reader or theater-goer believes the speech entirely, it provides the master-perspective that shows the horrible this-worldly error of every single character we have met up to this point – and of most audience members, as one does not have to be an incestuous or murderous adulterer to fall under the Cardinal's condemnation of those who lose track of the next world in the pleasures of this one. On the other hand, the Cardinal's invocation of sin and eternal death may be just another expedient perspective used by a character who wants someone to do something – the kind of persuasive recontextualization we have seen over and over again in the play. In either case, the Cardinal's speech instantly influences his brother the Duke, but not in exactly the way the Cardinal intends. The Duke vows to sin no more. As soon as the Duke is alone, he comments on Bianca and his vow:

> She lies alone tonight for't, and must still,
> Though it be hard to conquer; but I have vowed
> Never to know her as a strumpet more,
> And I must save my oath. If fury fail not,
> Her husband dies tonight, or at the most
> Lives not to see the morning spent tomorrow.
> Then I will make her lawfully mine own,
> Without this sin and horror.
>
> (4.1.267–274)

So marriage conveniently erases the sin and horror of illicit sex, never mind the collateral damage to Leantio, first in forcibly appropriating his wife, and now in arranging his death. Hippolito obligingly kills Leantio in a duel the next morning, fuming at what he takes (wrongly) to be Leantio's public bragging – Leantio, after all, told only his own wife about Livia, not the world at large. The Duke immediately announces a wedding ceremony. What neither he nor Hippolito has reckoned on is the fury of Livia at her lover Leantio's death, and her instant vengeful announcement to Guardiano that Hippolito is having sex with Isabella, and to Isabella that despite what Livia told her before, Hippolito is in reality her uncle. This parts Hippolito and Isabella, fills Isabella with hatred of Livia, does nothing to assuage Livia's hatred for Hippolito, and fills Guardiano with the need for vengeance on behalf of the cuckolded Ward.

All these vengeful purposes meet at the wedding masque Livia and Guardiano stage for the Duke and Bianca, one of the most overdetermined scenes in Renaissance drama. But before the masque, the Cardinal interrupts the wedding procession to denounce his brother once again, this time for imagining that marriage can make his relation to Bianca acceptable: "Grow not too cunning for your soul, good brother; / Is it enough to use adulterous thefts, / And then take sanctuary in marriage?" (4.3.35–37). The Cardinal objects to the Duke's motives and says that after death the Duke will learn how wrong he was: "Then you'll perceive what wrongs chaste vows endure / When lust usurps the bed that should be pure" (4.3.45–46). Bianca's response to the Cardinal is the final note of unconventional moral flexibility in this play that has enacted apparently successful accommodations of unusual intimacy only to bring them near destruction:

> Sir, I have read you over all this while
> In silence, and I find great knowledge in you,
> And severe learning; yet 'mongst all your virtues
> I see not charity written.
>
> (4.3.47–50)

Charity, she suggests, should rejoice at her reclamation from a sinful relation:

> If ev'ry woman
> That commits evil should be therefore kept
> Back in desires of goodness, how should virtue
> Be known and honored? From a man that's blind
> To take a burning taper, 'tis no wrong,
> He never misses it; but to take light
> From one that sees, that's injury and spite.
>
> (4.3.58–61)

This comment links itself to the torches the Cardinal used to supply allegorical backup for his condemnation of the Duke's lust: Bianca says, in effect, now we see what you wanted us to see, so why do you still condemn me, and all women who have erred but seek to redeem themselves? Bianca finishes her speech very powerfully, in terms that remind readers of the Courtesan's great speech at the end of *A Trick to Catch the Old One*, quoted earlier in this part:

> Pray, whether is religion better served
> When lives that are licentious are made honest
> Than when they still run through a sinful blood?
> 'Tis nothing virtue's temples to deface;
> But build the ruins, there's a work of grace.
>
> (4.3.65–69)

We should notice how the reclamation of apparent disasters in intimacy that has characterized Livia's interventions hitherto – fixing things for her brother, fixing things for the Duke, fixing things for Leantio so that his heartbreak may be well-compensated – is here seen as at least analogous to charity.

But too much blood has already passed under the bridge. Vengeful mayhem has been elaborately orchestrated. Moreover, as if in order to assuage our uncertainty about how to take Bianca, the philosophical stolen bride turned strumpet turned moralizing duchess, Middleton unexpectedly gives Bianca a new incarnation as a poisoner. Bianca is viewing an allegorical marriage masque during which Livia, appearing as Juno Pronuba (the goddess of marriage), destroys Isabella, appearing as a nymph, by dropping molten gold into her lap; and during which, if he can wait for his cue, the Ward will open a trapdoor to drop Hippolito onto a poisoned caltrop (a spiked ball), with Cupids with poisoned arrows providing backup for this vengeance killing on Guardiano's part; during which, however, Isabella's nymph presents Livia's Juno with an incense burner that produces poisoned smoke that kills Livia in turn; and during which the Ward misses his cue and drops Guardiano rather than Hippolito onto the poisoned caltrop; during which, further, Hippolito, obediently shot by the poisoned arrows of the Cupids, and loudly confessing his incest, impales himself on the halberd of a ducal guard. While all this is happening on, above, and under the masquing stage, pages costumed as Ganymede and Hebe bring cups of nectar to the masquing audience, consisting of the Duke, the Cardinal, and Bianca. Bianca informs us in an aside that she has poisoned the one for the Cardinal. But in fact Hebe slips up and gives that one to the Duke. As the Duke dies, Bianca kisses him to take in poisoned breath, then drinks off his cup to make sure of things. The Cardinal alone survives to deliver a final moralizing comment on sexual desire: "where lust reigns, that prince cannot reign long" (5.2.528).

Often described as the most over-the-top vengeance masque in Early Modern English revenge drama, this sequence is very difficult to stage and is usually simplified or truncated in performance. Nevertheless, it supplies a remarkably powerful image of what happens when unconventional intimacy, rather than being recontextualized and accommodated, is violently expunged as dishonor and sin. Livia's past manipulations, and Bianca's reflections on them, seem civilized by comparison.

2.6   Familiar and Familial: Incest in 'Tis Pity She's a Whore

W.H. Auden's poem, "Herman Melville," (1939) proclaims "Evil is unspectacular and always human, / And shares our bed and eats at our own table" (ll.17–18). This is certainly true of John Ford's 1633 tragedy, 'Tis Pity She's a Whore, which centers upon evil that is at once both familiar and familial: incest. In 'Tis Pity, brother and sister confront an external sphere that is filled with ugliness, ignorance, duplicity, and injustice, and so they turn inward toward a domestic space associated with the warmth, affection, and intimacy found in the bedchamber. But as the outside world closes in on the lovers, the bed too becomes corrupted and is transformed into an operating theater where the innermost recesses of the body and their illicit relationship are laid open for public scrutiny.

The play follows a trajectory from the outside to the inside, from multiple plots and subplots toward two interconnected storylines focused on the love triangle that develops among the lover-siblings, Giovanni and Annabella, and Annabella's husband, Soranzo, ultimately ending inside of Soranzo's home. And yet, while the narrative moves from complexity to simplicity and the spatial orientation shifts from exterior to interior locales, the doomed brother and sister are remarkably self-contained from the earliest moments.

As the play begins, Giovanni appears to be debating with his friend and mentor, Friar Bonaventura, about the nature of incest and whether it is,

in fact, always a sin. But it is clear that what Giovanni presents as inter-
rogatives are actually rhetorical questions:

> Must I not do what all men else may: love?
> […]   Must I not praise
> That beauty which, if framed anew, the gods
> Would kneel to it, as I do kneel to them?
> […]   Shall a peevish sound,
> A customary form from man to man
> Of brother and of sister, be a bar
> 'Twixt my perpetual happiness and me?
>   (1.1.19–27)

Friar Bonaventura's efforts to answer, and to contradict the implicit arguments imbedded in Giovanni's questions, are simply met with more rhetorical twists; even the friar notes that this is neither a conversation nor a debate:

>   Nice philosophy
> May tolerate unlikely arguments,
> But heaven admits no jest; wits that presumed
> On wit too much, by striving how to prove
> There was no God, with foolish grounds of art,
> Discovered first the nearest way to hell.
>   (1.1.2–7)

Like Hamlet in his "To be or not to be" soliloquy, Giovanni is engaged in
internal deliberation, but unlike Shakespeare's hero, Giovanni has already
come to a conclusion that is also the starting place for this argument: that
he is the exception to the rules about incest. Giovanni stays stubbornly fixed
upon his own desires within his private world. Unfortunately, Bonaventura
unwittingly encourages this by counseling Giovanni to meditate further upon
these unnatural yearnings within the very location that gave birth to them:

> Hie to thy father's house. There lock thee fast
> Alone within thy chamber, then fall down
> On both thy knees and grovel on the ground.
> Cry to thy heart … .
>   (1.1.69–72)

It is Giovanni's isolation from the rest of society that has fed his incestuous
passion. He has spent too much time engaged in the introspection associated
with study, and in constant companionship with the solitary Bonaventura,
causing him to look within, rather than without, for an equal. What he
finds is that no one outside of himself can serve as an appropriate mate for
one, as the friar puts it, whose "government, behavior, learning, speech, /

Sweetness" are so highly esteemed (1.1.51–52). All that is left for Giovanni
is to look closer to home:

> Say that we had one father, say one womb
> (Curse to my joys!) gave both us life and birth;
> Are we not therefore each to other bound
> So much the more by nature? By the links
> Of blood, of reason? Nay, if you will have't
> Even of religion, to be ever one,
> One soul, one flesh, one love, one heart, one all?
> (1.1.28–34)

Here, Giovanni literalizes the sentiments found in the Christian nuptial rite
which imagines the creation of a spiritual and physical union through the
sacrament of marriage, envisioning himself as another Adam who draws his
companion from out of his own body (Genesis, 2: 21–24).

Giovanni's interpretation of the situation is at once both egotistical and
rational. His love for his sister is a kind of self-love, a narcissistic impulse
to shun exogamous marriage and the centrifugal pressures associated with
early modern patriarchal culture. And yet, the play also confirms Giovanni
and Annabella's beliefs that the realm beyond the unfortunate couple is corrupt and vile. The friar may tell Giovanni to "Look through the world, /
And thou shalt see a thousand faces shine / More glorious than this idol
thou ador'st"(1.1.59–61), but within the world of the play this is hardly
the case. In terms of class, character, and age, no woman but Annabella is
a suitable match: Annabella's "tut'ress," Putana, is not only too old, but
strikingly low and carnal – unsurprising for a woman whose name literally
translates as "whore"; the widowed Hippolita is an acknowledged adulteress
whose vengeful bitterness leads her to the attempted murder of her seducer,
Soranzo; only Philotis, the meek niece of Hippolita's disguised husband,
Richardetto, is seemingly virtuous, but her fondness for the dullard Bergetto
casts doubts on her discernment. Only Annabella possesses beauty, virtue,
and affinity – in both senses of that word. She is the only mate for Giovanni.

The obverse is also true. At the start of scene 2, we are introduced to
the men who are vying for the hand of young Annabella, and it is immediately apparent that they are inadequate. Just like Portia in *The Merchant
of Venice*, Annabella is faced with three suitors striving to prove themselves
worthy of the lady and the fortune that will accompany her. While these men
do not face a riddle meant to test their mettle/metal as the wooers encounter
in *Merchant*, they are assayed by Annabella and Putana, who find them
wanting: Grimaldi, the soldier, is a boastful and splenetic coward; Beregetto
is an obtuse man-child interested in little more than puppet shows and prostitutes; and Soranzo is an inconstant and manipulative lothario who lures

Hippolita to unchastity with promises of marriage only to renege and label her "whore" for their shared sin. Putana informs her mistress that "you have choice fit for the best lady in Italy" (1.2.73–74), which does not bode well for Italian ladies. Even casting beyond her hometown of Parma, the best there is to offer is the Roman, Grimaldi – a man potentially hiding "some privy maim" (1.2.82) such as syphilis. Under the circumstances, Annabella and Giovanni's mutual affection seems comprehensible, even if uncomfortable. We see why her "thoughts are fixed on other ends" (1.2.70) when the more appropriate – extra-domestic – choices are thoroughly unfit.

Giovanni imagines this coupling as inevitable, because as manfully as he labors *not* to love his sister, his feelings endure: "The more I strive, I love; the more I love, / The less I hope. I see my ruin, certain" (1.2.145–46). Unrelentingly circular, Giovanni's passion not only does not dissipate, it is constantly renewed because it is at the center of his being, as he says, "I am still the same" (1.2.157). This circularity/insularity is also apparent in the exchange between the siblings when Giovanni declares his love. Lost in his own thoughts, Giovanni fails to hear his sister call to him; when he is gently chastised for his inattention, he responds with, "How d'ee, sister?" (1.2.167). After informing Annabella that he wants to speak with her without Putana's supervision – "Sister, I would be private with you" (1.2.171) – Giovanni again asks, "How is't with 'ee?" (1.2.182). This sort of repetition frequently marks agitation or psychological unrest in Shakespeare's plays – appearing in the anxious utterances of characters such as Lady Macbeth, Othello, and the ersatz madman, Poor Tom of *King Lear* – and even Annabella notes it: "I trust he be not frantic" (1.2.183).

The language that Giovanni deploys as he attempts to woo his sister is similarly narrow and circular. Using the relatively rigid form of the blazon, Giovanni constructs a vision of Annabella that deploys the standard lexicon of love poetry and an almost cartographic mapping of her body – starting at her head and moving downward toward the most intimate regions. But although he begins by comparing Annabella's brow to the goddess Juno's (1.2.193–95), her eyes to "a pair of stars" (1.2.196), and her complexion to the "lily and the rose," (1.2.200), Giovanni's description of her hands begins a process of movement from her body to his body – completing a circuit. Observing that "such hands as those / Would make an anchorite lascivious" (1.2.202–203), Giovanni invokes both holiness tempted to sin, but also an isolated, circumscribed body craving human contact only attainable through self-stimulation, as an anchorite, by definition, lives in seclusion, sometimes even confined in a lonely cell. The anchorite in this line is both himself and Annabella, and his collapse of their two identities is further reinforced by a shift from a poetic exposure of *her* body to a literal uncovering of *his* own body. While the blazon tradition associated with Petrarch would customarily move toward a description of the beloved's ivory breast, Giovanni literally bares his, declaring,

> And here's my breast. Strike home!
> Rip up my bosom; there thou shalt behold
> A heart in which is writ the truth I speak.
>
> (1.2.209–211)

Annabella's response, "If this be true, 'twere fitter I were dead" (1.2.220), suggests their connection as well; however, it is their interchange beginning at line 232 that reveals the level of their link:

> ANNABELLA   You are my brother, Giovanni.
> GIOVANNI   You
> My sister, Annabella. I know this,
> And could afford you instance why to love
> So much the more for this; to which intent
> Wise Nature first in your creation meant
> To make you mine; else 't had been sin and foul
> To share one beauty to a double soul.
> Nearness in birth or blood doth but persuade
> A nearer nearness in affection.
>
> (1.2.232–240)

The shared line at 232 not only indicates a profound verbal intimacy between the pair, "You" completes the line – suggesting a melding of "Giovanni" and "You" Annabella into a single entity, a notion supported by the repeated images of doubles becoming one in Giovanni's speech and the two forms of the word "near."

The intimacy of the relationship and the rhetoric becomes more obvious after Annabella declares her love for Giovanni. As they enact a parodic version of the marriage ceremony, the siblings mirror each other's speech and gesture.

> ANNABELLA   On my knees,   *She kneels.*
> Brother, even by our mother's dust, I charge you,
> Do not betray me to your mirth or hate.
> Love me, or kill me, brother.
> GIOVANNI   On my knees,   *He kneels.*
> Sister, even by my mother's dust, I charge you,
> Do not betray me to your mirth or hate.
> Love me, or kill me, sister.
>
> (1.2.253–259)

The vows differ only in regard to the gender of the sibling, and both brother and sister complete each other's verse lines. The circularity of the oaths also operates on a deeper level as the pair swear fidelity to one another by invoking their "mother's dust" (1.2. 254, 257). By using "dust," as opposed to synonyms such as grave or earth, Annabella and Giovanni are conjuring up the body from which both sprung, in essence, showing how each desires to return to the point of origin. And as the scene ends, the two are thoroughly enmeshed in each other, so that as they prepare to consummate their union, literally making their two fleshes into one, Annabella's speech is encompassed by her husband-brother's; they are no longer separate individuals:

> GIOVANNI   What must we do now?
> ANNABELLA   What you will.
> GIOVANNI   Come, then;
> After so many tears as we have wept,
> Let's learn to court in smiles, to kiss, and sleep.
>   (1.2.265–67)

After their first sexual encounter in 2.1, Giovanni remarks that nothing has changed between them, even echoing his own words from 1.2 when he tells Annabella, "'tis nothing, / And you are still the same" (2.1.11–12). And to a certain extent this is true; in the confined space of the bedchamber, they maintain their status as siblings and lovers. But, beyond this minute sphere, both are altered – especially Annabella. Their congress carries real consequences for her because of the threat of pregnancy and consequent damage to familial reputation, even setting aside the dire public scandal that might ensue were their incest to be revealed. The "dream" (1.2.252) of this unchanged and unchanging love can only exist within the confines of the bed in their father's home. When an ebullient Annabella refers to the "paradise of joy" she has "passed over," an astute Putana retorts:

> Nay, what a paradise of joy you have passed under! Why, now I commend thee, charge: fear nothing, sweetheart. What though he be your brother? Your brother's a man, I hope, and I say still, if a young wench feel the fit upon her, let her take anybody, father or brother, all is one.   (2.1.43–49)

Putana brings the lovers' assignation out of the ether and down to earth by not only highlighting the carnal nature of the relationship, but by suggesting that all sexual prohibitions are inconsequential. In this scenario, Giovanni is not a soul mate, another half, but simply "a man." Annabella's reaction registers her own awareness of the vulnerability of her union with her brother: "I would not have it known for all the world" (2.1.50). The home is one thing, but the world another – and "the speech of people" (2.1.51) is especially dangerous in the public sphere which threatens to encroach upon the private one.

Although Giovanni continues to believe in their unanimity, their oneness, it is wholly dependent upon isolation and secrecy. While Bonaventura knows about the illicit relationship, he is bound by the confessional and his bonds to Giovanni and so operates as an extension of Giovanni's conscience – however inadequate. Giovanni can suppose that the incestuous affair will continue indefinitely because, "She is like me, and I like her resolved" (2.5.67). But as the first signs of pregnancy materialize in one of the public spaces within Florio's house, the insularity of the relationship is threatened. Although Annabella's swooning is initially read by Soranzo and his servant, Vasques, as "maids' sickness, an overflux of youth" (3.2.81), this misdiagnosis cannot be maintained. Like John Webster's Duchess of Malfi, Annabella now "wanes i'th'cheek and waxes fat i'th'flank" (*Duchess* 2.1.67). While she is taken "to her bed instantly," the intrusion of the doctor, Richardetto, into Annabella's private space means that the affair and the pregnancy cannot stay hidden. As Putana says, attributing rather more science to Renaissance medicine than it possessed, "If you let a physician see her water [urine], you're undone" (3.3.16–17).

Annabella's physical transformation from individual to double being, marks a realignment within her relationship with Giovanni. Although the child within her comes from her brother, it also separates her from him as she literally expands beyond the limits of their private space. She begins to seek counsel beyond Giovanni, even asking Friar Bonaventura for absolution. The narrative of damnation he offers pulls Annabella further away from the bed she shares with her brother because of Bonaventura's reclassification of the domestic space as a diabolical one:

> There stands these wretched things
> Who have dreamt out whole years in lawless sheets
> And secret incests, cursing one another.
> Then you will wish each kiss your brother gave
> Had been a dagger's point; then you shall hear
> How he will cry, 'Oh, would my wicked sister
> Had first been damned, when she did yield to lust!'
> (3.6.24–30)

As Putana did in 2.1, Bonaventura denigrates the romance by focusing on the sexual aspects of the relationship – especially through his emphasis on "sheets" and the penetrative violence of the "dagger's point." What is also noteworthy is that the friar blames Annabella, not Giovanni for the sin – in other words, it was not the brother's desire, but the sister's yielding that leads to damnation, and, of course, it is her body that bears the proof of their sin.

Knowing that her bed and her body can no longer conceal her transgressions, Annabella – at the friar's urging – assents to a joining with Soranzo. Yet, while she vows to "live with you and yours" (3.6.53), she does not promise her new husband love, or even sexual access. Like Evadne of *The Maid's Tragedy*, Annabella hopes to simply use the marriage as a way to legitimize her unborn child and to allay suspicions of unchastity: she has relocated, but carries her "lawless sheets" with her to the new domestic space of Soranzo's house. Annabella's inability to see the improbability of this scenario harkens back to Giovanni's deluded daydreams about the relationship in the opening moments of *'Tis Pity*, but by this point, both should know better, especially as a dying Hippolita curses Soranza and Annabella at their wedding:

> Yet ere I pass away – cruel, cruel flames! –
> Take here my curse amongst you: [*To Soranzo*] may thy bed
> Of marriage be a rack unto thy heart!
> Burn, blood, and boil in vengeance! –
> [...]   Mayst thou live
> To father bastards; may her womb bring forth
> Monsters, and die together in your sins,
> Hated, scorned, and unpitied!
>
>   (4.1.92–99)

The curse becomes a prophecy fulfilled as Soranzo discovers that Annabella is pregnant even though he has yet to enjoy his spousal privilege. Calling her "Whore of whores!" and decrying her "belly sports" (4.3.20, 12), Soranzo threatens to murder his new wife for befouling his name and turning her bed (and his) into a common space. Despite Annabella's earlier assertions about the fear of exposure, she not only confesses to be with child, she also declares, that "the man / The more than man that got this sprightly boy ... was in every part / So angel-like, so glorious, that a woman / Who had not been but human as was I / Would have kneeled to him and have begged for love" (4.3.30–32, 37–39). While she stops short of naming Giovanni, she publishes and, therefore, publicizes the relationship, bringing it from a restricted private space into an open one, which invites Soranzo and Vasquez to call her "cunning" (4.3.169). But even they see the need for "privacy," and for her to "make no show / Of alteration" (4.3.268, 142–43).

Remarkably, it is Giovanni who forces the publication of their sin once he understands that their intimate space has been breached. While the affair has continued even after Annabella's wedding, and Giovanni initially sees "no change / Of pleasure in this formal law of sports," noting, "She is still one to me, and every kiss / As sweet and as delicious as the first / I reaped" (5.3.6–10), he comprehends the "change" when he reads a letter written in his sister's blood. Their "two united hearts like hers and mine" are rent apart because their relationship is "discovered" (5.3.12, 34). Although Soranzo plans to have his wife and brother-in-law murdered by hired banditti, he hopes to cover his own involvement by having the crime occur during his own birthday party. His desires for simultaneous exposure and containment, however, are impossibly contradictory. And while Soranzo hopes to damn his "much-loved brother" while he "glut[s] himself in his own destruction" (5.4.35, 45), Giovanni has other plans.

Maddened by the prospect of being cut off from his other half, Giovanni reacts violently. As 5.5 begins, Giovanni and Annabella are presented on a bed for the first time in the play. While offering the suggestion of a sexual assignation, the "liberty" that Soranzo and Vasques plan for, it also conjures up a parallel bed scene at the end of Shakespeare's *Othello*. Like Desdemona, Annabella has been outfitted in the "gay attires" she sported for her wedding, and is "chambered here alone, / Barred of my guardian or of any else" (5.5.20, 23–4). But while the threat to Desdedmona comes from her husband, it is Annabella's brother who offers the genuine peril. Spurred on by jealousy and his own fears at loss of integrity, Giovanni seeks to master the part of him that tries to gain independence and bring another into their intimate space. Just as Othello does, Giovanni instructs his lover to pray so that when he kills her, her soul will go to heaven; and, as in *Othello*, Giovanni continues to kiss his sweetheart as he reluctantly parts from her. As he stabs Annabella, Giovanni declares, "Thus die, and die by me, and by my hand" (5.5.85) – affirming his ownership of her body and his power over it, the repetition of "me" and "my" signaling his conception of her flesh as an extension of his own. Regarding the lifeless body, he meditates on the other part of himself he has destroyed,

> The hapless fruit
> That in her womb received its life from me
> Hath had from me a cradle and a grave.
> (5.5.94–96)

Giovanni constructs a world of Russian nesting dolls, in which his own mother gives birth to him, who in turn gives birth to Annabella, who is the repository for another Giovanni.

When Giovanni enters the birthday feast at the start of 5.6, with Annabella's heart on the end of his bloody dagger, it is a defiant and arrogant act meant to demonstrate his mastery over Annabella, Soranzo, the church, and society. Because he cannot maintain the intimate character of his relationship with Annabella, Giovanni not only makes it public, he turns it into a spectacle. He usurps the social occasion associated with celebrating Soranzo's birth, and turns the event into a convoluted mixture of wedding, birth, and funeral ceremony. Announcing his incest, he constructs himself as Annabella's husband, "A happy monarch of her heart and her" who secretly "enjoyed / Sweet Annabella's sheets" (5.6.45, 44). But by also declaring that he occupied her bed "For nine months' space" (5.6.43), Giovanni links his union with pregnancy and parturition. What is more, his declaration that "This dagger's point plowed up / Her fruitful womb" (5.6.31–32) presents Giovanni as a kind of man-midwife – a figure associated with the forcible extraction of the baby from his mother's womb, and whose presence usually meant the death of both mother and child.

In the end, Giovanni anatomizes his relationship with his sister and reveals all that he believes is remarkable about their love – their miraculous interconnectedness. He presents her heart to the audience in attendance – and to the audience off stage – to expose his own. As he says, "'Tis a heart, / A heart, my lords, in which mine is entombed," but he also must insist upon his mastery over Annabella by proving that "These hands have from her bosom ripped this heart" (5.6.26–27, 59). And in his final act of dominance, he uses his dagger to stab Soranzo through the heart. Giovanni refuses to allow the incest, the adultery, the pregnancy or the murder to go unnoticed; instead, he bares his own vices, reveling in their presentation. He wants those watching to observe and be amazed – once this has happened, he is content to die.

Ironically, those few who remain alive at the play's end fail to appreciate the exhibition Giovanni has offered. One of the only witnesses to all of the events, Putana, has had her eyes put out as punishment for her part in the tryst, and is sentenced to public execution by burning – she has seen, but cannot report what she has seen. What is more, when all the "slaughtered bodies"(5.6.149) are cleared away, it is not Giovanni but Annabella who is imagined as the center of this spectacle. It is her body, her bed that is viewed as the "heart" of the tragedy, so that the final lines of the play, delivered by the Cardinal, the representative of the church in the play, pronounce

> Of one so young, so rich in nature's store,
> Who could not say, 'Tis pity she's a whore?
> (5.6.160–61)

While Annabella consistently seeks privacy, an intimate space for herself and her brother, the world around her demands she live and die in a public realm where virtue can and will be judged. And Giovanni, who imagined his sister as simply an extension of himself, or his private desires, is finally eclipsed by her and the body that he opened for public view.

Part 3

Society, Politics, the City, and the State

In the course of this book, we have worked our way outward in terms of the representations Early Modern drama undertakes, from the inner self, to intimacy, to the family, to social determinants like rank and location. In this part, we turn to the ways Renaissance drama treats large-scale structure: the city, war, politics, and the state. In some ways these are difficult themes to encompass in the concentrated and personalized arena of drama. At the same time, given that tragic drama especially has always focused on what communal obligation calls forth or stifles in individual lives, it is natural to drama to engage broad sociopolitical forces. Moreover, in the climate of interpretation that has emerged in the past 25 years or so, we ask of art we admire that it take on issues that go beyond contemplative selfhood and personal relationship to offer commentary on the operations of social power.

In some ways, what we ask of art now is parallel to something new we ask of ourselves as interpreters. In our lifetimes as scholars, writing about Renaissance drama has changed. It is no longer dominated by the experience of the well-informed individual reader in the study, trying to make sense of a difficult text – long a norm for academic exercises, which after all focus on students, who are expected to cultivate intellectual individuality through reflective reading. Most criticism is still written by individuals who work in studies and who read things and care about what they mean. But ways of framing the idea of drama that reduce emphasis on the problems of individual readers reading, and increase emphasis on the variety of purposes and forces that converge on a play in performance at a particular time, have led to a strong reformulation and expansion of the contextual aspects necessary to take into account when writing about a play. Indeed, a great deal of writing about plays now takes place in the course of writing about some larger or broader cultural phenomenon that the play is seen to

Studying Shakespeare's Contemporaries, First Edition. Lars Engle and Eric Rasmussen.
© 2014 Lars Engle and Eric Rasmussen. Published 2014 by John Wiley & Sons, Ltd.

participate in. This has, in its turn, transformed the imaginative position of the individual critic with respect to his or her activity: often an intensity from contemporary politics, broadly understood to include issues of gender, race, and class, enters into the reading and writing in explicit ways. This impact is widely seen, and has been evident in the previous parts. But nowhere is it clearer than in the ways we discuss relations between drama and large social structures: cities, states, empires, and what Foucault encouraged us to think of as discursive regimes. This part will deal with the ways in which urbanity, the national economy, class, politics, and the state feature in Thomas Middleton and Thomas Dekker's *The Roaring Girl*, Thomas Dekker's *The Shoemaker's Holiday*, Philip Massinger's *A New Way to Pay Old Debts*, Francis Beaumont's *The Knight of the Burning Pestle*, Thomas Kyd's *The Spanish Tragedy*, Christopher Marlowe's *Edward II*, Francis Beaumont and John Fletcher's *The Maid's Tragedy*, John Webster's *The Duchess of Malfi*, Thomas Middleton's *The Revenger's Tragedy*, and Ben Jonson's *Sejanus*. Drama works through particular speaking human bodies who usually, in Renaissance plays, represent individuals rather than impersonal entities or classes. But even though it thus perforce personalizes institutions, it also can focus with emotional power and analytic insight on the large impersonal structures and institutions that call various forms of individual identity forth, making some thrive and others wither.

While it is standard to argue that the engines of intellectual change in this period are the Reformation, the rediscovery of classical culture, and the discovery of the New World, while the engines of political change are the centralization of military power in nation–states aspiring to a monopoly of force (partly through the development of firearms, especially cannons) and the conversion of a relatively independent feudal aristocrats into courtiers intriguing to be as close as possible to a monarch, probably the most visible transformation to the dramatists we are writing about here was the development of London. So we start this part with a great London play.

3.1   Dreaming Up the Free City: *The Roaring Girl*

What is the magic in the proper nouns "Paris," "New York," "Tokyo," "London"? What makes a great city a magnet for talent and a crucible of the new? Can there be a great nation that does not contain a great city?

While none of these questions is directly addressed by Thomas Middleton and Thomas Dekker's *The Roaring Girl*, the play's interest and charm derive from its presentation of a London that can accommodate its unusual heroine and can serve as a life academy for its inhabitants, old as well as young. London in 1611, when *The Roaring Girl* was first performed at the Fortune, had a population of about 225 000, equal to that of contemporary Reno and half that of contemporary Tulsa, the cities of the authors of this book. But early seventeenth-century London conferred a cultural cachet on its inhabitants that Tulsa and Reno, despite their attractions, do not. The London in 1611 was by a huge margin the largest city in Britain and by a narrow head the largest in Western Europe. Moreover, it was growing visibly. The remarkable change in London's population, from around 70 000 in 1550 to around 200 000 in 1600 to around 400 000 in 1640, fueled the establishment of new institutions like public theater and encouraged Londoners to be aware that they were part of something both important and mutable (Wrightson, 2000: 164). Thus in imagining the cultural life of early seventeenth-century London, we need to take into account the opportunities for personal familiarity with those of shared occupation or interests or status afforded by life in what would now be quite a small city, while also recognizing that London had an absolute and uncontested cultural and economic and political centrality for English speakers that very few if any gigantic capital cities now possess (Paris, perhaps, for Francophones, but early seventeenth-century Boston was no Montréal or Abidjan). The demographic data tells even more when one notes that throughout this sixteenth and seventeenth-century population explosion many more people died in London than were born there. An unhealthy place, it thrived on immigrants, British and foreign, drawn by its opportunities, but also served as a place the desperate driven by economic dislocation in rural Britain came to die. So Renaissance London offered its inhabitants, many of them newcomers, a spectacle of heightened competition and accelerated change that we tend to associate with the creative destruction of capitalist modernity: this is one of the reasons that English city comedy seems particularly modern in spirit.

Part of London's cultural centrality was its new role as a center for theater. An enterprise that had been dispersed among traveling companies moving from town to town and noble household to noble household acquired a local habitation and a (set of) names when fixed public theaters were built in London in the 1570s, began to thrive in the1580s, and drew great literary talents like Marlowe, and a decade later Middleton, from the universities into their not entirely respectable orbit. Indeed, the expensive new theaters built in the late 1590s, the Globe by the Lord Chamberlain's men in 1599 and the Fortune by the Lord Admiral's in 1600, may have in their names evoked both the emergence into lucrative success of a large new public enterprise, and the new security and potential respectability for those two companies that came from their special license to perform for royalty, explicitly granted in 1598 (Dutton, 2009b: 371). The genre of English city comedy that arose at the end of the 1590s to participate in this exploding urbanity – a genre Middleton helped develop – is not, on the whole, entirely celebratory of the London scene. But *The Roaring Girl* declares from the outset that it intends to look on the bright side of its brawling, streetwise, cross-dressing, proto-bohemian heroine, Moll Cutpurse, alias Captain Jack, alias Mad Moll, based on a notorious living Londoner named Moll Frith. Discussing various disreputable genres of female Londoner who might be imagined from the title *The Roaring Girl*, the Prologue says "None of these roaring girls is ours: she flies / With wings more lofty" (Prologue 25–26). The play's London takes flight too.

While cities open new paths for those coming to them or coming of age in them, we should not expect these paths often to be original ones. Just as social inequality may seem a tediously repeated aspect of descriptions of the social order, but is discovered anew as individual pain and struggle by each person born on the wrong side of it, so self-urbanization may follow standard patterns yet feel new to each immigrant to London who experiences it. Most city comedy characters, like most people, have conventional expectations and standard desires, and most comic plots channel their protagonists along well-traveled routes, many of them as old as comedy itself, to provisionally satisfying closure. Although cities manufacture new desires by churning fashions in dress and behavior, these too become city comedy tropes, as continual attention to whether one is fashionable becomes a convention of urban life and of urban drama. "You change the fashion," says the Tailor who bustles around Moll attempting to measure her very substantial thigh for a new and ampler set of trousers: "You say you'll have the great Dutch slop" (2.2.85–86). While Moll Cutpurse's breeches disrupt gender norms, an exchange between a tailor and a Londoner concerned to keep up with imported fashion is standard in this sort of play. *The Roaring Girl*, then, sets Moll, a genuinely unusual heroine, amid quite conventional city-comedy types with quite conventional city-comedy problems: Sebastian Wengrave and Mary Fitzallard trying to outwit a blocking father, or the Gallipots, Tiltyards, and Openworks negotiating their more or less satisfactory mercantile marriages amid sexual predation from the prodigal gallants Laxton and Goshawk. Two of the three main plot questions – will Sebastian and Mary be able to marry despite paternal opposition? will the Gallipot and Openwork marriages survive Mrs. Gallipot's dalliance with Laxton and Mrs. Openwork's jealousy, which Goshawk seeks to exploit? – are familiar from any number of London comedies, and the first of them would have seemed entirely familiar to theatergoers in ancient Athens and Rome. The third plot question – will Sir Alexander succeed in entrapping Moll in a crime for which he can have her tried and executed, thus rescuing Sebastian from the marriage to Moll Sebastian claims to intend? – is the center of the play's originality. Moll and her antagonist Sir Alexander are the figures who turn the play into a celebration of the city as a magnet for life-experimentation, a challenge to censorious conventionality, and, potentially, a showcase of diversity and tolerance.

Commentators on *The Roaring Girl* often count Sir Alexander among the conventional comedy types who form a background for the extraordinary figure of Moll (see Orgel, 1996: 152; Maus, 2002: 1375; Kahn, 2007a: 723). He does indeed conform to the New Comedy senex whose greed, selfishness, and refusal to age gracefully make him arbitrarily oppose the desires of his child (Hermia's father Egeus in Shakespeare's *A Midsummer Night's Dream* offers a classic example). But Sir Alexander seems more idiosyncratic than this, in ways that turn out to contribute to the play's representation of the city.

When we first meet him, he is displaying his own mastery of the urban scene to an assembly of guests in his house, some of his own generation and some of his son's. He repudiates their chorused thanks for the dinner he has just provided:

> OMNES   Thanks, good Sir Alexander, for our bounteous cheer.
> SIR ALEXANDER   Fie, fie! In giving thanks you pay too dear.
> SIR DAVY   When bounty spreads the table, faith, 'twere sin
>   At going off, if thanks should not step in.
> SIR ALEXANDER   No more of thanks, no more. Ay, marry, sir
>   Th'inner room was too close. How do you like
>   This parlor, gentlemen?
>
> (1.2.1–7)

What might seem like a way of extracting more expressions of gratitude, more "payment," seems also to be a humorous incapacity for sustained contentment at arrangements he himself has made and a nagging moral awareness that having guests "pay" for hospitality is at odds with the nature of hospitality. Moreover, Sir Alexander cannot entirely accept their account of his hospitality's value: "Th'inner room," Sir Alexander claims, "was too close" – too small or too stuffy. But he turns to something better: "How do you like / This parlor, gentlemen?" (1.2.6–7). After his guests, clearly accustomed to singing for the suppers Sir Alexander provides, have praised the parlor's size, the "sweet breath the air casts here" (1.2.8), its furnishings, and its view, Sir Alexander reflects fussily on how much it all cost, then once again turns on his own money anxiety in the name of hospitality: "Sir Davy Dapper, / The furniture that doth adorn this room / Cost many a fair gray groat ere it came here; / But good things are most cheap when they're most dear" (1.2.10–13). Having pushed his guests into the parlor, he then directs their attention to "my galleries, / How bravely they are trimmed up" (1.2.14–15). Here the actor playing Sir Alexander directs his onstage guests' attention to the original audience crowding the roofed "galleries" of the Fortune Theatre, stacked three high, framed in squares by the pillars supporting each angled gallery, and containing the more expensive seating that surrounded the open-air yard where the groundlings stood for a single penny (Gurr, 2009: 193–197). Sir Alexander once again anticipates his guests' responses: "you all shall swear / You're highly pleased to see what's set down there":

> Stories of men and women, mixed together
> Fair ones with foul, like sunshine in wet weather.
> Within one square a thousand heads are laid
> So close that all of heads the room seems made;
> As many faces there, filled with blithe looks,
> Show like the promising titles of new books
> Writ merrily, the readers being their own eyes,
> Which seem to move and to give plaudities.
>
> (1.2.15–24)

The gesture contains both a claim (or hope) that Dekker and Middleton's audience is happy, but also a more complex claim that the packed faces of Londoners together constitute a promising library of new stories which Londoners read out of one another's behavior and applaud. Thus it offers a cheerful version of Dekker and Middleton's urban representation, and of the city as a space of mutual spectators applauding one another's performance art. All this is something Sir Alexander, as owner and commissioner of these pictures or tapestries, displays to his guests as his vision of the city and requests their approval of. Yet the picture is not entirely a happy one:

> And here and there, whilst with obsequious ears
> Thronged heaps do listen, a cutpurse thrusts and leers
> With hawk's eyes for his prey. I need not show him;
> By a hanging villainous look yourselves may know him,
> The face is drawn so rarely.
>
> (1.2.25–29)

Sir Alexander notes that urban spectatorship can make one a victim of urban predators, here a pickpocket; he also claims that such predators are recognizable by their "villainous look" when "drawn" by an observer as sharp as Sir Alexander's artist. His portrait of these happy but vulnerable Londoners details the more affluent in the galleries; he then lumps together the standees in the yard as a medium or basis for the activity of the rest:

> Then, sir, below,
> The very floor, as 'twere, waves to and fro,
> And like a floating island seems to move
> Upon a sea bound in with shores above.
>
> (1.2.29–32)

The speech not only offers a rare actor's eye view of a public theater from within but also Sir Alexander's view of the London that he not only inhabits, and imaginatively offers to his guests, but also administers as a Justice of the Peace (see 5.1.11). Sir Alexander takes evident pride in his knowledge of the city, which seems to include a sense that he at least can recognize malefactors by their "villainous look."

The rather subtle depiction of Sir Alexander routinely second-guessing his own provisions for his guests, as well as their responses, frames his interference in his son's happiness. As Sebastian explains to Mary Fitzallard when she disguises herself as a seamstress and comes to interrogate the betrothed lover who has been ignoring her after "our fathers did agree on the time when" they should be married (1.1.77), Sir Alexander has turned on the marriage agreement immediately after making it:

> When the knight your father
> Was from mine parted, storms began to sit
> Upon my covetous father's brow, which fell
> From them on me.
>
> (1.1.81–84)

Sir Alexander evidently concludes – wrongly, so far as we can judge – that he has been taken advantage of in the customary marriage settlement that balances the bride's dowry (a cash payment at marriage to set the couple up as an independent household) against the groom's jointure (a legal obligation to provide later financial support, often in the form not only of a future inheritance settled on the groom, but also of guarantees that the dowry would be retained by the bride should the groom die before inheriting). Sebastian reports to Mary that Sir Alexander "scorned thy dowry of five thousand marks" (1.1.89) even though that sum was very substantial, equivalent to roughly half a million pounds today, but he also says, paraphrasing his father's evolution of thought,

> He reckoned up what gold
> This marriage would draw from him, at which he swore,
> To lose so much blood could not grieve him more.
> He then dissuades me from thee, called thee not fair.
>
> (1.1.84–7)

Clearly avarice is a partial motive here, but so are his desire to retain control of Sebastian (and thus not "lose … blood") and his suspicion that Sir Guy, Mary's father, has taken advantage of him. The rivalrous complexity of Sir Alexander's motives does not make him attractive, but it marks his relation to an urban scene that is both full of mutual observation and of contest for advantage. He veers between seeing the city as full of delighted eyes reading each other's faces, and as full of credulous marks being fleeced by villains. He wants to provide the first for his friends and family, giving them superiority in perspective and value judgment (thus he must persuade Sebastian that Mary is "not fair" once he has decided that Sir Guy has outmaneuvered him), and he also sees it as his duty to protect good citizens from predators.

This characteristic ambivalence on Sir Alexander's part emerges toward the end of his "pretty tale" (1.2.61) to his guests describing in transparent disguise his own situation as an essentially "good old man" (1.2.88) blessed with wealth and a sense of how to use it, "For, like a lamp / Fed with continual oil, I spend and throw / My light to all that need it, yet have still / Enough to serve myself" (1.2.100–103). This "good old man" Sir Alexander claims he has met complains of "a son that's like a wedge doth cleave / My very heart root" (1.2.105–106). The son does this by courting Moll, "A creature … nature hath brought forth / To mock the sex of woman" (1.2.128–129). As Sir Alexander abuses Moll, as much in his own voice as that of his surrogate the good old man, Sebastian takes it as his cue to intervene and bolster his appearance of Moll-besottedness:

> SIR DAVY   A monster. 'Tis some monster.
> […]
> SEBASTIAN [*aside*]   Now is my cue to bristle.
> SIR ALEXANDER   A naughty pack.
> SEBASTIAN [*aloud*]   'Tis false!
> …
> SIR ALEXANDER   What's false? I say she's naught.
> SEBASTIAN   I say that tongue
> That dares speak so, but yours, sticks in the throat
> Of a rank villain. Set yourself aside –
> SIR ALEXANDER   So, sir, what then?
> SEBASTIAN   Any here else had lied.
>   (1.2.136–142)

Piously exempting his own father from insult (and thus taking advantage of Sir Alexander's thin fiction that he recounts the family difficulties of a good old man he ran into yesterday), Sebastian defends Moll and exposes his father's intentions. As they unfold, Sir Davy, always a bit slow on the uptake, comments, "Why sir, 'tis thought Sir Guy Fitzallard's daughter / Shall wed your son Sebastian" (1.2.163–164). Sir Alexander, caught up in his self-portrait as generous father wronged by a son's utterly perverse choice, responds, "Sir Davy Dapper, / I have upon my knees wooed this fond boy / To take that virtuous maiden" (1.2.164–166). But of course he has done the opposite, as Sebastian immediately takes him aside to point out,

> SEBASTIAN   Hark you a word, sir.
> You on your knees have cursed that virtuous maiden
> And me for loving her, yet do you now
> Thus baffle me to my face? Wear not your knees
> In such entreats! Give me Fitzallard's daughter.
> SIR ALEXANDER   I'll give thee ratsbane rather!
>   (1.2.166–171)

Sir Alexander's fury here surely partly derives from being caught in such a contradiction, and forced into near awareness that his motives for thwarting his son will not really bear examination. He turns his malice on Moll, laying a series of plots to entrap her.

We have dwelt upon Sir Alexander's initial presentation to emphasize how important to his self-conception it is to be seen as a master of the urban scene in its full spectrum, from generous good living to monstrosity and predation. Middleton and Dekker, in our view, seek to establish Sir Alexander not entirely as a blocking figure and villain, but also as a Londoner of some moral range who resists having that range extended. Thus Sir Alexander's small aria later in the play on the educative virtues of debtors' prisons after his friend Sir Davy Dapper decides to put his prodigal son Jack Dapper in one in order to teach Jack a lesson. Jack is a genuine prodigal, one we see making dubious purchases, being sponged on by his friends, and being complained of for extravagance and dissipation by his own servant (2.1.128–131, 322–323, 404–407).

> Sir Alexander   Bedlam cures not more madmen in a year
>   Than one of the counters does; men pay more dear
>   There for their wit than anywhere. A counter,
>   Why, 'tis an university. Who not sees?
>   As scholars there, so here men take degrees
>   And follow the same studies – all alike.
>   Scholars learn first logic and rhetoric;
>   So does a prisoner. With fine honeyed speech,
>   At's first coming in, he doth persuade, beseech
>   He may be lodged with one that is not itchy,
>   To lie in a clean chamber, in sheets not lousy.
>   (3.3.85–95)

A prisoner graduates with rare honors, says Sir Alexander, "When, money being the theme, / He can dispute with his hard creditors' hearts / And get out clear, he's then a Master of Arts" (3.3.104–106). So Sir Alexander recontextualizes Sir Davy's cruelty to his son as the provision of an education, once again showing off his mastery of the London scene.

The prodigal's career, from waste to debt to arrest to misery in debtor's prison, seems to be in store for Jack Dapper, pursued at his father's suit by two grim arresting officers, Curtalax and Hanger, who justify their predatory occupation by characterizing London as a shark tank: "We are as other men are, sir... All that live in the world are but great fish and little fish, and feed upon one another" (3.3.143–146). But Jack Dapper is rescued by Moll Cutpurse, who disrupts the arrest and gives him time to flee. Like Sir Alexander, Moll can recognize urban threats on sight, as she says to Trapdoor – her servant, whom Sir Alexander has hired to entrap her:

> MOLL   I spy ravens.
>
> TRAPDOOR   Some poor wind-shaken gallant will anon fall into sore labor, and these men-midwives must bring him to bed i'the Counter; there all those that are great with child with debts lie in.
>
> (3.3.190–194)

Preparing to thwart Curtalax and Hanger, Moll comments that they resemble carriers of disease into the city: "They look for all the world like two infected maltmen coming muffled up in their cloaks in a frosty morning to London" (3.3.200–202). And Moll's role in this scene – preventing a cruel but standard urban process from proceeding in its normal course, partly by recognizing it and redescribing it – is also her role with respect to Mrs. Openwork's jealous accusations, to Laxton's sexual predation, and, most centrally, to Sir Alexander's attempt to impose his will on his son and on Moll herself.

Middleton and Dekker take pains to make the antagonists suggestively similar. Like Sir Alexander, Moll offers her many friends guidance to London's pleasures. Like Sir Alexander, her view of the great city is strongly self-inflected, and she responds to what she takes as insult with a combination of violence and strategy. Sebastian, as we have already seen, uses Moll from the outset, initially without her knowledge or permission, to teach Sir Alexander a lesson and shame him into blessing Sebastian's marriage to Mary. This is, however, a use to which Moll also puts herself, as she habitually teaches others lessons. Some of these are quite opposed to Sir Alexander's: Moll in general teaches people to let other Londoners alone to pursue their harmless unorthodox desires by their own lights. Like Sir Alexander, however, she also teaches people how to protect themselves in a great city, more often from the villains that are not immediately visible than from those Sir Alexander claims are instantly recognizable by their "hanging villainous look"(1.2.28). Sir Alexander creates personae for himself – the good old man, the grieved father, the warm generous host – and his patronage of the arts serves some of these personae, as we have seen in his reading of the pictures or hangings in his "galleries." Moll too performs various versions of herself, most notably by alternating between her unorthodox female identity as Mad Moll and her male identity as Captain Jack, but also by composing and singing songs that speak for her idiosyncratic life, and, toward the play's end, by demonstrating that she can look entirely convincing, and can attract even Sir Alexander, as a conventional upper-class bride.

> *Enter Moll [dressed as a woman], masked, in Sebastian's hand, and*
> *[Sir Guy] Fitzallard*
>   ...
> SIR ALEXANDER   Now has he pleased me right. I always counseled him
> To choose a goodly personable creature.
> Just of her pitch was my first wife, his mother.
>
> (5.2.132–136)

More typically, however, Moll teaches lessons to those who, like Sir Alexander in reading his pictures, assume that they know what she is by her "look." The most important of these is the shifty and landless but personable gallant Laxton. Laxton supports himself by sponging from the enamored Mrs. Gallipot while avoiding actually having sex with her: "I know she cozens her husband to keep me, and I'll keep her honest as long as I can, to make the poor man some part of amends" (2.1.142–144). This odd arrangement – *vis-á-vis* Mrs. Gallipot, Laxton is a chaste gigolo – would not in itself bother Moll, who models good-humored tolerance of varieties of behavior and desire, and appreciation of the city as a haven for such diversity. But she hates cruelty and dislikes being accused of impropriety simply because she cross-dresses, smokes, and wears a sword. When, in Laxton's presence, Mrs. Openwork, jealous of her husband's friendly greeting to Moll (who seeks "a shag ruff" (2.1.209–10) from the Openwork shop), takes Moll to be on "love terms"(2.1.232) with him, Moll, angry, feels thwarted:

> MRS. OPENWORK   I'll sell ye nothing. I warn ye my house and shop.
> MOLL   You, Goody Openwork ...
>   I wish thee for a minute but a man.
>   ... But as th'art,
>   I pity my revenge ...
>   Ha! Be thankful.
>   Now I forgive thee.
> MRS. OPENWORK   Marry, hang thee! I never asked forgiveness in my life.
>   *Enter a Fellow with a long rapier by his side.*
> MOLL [*to the Fellow, as she draws her sword*]   You, goodman swine's face!
> FELLOW   What, will you murder me?
> MOLL   You remember, slave, how you abused me t'other night in a tavern?
> FELLOW   Not I, by this light.
> MOLL   No, but by candlelight you did .... And I have reserved somewhat
>   for you. [*She strikes him.*] As you like that, call for more.
>
> (2.1.245 ... 264)

We have no idea whether the alleged tavern slander is real or merely an excuse for the violent displacement of Moll's anger at Mrs. Openwork. Laxton, watching, and already taken with Moll's look, finds it stimulating:

"Gallantly performed, i'faith, Moll, and manfully! I love thee forever for't" (2.1.270–271). Smitten with Moll in her semi-female attire (man's jacket and riding-skirt), and having ten gold coins as a love gift from Mrs. Gallipot, he proposes an assignation:

> LAXTON   Prithee, sweet plump Moll, when shall thou and I go out o'town
> together? ...
> MOLL   What to do there?
> LAXTON   Nothing but be merry and lie together. I'll hire a coach with four
> horses.
> MOLL   ... [T]hree horses will serve, if I play the jade myself.
> ...
> LAXTON [*He offers money.*]   There's ten angels in fair gold, Moll; you see I
> do not trifle with you ... .
> MOLL   Why, here's my hand I'll meet you, sir.
> LAXTON [*aside*]   Oh, good gold! – The place, sweet Moll?
>
> (2.1.282–301)

When Laxton in his coach comes to Gray's Inn Fields for this meeting, he does not find Moll, but is instead addressed by a man. Laxton, taking him for a lawyer from the Inn, says "You seem to be some young barrister. / I have no suit in law; all my land's sold, / I praise heaven for't; 't has rid me of much trouble" (3.1.46–8). The play seems quite at home with the idea that London is full of people who get along stylishly with neither a visible means of support nor shame at its absence: Laxton's very name proclaims that he lacks property (and possibly also that he lacks testicles); the Lord Noland who appears at the play's end is another such. But it is Moll, unrecognized in male attire, who has met Laxton, and she draws her sword to teach him a lesson, producing ten gold coins of her own to match the ones Laxton offered for sex with her:

> MOLL   Ten angels of mine own I've put to thine
> Win 'em and wear 'em!
> LAXTON   Hold, Moll! Mistress Mary–
> MOLL   Draw, or I'll serve an execution upon thee
> Shall lay thee up till doomsday.
> LAXTON   Draw upon a woman? Why, what dost mean, Moll?
> MOLL   To teach thy base thoughts manners. Thou'rt one of those
> That thinks each woman thy fond flexible whore.
>
> (3.1.67–74)

"Win 'em and wear 'em" is a challenge to a duel for money: Moll is giving Laxton a fair chance (as she did the Fellow with the long rapier) to defend himself against her, and indeed to profit if he can beat her. But she seeks also to puncture his male conceit and his propensity for malicious gossip about his conquests (which he has demonstrated earlier: see 2.1.1–20).

> If [a woman] but cast a liberal eye upon thee,
> Turn back her head, she's thine ...
>   [N]ay, for a need,
> Wilt swear unto thy credulous fellow lechers
> That thou'rt more in favor with a lady
> At first sight than her monkey all her lifetime.
>
>   (3.1.75–81)

Although Moll herself may live freely and expressively, she is acutely aware, as we have already seen, of her own and all women's vulnerability to malicious misconstrual of expressive behavior as unchastity:

> How many of our sex by such as thou
> Have their good thoughts paid with a blasted name
> That never deserved loosely or did trip
> In path of whoredom beyond cup and lip?
>
>   (3.1.82–85)

Thus Moll's sword and words defend females from the male detraction that hems in their sociability. She fights for herself, but she also fights to make London a safe zone for female self-realization as it evidently already is for male self-realization. In doing so, she gives one of Renaissance drama's best sketches of female urban desperation:

>   What durst move you, sir,
> To think me whorish? ...
> In thee I defy all men, their worst hates
> And their best flatteries, all their golden witchcrafts
> With which they entangle the poor spirits of fools,
> Distressed needlewomen and trade-fall'n wives.
> Fish that must needs bite or themselves be bitten,
> Such hungry things as these may soon be took
> With a worm fast'ned on a golden hook;
> Those are the lecher's food, his prey.
>
>   (3.1.89–100)

Speaking thus for her "poor shifting sisters" (3.1.101), Moll nonetheless draws a sharp distinction between their weakness and her own militant independence as their champion and her own:

But howe'er
Thou and the baser world censure my life,
I'll send 'em word by thee, and write so much
Upon thy breast, 'cause thou shalt bear't in mind:
Tell them 'twere base to yield where I have conquered.
I scorn to prostitute myself to a man,
I that can prostitute a man to me,
And so I greet thee.
(3.1.108–114)

With this Moll attacks, wishing that "the spirits / Of all my slanderers were clasped in thine, / That I might vex an army at one time" (3.1.114–16). It is such moments that lead Katharine Eisaman Maus to remark aptly that Moll "owes something to the example of Edmund Spenser's Britomart" (Maus, 2002: 1375): she represents armed outraged chastity. Having wounded Laxton, and extracted an apology, she spares him:

LAXTON　　I ask thee pardon.
MOLL　　　　　　　I'm your hired whore, sir!
LAXTON　　I yield both purse and body.
MOLL　　Both are mine and now at my disposing.
LAXTON　　Spare my life!
MOLL　　　　　　　I scorn to strike thee basely.
(3.1.122–124)

But unlike Britomart, Moll does not conceal a secret passion that we know of; rather, she expresses a resolve to remain free and unattached:

Base is that mind that kneels unto her body,
As if a husband stood in awe on 's wife!
My spirit shall be mistress of this house
As long as I have time in't.
(3.1.138–141)

She has articulated the same position to Sebastian, when, under Sir Alexander's surveillance, he offers marriage:

I have no humor to marry. I love to lie o'both sides o'th'bed myself; and again, o'th'other side, a wife, you know, ought to be obedient, but I fear me I am too headstrong to obey; therefore I'll ne'er go about it .... I have the head now of myself, and am man enough for a woman. Marriage is but a chopping and changing, where a maiden loses one head and has a worse i'th'place.　(2.2.36–46)

Whether Moll's lying on both sides of the bed bespeaks active bisexuality, or whether it bespeaks contented role-playing celibacy, we can never be entirely sure: she seeks above all to retain her own freedom, which is partly a freedom to tease her spectators with their uncertainty about her sexual behavior. Indeed, as Nancy Bunker has argued, this ambiguity about what sort of challenge Moll presents is encoded in the contrast between the frontispieces of the first and second printings of the play (Bunker, 2005). The first printing, familiar to students of the play, shows a masculine, confrontational Moll; the second, much more rarely reproduced, shows a Moll who is considerably more feminine and friendly looking.

This second Moll seems, arguably, more like the one who charms Laxton and Sir Alexander, and who performs for Sebastian with the viol set between her knees. Her song is both suggestive and defensive. It begins with a roaming woman, probably a wife, in an unclear but suggestive relation to money, clothes, and urban mobility (Saint Kathern's is a not very respectable dockside district):

> I dream there is a mistress,
>   And she lays out the money.
> She goes unto her sisters;
>   She never comes at any.
> She says she went to th' Burse for patterns;
> You shall find her at Saint Kathern's,
>   And comes home with never a penny.
>   (4.1.105–111)

"That's a free mistress, faith," (4.1.112) remarks Sebastian, doubtless hinting that the woman has spent her money on hired sex with a sailor, and doubtless also speculating (as the hidden Sir Alexander explicitly does) that this is a portrait of "her that sings it" (4.1.114). But Moll then responds with another song, this one beginning with a sexually enterprising "trade-fall'n wife" (3.1.96) of the sort she represented as a victim to Laxton:

> Here comes a wench will brave ye,
>   Her courage was so great;
> She lay with one o'the navy,
>   Her husband lying i'the Fleet.
> Yet oft with him she caviled.
>   I wonder what she ails?
> Her husband's ship lay graveled
>   When hers could hoise up sails.
>   (4.1.116–123)

This speaks for the freedom of women to seek sexual satisfaction for themselves when they do not find it in marriage. But this possible self-portrait turns out to represent another of Moll's unworthy detractors: "Yet she began, like all my foes, / To call 'whore' first; for so do those. / A pox of all false tails!" (4.1.126–128). Moll thus enacts a fairly complex piece of performance art that encodes one of the chief attractions of a great city: people can do as they like sexually as long as they let Moll be and do not prey on the weak.

Obviously, part of the moral of this great play is the one Sebastian articulates to his father *vis-à-vis* Moll: "He hates unworthily that by rote contemns" (2.2.175). London needs to recognize itself as a place where life experimentation can proceed without rote censure.

Moll, however, takes this idea much further than Sebastian. She sees the urban scene as her opportunity to carve out a congenial role for herself: performance artist. She champions the oppressed, but largely as a guarantor of the rights of those who wish to experiment, however foolishly or expensively, with new forms of life. At the same time, she is moral in not allowing this bohemianism to undermine her strong sense of fairness. Indeed, she respects property and propriety, seeing scrupulous care in such matters as necessary if she is to be allowed the latitude she wants in other aspects of her life, despite violent anger on behalf of wronged women. Thus, *The Roaring Girl*'s Moll is a fairly appropriate hero for the modern and contemporary big city emancipation narrative that involves finding one's sexually or morally unconventional true self. When she walks through the city translating canting slang for Lord Noland and Sir Beauteous Ganymede, two London worthies whose names proclaim their nonconformity, Moll enacts the role she plays for modern audiences: tour guide to liberation. Moll indeed fits both the socioeconomic emancipation narrative of justice feminists and the gender-emancipation narrative of life-style progressives. No wonder we like this play.

3.2   *The Shoemaker's Holiday*

Thomas Dekker's *The Shoemaker's Holiday* begins with a disagreement between Sir Roger Oatley, the Lord Mayor of London, and the Earl of Lincoln. The two discuss the courtship between Oatley's daughter, Rose, and Lincoln's nephew, Rowland Lacy. Each man claims to object to the match out of deference to the situation of the other. Oatley says his daughter, a mere citizen, does not have the proper rank to wed Lacy: "Poor citizens must not with courtiers wed" (1.12). Lincoln derides his spendthrift relative, warning Oatley that, despite the Lord Mayor's financial resources, "One twelvemonth's rioting [from Lacy] will waste it all" (1.35). The direct conversation between the men displays nothing but courteousness, but asides and conversations with others reveal that they both see the "subtlety" afoot and the selfish motivations each has for objecting to the marriage (1.38). Lincoln indeed sees Rose as an unfit match for Lacy owing to her nonaristocratic roots, and Oatley wants to protect his fortune. Each has also taken steps to make sure the marriage cannot happen. Oatley "secretly conveyed ... Rose from London / To bar [Lacy] of her presence" (3.15–16) and Lincoln arranged for Lacy to ship off as "Chief colonel ... in those wars of France" (1.47, 49). As any savvy reader would suspect from a comedy, the young lovers overcome the machinations of their elders and marry each other by the end of the play.

Still, even seasoned audiences might have trouble predicting the role the King plays in that marriage. The need for royal authority to intervene in a marriage comes because the obstacles facing Lacy and Rose go far beyond family disagreements and represent some of the major social and political conflicts in late-sixteenth-century England. Lacy's aristocratic family has political influence – Lincoln secures Lacy's military appointment directly from the King (1.46) – but they have also lost over £1000 recently because of Lacy's extravagance. Oatley's lowborn, but wealthy, clan holds power within London, but lacks the hereditary position and national sway of Lincoln's. Together, these families represent the disconnection that capitalism enables between traditional power structures and emerging economic control. A conflict between national and local interests is another key factor in the plot, as exemplified by Lacy's desertion, motivated by a desire to marry Rose, and Ralph's impressed service, which endangers his existing marriage to Jane. The resolution of the play requires the King to mediate in these issues of class difference and varying systems of values. The resulting conclusion settles the problems within the play, while simultaneously highlighting the precarious nature of a settlement reliant on direct intervention from the highest authority in the realm.

As noted earlier, class differences take center stage from the first interactions within Dekker's play. Lincoln represents the aristocracy, and Oatley the London citizens – members of the trade guilds who amassed their fortune and influence through capitalism. Beyond Lacy's squandering of money, other examples in the play depict the aristocracy as reliant on citizens for money. Oatley, through London's Guildhall, allots the press money to the soldiers (1.63). When Simon Eyre becomes the new Lord Mayor at the end of the play, his wealth rather than the King's provides the final banquet (21). Conspicuous wealth attends London citizen, particularly Simon Eyre, throughout the play. From purchasing a ship (7.106–7), to using that wealth to pay for his advancement to sheriff (9.71–2), to the rich accoutrements of being the sheriff ("a gold chain for Simon Eyre" and "a French hood" for his wife (10.147–8)), Eyre's wealth and economic clout are far more conspicuous than those of Lincoln or any aristocratic figure. The divide between blue bloods and those with new wealth appears throughout the play, beginning with Lincoln and Oatley and ending with Eyre and the King. Although the King and Eyre have a much better rapport than Lincoln and Oatley, differences in values and aims persist.

National and local concerns bifurcate in much the same way as aristocratic and citizen issues. Before the King's entrance, Lincoln provides the voice of nationalism. In addition to wanting Lacy far from Rose, Lincoln sees the war as an opportunity to gain honor for his family through military service to the country. Lincoln speaks of opportunities to "Increase the King's love" (1.82) and Lacy, already intent on disguising himself in order to remain in London, flatters his uncle by saying, "I will for honor … So guide my actions in pursuit of France / As shall add glory to the Lacy's name" (1.86, 88–9). However, as evidenced by Lacy's romantic quest, what is needful for the nation and what is beneficial for the city or individual often do not align. Simon Eyre, the titular shoemaker in the play's title, first enters the play as he, his wife, and his workers attempt to persuade Lacy to let his apprentice Ralph out of his duty to serve in the army (1.133). The benefits of having Ralph stay are clear – he can remain with his new wife, Jane, and continue to work for Eyre. The purposes for which he would go to war, conversely, are nebulous. David Bevington, in the introduction to the play, notes, "We are never told why the two sides are fighting" (Bevington *et al.*, 2002: 487). Bevington attributes the lack of specificity about the war to its purpose as a plot device: "The exact time period doesn't really matter; wars occur, and young men go off to fight in them" (Bevington *et al.*, 2002: 487). The war gives Lacy a reason to take up the façade of Hans the shoemaker and remain in London while simultaneously taking Ralph away. Bevington correctly posits that the war advances the plot, but the ill-defined war additionally makes the audience share with Jane, Eyre, and Ralph's fellow workers a feeling that this war's purpose is far removed from the daily concerns of London life. Eyre and his associates value artisanal work, marriage, and economic advancement. They see Ralph's conscription, his national duty, as detrimental to these things and attempt to free him from his obligation.

Lacy, Ralph's captain, will not let allow the soldier-to-be to escape his journey to France, urging him to "hie to [his] colors" (1.203). Lacy emphasizes "His country's quarrel" as the greater cause (1.186) and points out that Ralph's superiors, the King who declared the war and the Lord Mayor who "pressed, paid, and set forth" the soldiers (1.148), require his service. Lacy's firm stance elicits a reply of hearty, if vague, patriotism. Eyre and his workers change their attitude immediately, from trying to help Ralph avoid his military service to praising its decorous merit and Ralph's martial ability (1.167–189). Ralph, rather than becoming the next "Hector of Troy … Hercules [or] Termagant" as Eyre predicts (1.169–70), returns home lame (10.63). The play does not show what happened to Ralph in battle, and Ralph never speaks of the details. From what the play reveals, amputation was the only result of his military service. Certainly, his fellow shoemakers only desire to return his life, as much as possible, to the way it was before his journey to France by restoring his vocation and wife – to return what was taken away in the war. The only consequences of war the play depicts are negative, producing no tangible benefits for the London craftspeople.

Lacy's desertion underscores the detachment between local and national values. Lacy, despite his words to Ralph and his uncle, remains unmoved by his own arguments about military duty and the honor it could bring his family. Instead, Lacy abandons his post as colonel, placing Askew in charge of the troops (1.102–3), and disguises himself as Hans the shoemaker in order to "possess / The only happy presence of [his] Rose" (3.5–6). Lacy commits treason for a chance at the very benefits from which he has just deprived Ralph – a job in Eyre's workshop, a safe home in London, and a (potential) wife. Along with class warfare, the divergence between national and local welfare forms a major focus of the play.

This divergence often appears in Eyre's rise to Lord Mayor as well. Eyre does not hesitate to place his personal desires and those of London over national interests. Rather than hiring an English citizen to fill the vacancy left by Ralph's departure, Eyre hires "Hans," the disguised Lacy, because of his loyalty to his guild and his workers (4.71–3). Bevington notes that the play was written – although not set – during "an influx of unemployed workers from the countryside" (Bevington *et al.*, 2002: 483), increasing the controversial nature of Eyre's hiring practices. Eyre vastly increases his wealth by purchasing a ship clearly owned by someone who had run afoul of English authorities rather than helping to capture the criminal (7.17–18). Eyre uses this wealth to become sheriff, alderman, and eventually Lord Mayor. When Eyre does become Lord Mayor, he stays true to his roots by having a feast day for his "fellow prentices of London" (17.44). The apprentices come at Eyre's invitation, whereas the King has to instigate his own attendance at the banquet. Undeniably, Eyre and the King are on good terms when they meet in the final scene, which means London and England are allied, but this does not alter the many times where Eyre envisions himself primarily as a shoemaker or Londoner rather than an Englishman.

The jovial and friendly actions of the King in the final scene offer to resolve the major conflicts discussed thus far. To the extent that the nation and Londoners have different goals through much of the play, in the end, the King and his subjects are on good terms. The King even allows the shoemakers "To hold two market days in Leadenhall" (21.162) each week, providing national support for the capitalistic endeavors that previously appertained only to the Londoners. Another of the King's reconciliatory roles enables the love story between Lacy and Rose to have its happy ending. Previously, Lacy's disguise as Hans allowed him access to Rose (15). The two married successfully, but this did not stop Lincoln and Oatley from continuing to seek every means possible to destroy the match. They implore the King to "forbid the boy to wed / One whose mean birth will much disgrace his bed"

(21.61–62), even urging him to divorce them once it is discovered they have already married (21.75–76). Only the King, who describes marriage as "The sacred knot knit by God's Majesty" (21.66), provides an endorsement strong and binding enough to end the feud between the families of Oatley the grocer and the Earl of Lincoln. The play foreshadows the happy arrangement of this marriage with the successful defense of Ralph and Jane's marriage earlier. Ralph, wounded in war and unable to find Jane upon returning home (10.107–110), only discovers her whereabouts when asked to make a shoe for her wedding to a new suitor, Hammon (14.36–41). Jane, believing Ralph dead, has reluctantly agreed to marry Hammon (12.120–122), but with the help of the other shoemakers to keep Hammon from marrying Jane, that couple has been successfully reunited. With marriages secured, a lavish feast laid out for apprentices and aristocrats alike, and the King's blessing upon the joyous occasions, *The Shoemaker's Holiday* seemingly ends with a satisfying comic resolution in which the main divisive features of the play – class differences and a national/local rift – disappear.

Unfortunately, that statement is not quite accurate. Along with the King attending a feast with his subjects, the marriage of Lacy and Rose would, in most comedies, form part of a larger pattern of harmony. In Dekker's play, class differences and divided loyalties persist and litter the end of the play. The King's rousing defense of the newlyweds' happy union elicits only a response of, "I am content with what Your Grace hath done" from Oatley (21.119). Lincoln's follow-up, "And I, my liege, since there's no remedy" (21.120) hardly sounds more enthusiastic. If possible, these words demonstrate even less sincerity than appears on the surface, because a defining feature of both characters during the play is duplicity in their speeches – as when they both simulate concern for the other in the matter of Lacy and Rose's marriage. Oatley's "I am content" also echoes Shylock's forced acceptance of conversion in Shakespeare's recent *The Merchant of Venice* (4.1.401), perhaps written only a year or two prior to *The Shoemaker's Holiday* (Bate and Rasmussen, 2007: 416). Despite royal and implied heavenly approbation, the two characters who opposed Lacy and Rose's marriage owing to class differences at the beginning of the play end the play with their prejudices intact.

Another dark shadow covers the convivial feasting shared by the King, Eyre, and the gathered apprentices. The King has the final speech of the play. In it he praises Eyre, his "Friends of the Gentle Craft," the "Lady Mayoress," and the lords for the banquet and cheer (21.191–195). His inclusive praise points to unity and festivity until the final two lines of the play: "When all our sports and banquetings are done, / Wars must right wrongs which Frenchmen have begun" (21.196–197). These lines remind the audiences, both the one at the banquet and the one experiencing the play, that the war continues, and that the very people currently feasting may soon die in it.

Earlier, the king had stepped aside to speak with Lincoln about the need to "incorporate a new supply" of troops for the war effort (21.142). The other attendees with whom the King was feasting could soon become "food for powder," to borrow Falstaff's appropriately dismissive term, and the king chooses to not even wait for the revelry to end to inform them of the fact. Ralph's lame condition, having lost his leg in the battle, gives the audience one reminder of the horrors war provides for those serving on the ground. Another comes in the form of the casualty list Lincoln receives from the battle Lacy should have been leading:

> The lot of victory fell on our sides.
> Twelve thousand of the Frenchmen that day died,
> Four thousand English, and no man of name
> But Captain Hyam and young Ardington.
> (8.7–10)

Apprentices, when transferred from the caring presence of Simon Eyre and the guild system to the battlefield, become nameless pawns whose deaths by the thousands form part of what is considered a positive outcome. At the end of the play, harsh feelings persist between Lincoln and Oatley, the war that claimed Ralph's leg continues to require more fodder, and the King – although present – remains dispassionate about the repercussions of that war for the assembled multitudes.

Despite moving toward a comic resolution with a saved marriage, a new marriage, and the commendable mad shoemaker taking the highest office in London, the play appears to avoid a truly comic ending. Still, if comedies are supposed to end with the (re)establishment of proper order in society, this one ends with the King in total control. Royal power keeps in check the enduring animosity between Lincoln and Oatley. The war receives at least perfunctory justification, "Wars must right wrongs which Frenchmen have begun" (21.197), and the King's personal sanction to further its cause. Eyre, who initially sought to keep Ralph away from the war as a defender of his worker, will now take on Oatley's responsibility to make sure "The Londoners are pressed, paid, and set forth" (1.148). Eyre will actively support the war effort rather than just offering vague patriotic platitudes. Many causes of conflict remain the same at the beginning and end of the play, but the immediate presence of royalty subdues them all and forces what superficially looks like a happy resolution. Perhaps the staging of the play "before the Queen's most excellent Majesty" (Epistle 49) helps explain why the proper world at the end of the play is one made "ideal" by the monarch. Unlike in many city comedies, where monarchs are often absent and the plays focus exclusively on local issues, Dekker has his play celebrate the resolution absolute power can provide. This would suit the play's opening-night royal audience, but what about others who could not count on the Queen showing up to solve their problems and eat pancakes? The persistent remnants of discord in the play – class rivalry, war, contradictory national and local objectives – reveal real social anxieties that could be very troubling to playgoers who do not have the promise of direct royal intervention.

3.3   *A New Way to Pay Old Debts*

As the title of Philip Massinger's *A New Way to Pay Old Debts* suggests, time is intimately connected with money. More specifically, conceptions of indebtedness and compensation are entirely dependent upon whether one is rooted in the older traditions of the past or disposed toward the novel practices of the present and future. These competing understandings of economics, and the accompanying visions of the rights and responsibilities associated with class, serve as the central theme of the play and a central concern of England in the first half of the seventeenth century.

The same year that *A New Way to Pay Old Debts* was entered into the Stationers' Register, 1632, Thomas Powell's tract, *The Mystery and Misery of Lending and Borrowing*, declared that through "lending and borrowing ...the soule of traffique is breathed into the body of a commonwealth." Credit, in other words, is the animating force of the economy and the culture – in terms of its literal place in financial transactions, as well as in its figurative associations with honor and recognition. Both sorts of credit animate Massinger's play, providing the ground for conflict as modern urban values based in profit and self-seeking behavior threaten the traditional rural mores tied to exchange and fellowship. The extravagance and avariciousness normally linked with London find their way to Nottingham, presenting an occasion for interrogating the imbrication of city and country, nobility and gentry, debtor and credit, old and new.

The play begins with the profligate gentleman, Frank Wellborn, quarreling over his bar tab and the blocking of his access to "booze" and tobacco. Having lost all of his money through drinking, smoking, whoring, and gambling, Wellborn's well has dried up as alehouse keeper, Timothy Tapwell, denies his customer even "a suck" of liquor, "Nor the remainder of a single can / Left by a drunken porter" (1.1.1–3). The heart of the conflict is not simply a difference of opinion about ale, however; it is a fundamental disparity in views about class in a changing economy where feudalism and patronage are being replaced by social mobility and nascent capitalism. From the start, Wellborn quibbles with the very notion that he can be cut off by Tapwell, that he can be ruled by an underling – even in that underling's own establishment – whereas Tapwell sees money as the great equalizer that has led to Wellborn's diminishment and his own elevation, which ultimately makes him his own master.

Throughout 1.1, Wellborn seeks to put Tapwell and his wife, Froth, in their right place, not only flinging insults such as "dog," "brach," and "Slave" at the pair, but also reminding Tapwell of his former position as a servant: "Wert thou not / Born on my father's land, and proud to be / A drudge in his house?" (1.1.27–29). Tapwell's perspicacious response – "What I was, sir, it skills not. / What you are is apparent" – highlights that times have changed, and so have their respective fortunes, so that "Late Master Francis" is "now forlorn Wellborn" (1.1.29–30, 39).

Both men view themselves and their world through contradictory systems of accounting. Wellborn asks for recognition – credit – for frequenting the alehouse, and considers Tapwell an "unthankful villain" for failing to see him as his patron as Wellborn's "riots fed and clothed" him (1.1.23, 27). In fact, Wellborn presents himself as a kind of silent partner in Tapwell's business: "Did not I / Make purses for you? ... 'Twas I that, when I heard thee swear if ever / Thou couldst arrive at forty pounds thou wouldst / Live like an emperor, 'twas I that gave it / In ready gold" (1.1.74–75, 77–80). Tapwell, on the other hand figures the situation differently. Since Wellborn originally furnishes the capital for the alehouse as a "gift," the money is not figured as a debt that must be repaid, or as Tapwell puts it, "I find it not in chalk, and Timothy Tapwell / Does keep no other register" (1.1.25–26). Honor and gratitude are immaterial, and, therefore, are not counted amongst one's debts which is why

> from the tavern to the taphouse, all,
> On forfeiture of their licenses, stand bound
> Never to remember who their best guests were,
> If they grew poor like you.
>
> (1.1.81–84)

Tapwell comes across as mercenary – and, in fact, he is: he relies on the *mercēs* or wages he receives from his customers. Because of his vulnerable economic position – one rung up the social ladder from a servant – he is reluctant to choose friendship over financial security, especially because Wellborn seems like a bad risk.

Tapwell's entire narrative of his former master is focused on a subtraction of resources. While after Old Sir John Wellborn dies, his son inherits £1200 *per annum*, Tapwell reminds Wellborn that

> You were then a lord of acres, the prime gallant,
> And I your under-butler. Note the change now.
> You had a merry time of't – hawks and hounds,
> With choice of running horses, mistresses

> Of all sorts and sizes – yet so hot
> As their embraces made your lordships melt.
> Which your uncle, Sir Giles Overreach, observing,
> Resolving not to lose a drop of 'em
> On foolish mortgages, statutes, and bonds,
> For a while supplied your looseness, and then left you.
>
> (1.1.42–51)

According to this report, not only has Wellborn been a spendthrift, squandering his legacy, he has reached his current predicament through the purchase of items meant to demonstrate wealth and rank – hawks, hounds, horses, and mistresses – all used in activities associated with men of leisure.

References to the "hot" embraces that have melted his "lordships" do suggest that Wellborn has gained something from his expenditures: syphilis – a reading supported by Wellborn's exchange with one of his creditors later in the play:

> [*To Third Creditor*] Oh, I know thy face;
> Thou wert my surgeon. You must tell no tales;
> Those days are done. I will pay you in private.
>
> (4.3.98–100)

Associated with both the administration of mercury in sweating tubs and the excision of syphilitic lesions, the presence of a barber–surgeon suggested moral and physical corruption, so it is no wonder that Wellborn requests discretion from his creditor and seeks a private audience to disburse his debts. This antipathy toward the profession, and more specifically toward their connection with the treatment of sexually transmitted disease, is graphically represented in Francis Beaumont's comedy, *The Knight of the Burning Pestle* (1607), where the barber–surgeon Barbaroso is presented as a "foul beast [who] / Hath scorched and scored" (3.4.81–82) the diseased knight, Sir Pockhole, instead of as a healer attending to his patient. Commonly linked with loss – whether in terms of the vast financial outlay required for treatment of the pox or the amputations of appendages ravaged by the disease – syphilis features as a deficit for Wellborn, marking him as an unsound investment.

As Craig Muldrew's *The Economy of Obligation* suggests, in the early seventeenth century, "social relations were not only reinterpreted in terms of judgement about credit," but as the culture grew more litigious, especially in regard to the dispensation of debts, there was an "increasing emphasis on the contractual nature of interpersonal relationships" (Muldrew, 1998: 315–16). Tapwell's unwillingness to extend Wellborn credit shows that the he has put profit above "interpersonal relationships," and that he would rather cater "to whores and canters, / Clubbers by night" who "had a gift

to pay for what they called for" than the cashless gentry (1.1.62–63, 65).
Further, Tapwell reckons that

> The poor income
> I gleaned from them hath made me in my parish
> Thought worthy to be a scavenger, and in time
> May rise to be overseer of the poor –
> Which if I do, on your petition, Wellborn,
> I may allow you thirteenpence a quarter,
> And you shall thank My Worship.
>
> (1.1.65–71)

While the source of the funds may be distasteful, Tapwell knows that the
provenance of the money matters less than its propagation, and an increase
in wealth leads to a broadening of one's social landscape. And although being
named a "scavenger" or garbage man does not appear to be a boon, it was
a position as overseer for street cleanliness and public hygiene, not a hands-
on filth-collecting job, which as such makes it a good place for Tapwell to
begin his social climb – so that he will ultimately be in a position to look
down upon his former master. Tapwell denies personal charity, and defers
any charity until the humiliating moment that he will be able to administer
public alms to Wellborn as a parish officer.

Alexandra Shepard points out that "if a man's worth was doubted, he
lost his credit and economic standing and was excluded from the relations
of trust which both bound communities and accorded status and agency."
(Shepard, 2000: 87) Because of a loss of both personal confidence and a
broader sense of public trust, Wellborn's status as "true gentry" is interro-
gated, and the man himself found wanting (2.1.89). It is for this reason that
Tapwell dares to strive for the title "Worship," as Wellborn's behavior, as
well as his loss of the estates that made him *landed* gentry, has removed the
need for reverence of this title or his person. In essence, Tapwell sees the
situation as a simple computation: Wellborn's loss is his gain. Indeed, this
zero-sum relation is encoded in their names: Tapwell has tapped into the
well-being Wellborn was born into and has drained it away.

Tapwell imagines himself as the spiritual heir of Wellborn's deceased father,
as he, unlike the flesh-and-blood heir, not only attempts to improve his
circumstances but tries to improve the community at large. As Katharine
Eisaman Maus suggests in her introduction to *New Way*, Tapwell "lives
a lowly parody of Wellborn's father's civic commitments" where he gains
prestige through marriage, hard work, and a gradual ascent to local government offices (Bevington *et al.*, 2002: 1833). While it is tempting to read
Tapwell and his wife as characters with stunningly low expectations for
advancement, and therefore as worthy of derision, Tapwell's encomium to

Old Sir John Wellborn indicates not only a keen understanding of the gentleman's virtues, but an acute grasp of the limitations of the new generation of gentry – their spurning of civic responsibility and their withholding of charity. As Tapwell states,

>   Your dead father,
> My quondam master, was a man of worship ...
>   Justice of Peace and Quorum,
> And stood fair to be *Custos Rotulorum*,
> Bare the whole sway of the shire, kept a great house,
> Relieved the poor, and so forth ... .
>
>   (1.1.32–37)

Because Sir John knew his place, knew his duty to the poor and to the shire, the country was in balance; it is only *after* Frank wastes his inheritance and shirks his responsibilities that Tapwell steps in to take his place. In this way, Tapwell is actually a relatively conservative character as he wants to carry on Sir John's charitable acts; his radicalism comes from his desire to use that charity as a cudgel to beat down his former master and from his refusal to grant charity *within* the alehouse. Unlike Sir John, Tapwell keeps his business separate from his civic obligations because he, as a servant turned small businessman, literally cannot afford the *noblesse oblige* associated with the aristocracy and landed gentry – the proffering of charity might mean that Tapwell himself would be in need of alms, so he chooses to live by the axiom "charity begins at home." Given Wellborn's current financial fix, extending credit would be tantamount to charity as the sum would, most likely, be classified as "desperate debt" – the severest category of debt in the period, "of which there was little chance of recovery" (Muldrew, 1998 176). While sympathetic to the old system, Tapwell cannot benefit from it, and, therefore must, out of necessity, reject it and Wellborn – especially as the powerful and vengeful Sir Giles Overreach has threatened to destroy Tapwell if he does not reject Wellborn.

Wellborn himself seems to have an ambiguous relationship with his own status as he is forced into the position of asking for the extension of credit from a social inferior – and perhaps this is one of the reasons for the vehemence of his response to the curt denial as well as a justification for his demand that Tapwell and Froth must "vanish, creeping on their knees" to avoid a severe beating (1.1.93). Less than a hundred lines later, Wellborn refuses a gift of "eight pieces / To put [him] in better fashion" (1.1.171–172) offered by his friend, Tom Allworth – a young gentleman who is employed as a page to Lord Lovell. Wellborn gives two reasons for the rejection: Allworth is younger, and, therefore a social subordinate; and Tom's fortunes are severely curtailed because he depends upon "the devotion of a stepmother / And the uncertain favor of a lord" (1.1.174–75).

While both Tapwell and Allworth are financially vulnerable – and face the possibility of ruin through lending to Wellborn – it is Allworth who faces the greatest peril because, unlike Tapwell, Tom is not his own master. His reliance on the old system of preferment and service to nobility means that Allworth's prospects are dubious, linked, as they are, to the whims of Lord Lovell and to the notion of "credit" as recognition. Because Allworth's future happiness is contingent on others giving credit where credit is due, he himself extends credit to Wellborn as a mark of faith in that system – but to *his* credit, Wellborn acknowledges his lack of desert for this confidence, declaring

> Although I thank thee, I despise thy offer.
> And, as I in my madness broke my state
> Without th'assistance of another's brain,
> In my right wits I'll piece it; at the worst
> Die thus, and be forgotten.
>
> (1.1.181–85)

In order to "piece it," Wellborn will have to exploit elements of both the old and the new economies – learning lessons from Tapwell, Allworth, and his immoral uncle, Sir Giles Overreach – as he attempts to regain not only his title but his manhood. Shepard reminds us that in early modern England, "to be worth nothing was to be economically impotent and by implication less than a man" (Shepard, 2000: 86). Wellborn's taking up a cudgel to beat Froth and Tapwell into submission and to improve their "memory" of his former status is telling, as is his referring to his club as a "scepter" – a word that suggests not only sovereign power but is also meant to contradict the "potent monarch called the constable" that Tapwell threatens to unleash on Wellborn (1.1.88,92,13). But the threat of violence appears feeble, and as with all of the threats of violence in the play, a sign of desperation and, ultimately powerlessness.

It is art not aggression that provides Wellborn his *New Way* to regain his old glory – and it is art that allows Allworth to obtain his heart's desire – the hand of Margaret Overreach. And the remainder of the play features both Wellborn and Allworth working, in two separate but related plots, to thwart the desires of their common enemy, Sir Giles Overreach. For Wellborn, this is accomplished through enlisting the aid of the virtuous widow, Lady Allworth – Tom Allworth's stepmother – and her solicitous servants to intimate that Master Francis is to become her next husband, not only giving Wellborn access to credit, but offering him the opportunity to regain the lands he has forfeited to his uncle. For Allworth, it is achieved by recruiting his master, Lord Lovell, to woo Margaret in his place, much as Don Pedro courts Hero for Claudio in Shakespeare's *Much Ado About Nothing* (1600) – although Allworth's proxy is used, not because of diffidence but because of a need to thwart Sir Giles' social overreaching: he wants his daughter to marry into the aristocracy. In both storylines, these down-on-their-luck gentlemen must depend on their social superiors to look toward the past – to former service and familiar reputation – in order to gain future happiness. Both must appeal to a patronage system and a societal structure built upon acknowledgment of deeds or credit.

Although Lady Allworth initially rejects Wellborn as a "son of infamy," and commands him to "forbear my house" (1.3.81), her tone softens when Wellborn reminds her of the literal and symbolic debt both she and her deceased husband owe him:

> That husband, madam, was once in his fortune
> Almost as low as I. Want, debts, and quarrels
> Lay heavy on him. Let it not be thought
> A boast in me though I say I relieved him.
> 'Twas I that gave him fashion; mine the sword
> That did on all occasions second his;
> I brought him on and off with honor, lady.
> And when in all men's judgments he was sunk,
> And in his own hopes not to be buoyed up,
> I stepped unto him, took him by the hand,
> And set him upright.
>
> (1.3.100–110)

Not only does Wellborn point to financial support of Lady Allworth's husband, he also alludes to the debt of honor associated with dueling – again alluding to an older England associated with courtly traditions and masculine virtue. It is telling that the widow initially offers money, "A hundred pounds," as payment for these former deeds – a thoroughly modern attempt to convert services to cash value – but Wellborn declares, "No, madam, on no terms. / I will not beg nor borrow sixpence of you" (1.3.121–122), showing his unwillingness to enter into another financial contract. His rejection of "terms" signals a denunciation of the emerging "capitalistic, cash-nexus society" (Neill, 2000: 74) that places a specific monetary value on goods and services. Instead, Wellborn seeks a suit "which you deny not / To strangers": charity (1.3.124–125). What Tapwell denies or defers is what Wellborn demands, which not only promises to return to the ways of Old Sir John Wellborn, but also removes him from a system in which he is presently unable to compete. The £100 that Lady Allworth tenders is insufficient to repair his fortunes or improve his prospects, for as Shepard reminds, "One of the preconditions of male credit in its patriarchal sense was householding status" (Shepard, 2000: 96). Until Wellborn can reclaim his estates from Sir Giles, he is no man and can gain no economic credit. Wellborn's only chance is to use Lady Allworth's credit – in terms of both her good reputation and her wealth – to improve his own, by convincing Sir Giles and the rest of the community that Lady Allworth has agreed to marry him. Wellborn's access to her credit allows him to regain the outward signs of respectability, which ultimately lead to his readmittance to the gentry.

Borrowed honor is also the means by which Allworth gains both love and financial independence. Because Sir Giles Overreach is determined that his daughter, Margaret "must part with / That humble title," of mistress, and instead "write 'Honorable' ... daughter," Lord Lovell has become his "main work" (2.1.74–75, 68). Allworth, although a man of great integrity and personal "worth," lacks both the economic security and rank to ensure that Margaret is "well attended" (2.1.78). Lovell is, as Allworth suggests, "Above my merit," but, then again, he is also above Margaret's (3.1.20). As Lovell confides to Lady Allworth,

> Were Overreach' states thrice centupled, his daughter
> Millions of degrees much fairer than she is,
> Howe'er I might urge precedents to excuse me,
> I would not so adulterate my blood
> By marrying Margaret, and so leave my issue
> Made up of several pieces, one scarlet
> And the other London blue.
>
> (4.1.219–225)

Lovell imagines the union as miscegenation or pollution, but even more than that, he sees the City and its values infiltrating the traditions of England that are embodied in the country. Overreach and his daughter "come from the city" and have acquired their status through industriousness, exploitation of the legal system, and the accumulation of capital *in* the capital (2.1.81). Their credit, in Lovell's estimation, is simply a matter of money, not merit – and even Margaret's apparently strong character cannot make up for her connections with her father's geographical and genealogical shortcomings. Within the older patriarchal system, blue blood cannot mix with the London blue worn by the working class – the status quo must be maintained: which is one reason why Lovell is willing to pretend to pursue Margaret – so that she will stay within the rank of gentry through marrying Allworth. While Allworth's birth is superior to Margaret's, her father's status as "Sir" Giles Overreach puts them on relatively equal footing, and the wealth that Allworth will gain from the match will allow him to attain a position similar to that enjoyed by his late father – in essence, offering a return to former times, especially if this results in the diminution of Overreach's fortunes.

Like Wellborn, Lovell and Allworth desire a reversion to the old days and the old ways to pay old debts. All three men explicitly reject Sir Giles Overreach and the tenets he represents: guile, treachery, and gain through another's losses. And yet, all three men practice the kinds of Machiavellian intrigues for which they despise Sir Giles. Wellborn not only pretends to be betrothed to Lady Allworth, he takes money from his uncle under the pretext that it is a loan, and he exploits the dissatisfaction of Overreach's lawyer and minion, Jack Marall, to regain the deed to his lands – and as payment, Marall is barred from practicing law. Lovell feigns interest in Overreach's daughter and thus manipulates the man in order to give Allworth access to his daughter; Allworth woos Margaret and marries her without the consent of her father, although he justifies it through a series of machinations and obfuscations. Sir Giles Overreach is presented as the villain because he "leave[s] religion and turn[s] atheist," that he believes that "Words are no substances" (5.1.382; 3.2.129). But, of course, the words of the other heroic characters have "no substances" either as they are engaged in as much dissimulation and deceit as Overreach. What really seems to mark Overreach as a "bold, bad man" (4.1.59) is not his scheming, but his understanding that nobility itself is a word that no longer retains the "substance" it once possessed (4.1.159). He realizes that titles are for sale, and that they do provide a kind of credit that negates the titles associated with naked capitalism: "Extortioner, tyrant, cormorant" (4.1.122); in other words, to be labeled "Right Honorable" provides a veneer that covers all villainies – something borne out by the play itself. Sir Giles Overreach's crime, then, is that he reaches for the cultural cover that aristocracy has traditionally provided.

The purportedly heroic characters in *A New Way to Pay Old Debts* resort to the kinds of witty scheming used by characters in Elizabethan and Jacobean city comedy, such as Rowland Lacy of Thomas Dekker's *The Shoemaker's Holiday* (1600) – a play whose main plot is remarkably similar to *New Way*. But, in this Caroline country comedy, the scheming is not performed for the purposes of invigorating the culture through the union of class (associated with men) and cash (connected with women), but with the reestablishment of older social values that confine marriage and money to narrowly defined class boundaries. In Dekker, the hero struggles against his uncle's desire that his nephew marry within his station. In *New Way*, Wellborn is a confirmed bachelor who desires no women at all; the role of thwarted lover is played by Allworth who only yearns for one of his own class – it is her father who has pretensions to one of greater rank. Nottingham is not London, and mobility is not lauded: old ways are still the best ways on the periphery of the commonwealth.

And yet, while it is easy to read the play, and the author, as ideologically conservative – punishing, as it does, those who attempt to elevate their station through fraud, litigation, and marriage – the extremity of the reaction to social mobility appears parodic rather than exemplary. Wellborn's exchange with his creditors is instructive in this regard. After rejecting Tapwell and Froth's petition to be repaid, Wellborn turns to the three men seeking recompense: a wine merchant, a tailor, and a surgeon. As part of their petitions, the merchant and tailor remark upon the hardships they have endured because they have not made use of the legal system to secure what is owed them. In fact, the first creditor declares that he is

> A decayed vintner, sir,
> That might have thrived, but that Your Worship broke me
> With trusting you with muscadine and eggs,
> And five-pound suppers, with your after-drinkings,
> When you lodged upon the Bankside.
>
> (4.2.83–87)

The tailor tells a similar tale, informing that once he was an aspiring entrepreneur,

> … but now mere botcher.
> I gave you credit for a suit of clothes,
> Which was all my stock, but, you failing in payment,
> I was removed from the shop board, and confined
> Under a stall.
>
> (4.2.92 95)

Both men lost their social footing, sliding from positions of relative security to poverty and degradation as a direct result of Wellborn's economic and moral failures. After all, the debts that Wellborn has racked up are related to his licentious lifestyle. The "suit of clothes" was purchased as a display of his wealth and stylishness. The food and drink were procured at the vintner's Bankside establishment, suggesting that less wholesome activities accompanied these "five-pound suppers" as London's south bank was associated with brothels as well as bars – something further hinted at by the presence of the silent third creditor: the surgeon. Unlike Tapwell, these men extend credit, but in the short run are repaid only with financial ruin. While Wellborn's change in circumstances allows him to pay what he owes the men, his suggestion that he will "set thee up again" (4.2.90) rings false as his economic troubles and theirs not are equivalent. With £1000 and the retrieval of his clothing from pawn, Wellborn is able to quickly return to his former station and the respect and credit that accompany the title "gentleman." The creditors' recoveries will not be as easy. As the tailor says, "I was removed from the shop board, and confined / Under a stall." Customarily, these lines are read as an indication that the tailor loses his place in a shop and must ply his wares outdoors in the market. This reading is certainly correct, but it fails to take into account the class dimension. As well as being a booth used for the sale of wares, "stall" has an alternate meaning: standing or degree of rank (*OED* 1). Because the tailor is denied a place to serve his affluent and exclusive clientele, he loses both his vocation and his identity, so that now he is "Under a stall" or beneath a rank.

Wellborn does not care about the injuries that his profligacy has caused. In fact, he mocks the tailor's declaration about not requesting interest on the debt. As Wellborn says, "Such tailors need not; / If their bills are paid in one-and-twenty year" (4.2.96–97). In other words, a gentleman's time and money are not the same as a laborer's – the working man should be happy to receive payment at all. And this does seem to be the message that Wellborn is sending to his creditors – because they have not sought out payment, they ultimately collect it, but not before the damage is done. Tapwell is bankrupted as punishment for extending credit to a wastrel, but the vintner and tailor are destroyed too. In essence, there is no way for the lower classes to succeed as both denying and extending credit lead to loss.

This scene can be read as the portrayal of characters ending up in their "right place," and yet, it is important to note that Wellborn's restoration is not only born from the kinds of Machiavellian manipulation exhibited by his uncle, Sir Giles Overreach, but he also resorts to extortion just as his uncle does. As we find out later in the play, it is Sir Giles who forces Tapwell and Froth to rebuff Wellborn.

The play's dénouement is highly problematic even as it is presented as a happy ending. The unexpected betrothal of Lady Allworth and Lord Lovell reminds us of the economic advantages of the match – after all, Overreach intended to acquire her lands when he believed she was to marry Wellborn, and he meant to give this valuable estate to Lovell; so, the canny aristocrat seems to have simply cut out the middle man. With neither of them exhibiting much in the way of affection or warmth, the pairing evokes that of the Duke and Isabella from Shakespeare's *Measure for Measure* (1604). The union of Allworth and Margaret is more conventional, less knotty except as it shows the bride's filial impiety. But as with Jessica, the daughter to *The Merchant of Venice*'s Shylock, Margaret can present her father's crimes as justification for daughterly disobedience. And yet, it is important to note that while critics frequently equate Overreach with Shylock, and liken *New Way*'s emphasis on old versus new economics with *Merchant*'s portrayal of vengeful Jewish "justice" versus attractive Christian "mercy," in *New Way* it is status not bloodshed that Overreach seeks, nor is Margaret's deception of her father nearly as flagrant as Jessica's (Neill, 2000: 96–97). Certainly, Overreach is wrong in encouraging his daughter to give up her chastity to gain a husband, but he is not wrong in his understanding that her credit, her value, is related to her sexual attractiveness and her dowry.

For this reason, Sir Giles Overreach's punishment seems extreme. Not only does he lose his wealth but he is denied the ability to fight and thus confirm his masculinity. Lady Allworth keeps her intended from dueling with Overreach by scornfully asking Lovell if he will "Contest with one distracted?" (5.1.305). Marked as a madman and one unworthy of confrontation, Overreach is publicly discredited, and his only course of action is to lash out and try to destroy those who have stolen his daughter, his money, and his dignity. In a final emasculating act, he is overwhelmed by Lady Allworth, who "sits upon mine arm / And takes away the use of't, and my sword" (5.1.363–64). This moment graphically illustrates the loss of patriarchal power, as his hand – associated with strength and power – and his sword – linked with phallic might and the threat of violence – are stayed by a widow. Overreach's thwarted aspirations turn to insanity, and like Malvolio in *Twelfth Night* (1602) he must be taken "to some dark room … for his recovery" (5.1.378–379). The danger he poses is more psychological than physical as he himself notes that "I am feeble" (5.1.362). His very name hints at the real threat – that a desire to reach above and beyond present circumstances is inherent in him, and in English culture.

Wellborn's final assertion that he must "do something" (5.1.400) to regain his own masculinity is telling, coming, as it does, on the heels of Overreach's collapse. The destruction of a patriarch – and one related to him – serves as a warning. Wellborn's desire to be of "service / To my king and country" (5.1.399–400) is a retreat to the old ways of credit as reputation. But as his dealings with his creditors have shown, patrons can be fickle and reward often slow. Just as Tapwell's hopes for betterment were dashed by the whims of a powerful superior, so are Wellborn's fortunes tied to an old way that promises new debts and an old uncertainty.

3.4   *The Knight of the Burning Pestle*

Francis Beaumont's *The Knight of the Burning Pestle* actually contains three separate plays. *The London Merchant* is the name of the play ostensibly about to begin in Act 1, Scene 1. George and Nell, two audience members upset with the subject matter of the evening's entertainment, request a play that does not "have … girds at citizens" (Induction.8). George is a citizen, a member of the grocers' guild, and he fears that this play will mock him. The portions of *The London Merchant* that appear in Beaumont's play justify George's fears, depicting the merchant, Venturewell, as a cruel father and foolish matchmaker. George and Nell request what they consider to be a proper play, a chivalric romance. When the Prologue suggests that they do not have the preparation time or extra actors to put on a play other than *The London Merchant* (Induction, 32–33, 59–60), George agrees to supply the plot and another actor, his apprentice Rafe. The Prologue gives a title to Rafe's play: *The Knight of the Burning Pestle* (Induction.95), after the heraldic symbol on Rafe's shield. Beaumont's play, also called *The Knight of the Burning Pestle*, presents the dueling stage presences of *The London Merchant* and Rafe's *Knight*. Additionally, it portrays the machinations that produce these plays by depicting the complex interaction between the company actors, the amateur actors that Rafe's play introduces, and the in-text, onstage audience (particularly George and Nell).

Generic familiarity informs George's hostile attitude toward *The London Merchant*. The play belongs to the genre of "city comedy," in which identifiable London places, events, and characters are prominent, along with stock characters from Roman New Comedy in updated forms. *The London Merchant*, for example, contains a self-interested father (Venturewell) trying to set up his daughter (Luce) with an unfit mate (Humphrey) rather than her true love (Jasper), with the young lovers triumphing in the end. George rightly anticipates that the victim of the lovers' plot, the unsuccessful Venturewell, will be a merchant like himself – and George has no intention of sitting through a play in which a citizen of his position and rank becomes the butt of the joke.

However, the mocking of the merchant class was standard fare at The Blackfriars – the setting of *The London Merchant* and actual venue for Beaumont's *Knight*. David Bevington characterizes George and Nell as "a kind of counterchorus or antichorus" (Bevington *et al.*, 2002: 1070), distinct from the majority of the patrons at this theater, who would have viewed merchants as *nouveau riche*, their wallets granting them entrance to an expensive, indoor private theater – where the price of admission was as much as six times that of outdoor public theaters such as the Globe – but their dramatic taste unrefined. The plays George lists as possible substitutions for *The London Merchant* were all presented at outdoor theaters; their plots honor London (*The Legend of Whittington, The Life and Death of Sir Thomas Gresham, with the Building of the Royal Exchange, The Story of Queen Eleanor, with the Rearing of London Bridge upon Woolsacks*) or England (*The Bold Beauchamps*). Although city comedies could be said to honor London in their own way, celebrating its colorful and diverse characters even while mocking them, George clearly wants the kind of unabashed civic pride and patriotism that he feels the public theaters provide. The Boy even comments that George's idea to have "the Sophy of Persia come and christen [Rafe] a child" will not go over well because "'Tis stale; it has been had before at the Red Bull" (4.1.30–32).

When economic and social class distinctions clash, Beaumont suggests that economic achievement wins out. George fails to stop *The London Merchant* from going onstage, but he manages to purchase a play custom made to his liking. The acting company indulges George's request for a play, Rafe's *Knight*, because he pays for it handsomely. At various points, George and Nell offer to pay extra to have specific theatrical elements: George sends for the "waits of Southwark" to be part of the performance (a musical ensemble that never appears, so the theater company may or may not really have parted with George's money to hire the group) (Induction.109); he agrees to pay if Rafe's May Day speech causes problems (Interlude 4.19–20); and Nell offers to pay for the additional costumes and props necessary for Rafe's Mile End scene (5.1.63–4). George's payments suggest that the theater is a primarily economic rather than artistic venture. Before Rafe's May Day speech, the Boy representing the company in negotiations with George explicitly acknowledges the danger to the plot of *The London Merchant* due to the unscheduled changes (Interlude 4.12-13), but as George will "pay for't," profitability trumps performance (Interlude 4.20).

In presenting an economically driven world, with its numerous guild members and money-driven plot lines, city comedies make the same claims about London that Beaumont makes about the theater. Quomodo in Thomas Middleton's *Michaelmas Term* is an archetypally greedy and unscrupulous merchant, and *The London Merchant* also has its fair share of shady capitalists. Venturewell's motivation for wanting his daughter Luce to marry Humphrey clearly originates with the suitors' economic and social status. Humphrey goes out of his way to demonstrate his affluence, including when he presents Luce with a pair of gloves by saying, "If you desire the price, shoot from your eye / A beam to this place ... / They cost me three and twopence, or no money" (1.2.78–9, 81). Venturewell wants Luce's marriage to serve economic ends as well as romantic ones.

Luce's chosen suitor, Jasper, comes from a family with a different relationship to money: Merrythought, Jasper's father, cares so little for it that it nearly brings his family to ruin. Merrythought is an endearing figure, a fun-loving person who enjoys each moment of his life regardless of circumstance; he sings the final song of the play, which brings together the casts of *The London Merchant* and Rafe's *Knight* as "a choir of hearts in one" (5.3.189) for a brief but happy resolution. Several moments, however, undercut the audience's ability to take Merrythought's side. Venturewell, after learning that Luce is with Jasper and planning on marrying him, visits Merrythought to ask his help in finding their children. Rather than expressing compassion, Merrythought continues his carefree jesting, even claiming he would sing if his sons were on the gallows (2.7.62); indeed, his treatment of his sons while they are still alive suggests this claim may convey some truth. Jasper receives an inheritance of ten shillings from his spendthrift father (1.4.96–8). The insignificance of this sum becomes clear when Jasper throws it away (2.2.87–89) and when George gives Rafe four shillings ninepence, nearly half the amount of Jasper's inheritance, to distribute among the actors as a prop when Rafe visits Lady Pompiona (4.2.58–67). Merrythought's wife and other son, Michael, realize that Merrythought cannot provide a secure future so they leave with the £1000 Mistress Merrythought saved (1.4.126–8; 2.3.16). The cold and practical mother here seems a superior parent to the mirthful and irresponsible father.

Unfortunately, as Mistress Merrythought travels with the money, Rafe's band – he is accompanied by two other apprentices, George and Tim, who play a squire and dwarf respectively – enters the stage. The unscripted entrance of armed men scares Mistress Merrythought away, and she leaves her money behind (and as the actor playing Mistress Merrythought in the scripted *London Merchant* goes off book, the rest of that play is necessarily improvised). This moment in which *The London Merchant* and Rafe's *Knight* collide profoundly alters the fortunes of Jasper and Michael. Michael, having lost his inheritance, seeks an apprenticeship as a tapster at the admonishment of his mother. To obtain this position, he must ask for help from Venturewell, but the grudge Venturewell holds against Merrythought for his dismissive attitude regarding Jasper taking Luce prompts him to refuse Michael's request (4.3.52–4). Following this turn of events, Mistress Merrythought sees only a bleak prospect of her and Michael having to do knitting as subsistence labor (4.3.57–9). Further degradation ensues when she and Michael find it necessary to return to Merrythought in desperation only to have him refuse their pleas unless they sing for him (5.3.57–9). Merrythought does not feel familial obligation, and his nonchalant attitude toward others parallels the increasing cultural insistence upon financial ties meaning more than social ones.

Jasper, however, profits where his brother loses. After having Luce taken from him by Venturewell, Humphrey, and some hired muscle, a beaten and distraught Jasper relies upon the £1000 he found, not realizing it was the same money his mother and brother lost (2.2.93–6). Jasper needs this money if he hopes to regain Luce. With it, he is able to pay "four lusty fellows" (4.1.2) to help in a scheme to fake his death. This plot enables him to gain entrance to Luce in a coffin by pretending to be a corpse, sneak Luce out in the coffin, and then – pretending to be a ghost – frighten Venturewell into a mood of reconciliation that enables the young lovers' marriage when Jasper reveals his still-living condition.

Rafe's interference, with its dire financial consequences, is ironic because he strives assiduously in his *Knight* to downplay the importance of money. Beginning his quest and becoming a "grocer-errant" displays a willingness to leave his profession for the pursuit of more idealistic and less materialistic rewards – honor and the love of Susan the milkmaid (1.3.49; 3.4.6–10). Despite knowing how much wealth Mistress Merrythought lost, Rafe offers to help her retrieve it without thought of monetary reward (2.3.25–8). Rafe even relies on principles of hospitality when he seeks refuge at the Bell Inn, offering thanks and reciprocal loyalty rather than money for lodging.

The Host at the Bell Inn fails to share Rafe's romantic ideals. When the Host demands payment and threatens to arrest Rafe, who has no money, plots of both Rafe's *Knight* and *The London Merchant* are forestalled. If Rafe and Mistress Merrythought remain in the Bell Inn scene, neither play can advance. Only when George comes from the audience and offers to pay Rafe's tab can Rafe and the other guests leave (3.2.41–3). The introduction of "real" money – from the perspective of Beaumont's *Knight* – into the onstage world of props and illusion seems like one of many examples of George and Nell's naiveté regarding the line between the real and theatrical worlds. Elsewhere, Nell implores George to "[r]aise the watch at Ludgate" when Jasper threatens Luce, and George uses "his knowledge of archery exhibits at Mile End" in an attempt to demonstrate historical knowledge (3.1.92; fn. 4.1.49). Alternatively, George's payment can be seen as just another instance in which he offers money to actors in order to see what he wants on stage. George wants Rafe's plot to continue, so he pays to see the next installment just as he unfruitfully paid to have the waits of Southwark supply the music.

Paying the Host highlights a paradox in George's theatrical tastes. He wants a play depicting the chivalric world where money has no meaning, but he needs vast sums of money in order to obtain it. Brian Gibbons posits several defining features of city comedy: "critical and satiric design, urban settings, and exclusion of material appropriate to romance, fairy-tale, sentimental legend or patriotic chronicle" (Gibbons, 1980: 11). It would be hard to describe the various portions of Rafe's *Knight* more accurately than by calling them "romance, fairy-tale, sentimental legend [and] patriotic chronicle." George wants to watch the antithesis of city comedy, but he obtains his goal through the means of the City. Even when Rafe sits in a tower with a princess, a scene straight from a fairy-tale romance, George insists that the proper end to the scene is for Rafe to give the princess and her household money – and George provides payment for that purpose. George's world and values have much stronger ties to *The London Merchant* than Rafe's *Knight*, and, as a result, those values infiltrate the supposedly noncapitalistic play he requests.

Even though fiscal transactions form part of Rafe's *Knight*, it remains highly distinct in its core values from *The London Merchant*. Rafe's *Knight* esteems deeds of renown, martial prowess, and nationalism in ways that the city comedy does not. When conflict arises, Rafe uses his mighty pestle as his preferred method of resolution. After Jasper beats Humphrey to win Luce's hand, George and Nell ask Rafe to defeat him in combat in order to teach the "unhappy boy" a lesson (2.4.58). Jasper easily defeats Rafe, beating him with his own pestle and mocking his antiquated language and practices as he does so.

> Come, knight, I am ready for you. Now your pestle
> *(Snatches away his pestle.)*
> Shall try what temper, sir, your mortar's of.
> 'With that he stood upright in his stirrups,
> And gave the Knight of the Calfskin such a knock
> *[He knocks Rafe down.]*
> That he forsook his horse, and down he fell;
> And then he leaped upon him, and, plucking off his helmet –'
> (2.4.97–104)

Rafe's defeat threatens to devastate his status in the chivalric world, with even Nell commenting, "I am afraid my boy's miscarried" (2.4.112–13). George consoles his wife by quickly concluding that Jasper must have been enchanted, making the fight unfair (2.4.116–17). As a chivalric hero, Rafe should not lose a duel.

In *The London Merchant*, triumphing in battle produces no tangible, positive results, and losing fails to produce the shock that accompanied Rafe's loss to Jasper. As the victor against both Humphrey and Rafe (2.4.26–29, 97–104), Jasper would gain his goal under the generic conventions of romance, but in *The London Merchant*, Venturewell and Humphrey just show up with more men and take Luce away (3.1.115–16). Honorable single combat has become less important than who can hire the most men, and despite Jasper finding the casket dropped by his mother, the wealthy merchants have greater resources. Despite the prominent place of money in the genre, city comedies rarely give ultimate victory to the richest character, who is often a cruel father or miserly ancient. The victors in such plays triumph more often through wit than through financial resources or physical toughness. Jasper's wily plan – faking his death, entering Venturewell's house in a coffin, sneaking Luce out in the coffin, and then gaining egress himself through playing a ghost who warns Venturewell to make amends – enables his successful marriage. Money plays a part, as he needs to buy a coffin and hire boys to carry it, but his victory comes mostly by way of cunning. Mental rather than physical prowess rules in the world of city comedy.

Early Jacobean England enjoyed relative peace. The absence of major national conflicts also allowed local issues to enter the forefront of people's minds. City comedies reflect this trend with their focus on London's locales, people, and concerns. When Michael asks, "Is not all the world Mile End?" (2.2.6), the question reveals the insular nature of *The London Merchant*. Rafe, despite being a member of the London guild system, often emphasizes his role as an English knight. The most prominent example of this occurs during his meeting with Lady Pompiona in 4.2. Beaumont's *Knight* as a whole includes 13 references to England (including words like "English" and "Englishmen") of which 5 occur in 4.2. The scene takes place in Moldavia, and Rafe's national pride comes through as he describes his quest and English virtues like Protestantism: "I am a knight of religious order, / And will not wear a favor of a lady's / That trusts in Antichrist and false traditions" (4.2.36–38). Lady Pompiona seems eager to learn of Rafe's "brave countrymen" (4.2.23). Not surprisingly, references to England cluster around Rafe. He speaks of the country six times, including using a romantic tale about England, *Palmerin of England*, as the inspiration for his quest. Rafe's rousing May Day speech exists only to praise national history and practices, with Rafe calling out, "Rejoice, O English hearts" and praising traditional practices like morris rings and the hobbyhorse (Interlude 4.35, 40). On the contrary, the only two references to

England within *The London Merchant* occur in a single sentence as Mistress Merrythought explains to Michael what happens at Mile End. "Mile-End is a goodly matter. There has been a pitched field, my child, between the naughty Spaniels and the Englishmen, and the Spaniels ran away, Michael, and the Englishmen followed. My neighbor Coxstone was there, boy, and killed them all with a birding piece" (2.2.8–13). The description of the military reenactments here is done as a joke, with the genital jokes in the name "Coxstone" and the clearly underwhelming presentation with only one man representing a whole victorious army. Mistress Merrythought's speech provides humor rather than genuine patriotic zeal, but Rafe designs his scene at Mile End specifically to invoke national and civic pride.

Rafe's scene at Mile End comes across to the audience as an extended depiction of the same kind of humorous misadventures Mistress Merrythought describes. Greengoose's pathetic weapon and the ridiculous lack of discipline mock the military gatherings at Mile End, but the motivation for the scene comes from the sincere patriotism of George and Rafe. It is done for Saint George (5.1.84), but also for the City. In this way, Rafe's play demonstrates at least one similarity with city comedy – praise for urbanity and the city. Rafe's play even depicts his speaking from a conduit, a common sight during royal processions (Interlude 4.29). City comedy rarely takes the time to overtly praise the City, but rather draws upon its vivacity, variety, and uniqueness in ways that implicitly value these things. Money and wit may mean more in city comedy than civic or national pride, but urban(e) wit and city commerce receive this praise. In city comedy, London's inhabitants need money and wit to get by; in Rafe's play, they need patriotism. Nell's inclusive invitation for all present to enjoy "a pottle of wine and a pipe of tobacco" (Epilogue 6–7) at her house after the play reveals that London's society had space and a place for polyvocal views on money, hierarchy, the nation, and the City itself.

3.5   The State at War in *The Spanish Tragedy*

Thomas Kyd's *The Spanish Tragedy* is famed for its pioneering treatment of erotic passion and vengeful hatred, topics we have treated without reference to Kyd in previous parts. Here we want to discuss the play's presentation of war. For *The Spanish Tragedy* takes up, in a characteristically subtle way, issues about military honor, the nature of battle behavior, and the relations of both to love and erotic rivalry, that set all these in a large context of historical transformation.

The play opens with Don Andrea's soliloquy, which describes how after his death in battle and his burial by Horatio, his soul sought an underworld location. It was judged by Aeacus to deserve placement with lovers, and then by Rhadamanthus to deserve placement in "martial fields, / Where wounded Hector lives in lasting pain, / And Achilles' Myrmidons do scour the plain"

(1.1.47–49). Minos, the last and deciding voice on the three-judge panel, refers the matter to Pluto and Proserpine, and at Proserpine's smiling suggestion, Andrea returns to earth with Revenge to become part of the audience of *The Spanish Tragedy*.

The death of Andrea, as initially reported, does not seem an adequate basis for the presence of Revenge, and both Proserpine's involvement, "sealed ... with a kiss" (1.1.80) from Pluto, and Revenge's naming of Bel-imperia hint that the denouement will have more to do with rectifying the abrupt thwarting of Andrea's love life than with revenging something unorthodox about his death in battle:

> REVENGE   Then know, Andrea, that thou art arrived
> Where thou shalt see the author of thy death,
> Don Balthazar, the Prince of Portingale,
> Deprived of life by Bel-imperia.
> Here sit we down to see the mystery.[1]
>
> (1.1.86–90)

The play proper then opens with a nameless general's description of the battle between the armies of Spain and Portugal in which Andrea was killed. This is a long, detailed, plot-establishing, eye-glazing passage, from which most readers glean the facts that Balthazar killed Andrea, that Horatio in turn captured Balthazar, and that the Spanish won. But its details have a purpose. Rhadamanthus has already set a Homeric context for military behavior, and there is a good deal of Homeric individualism, complete with heroic boasting, in the Spanish General's report to the King:

> GENERAL   Don Andrea, with his brave lanciers
> In their main battle made so great a breach
> That, half dismayed, the multitude retired;
> But Balthazar, the Portingale's young prince,
> Brought rescue and encouraged them to stay.
> Herehence the fight was eagerly renewed,
> And in that conflict was Andrea slain –
> Brave man-at-arms, but weak to Balthazar.
> Yet while the Prince, insulting over him,
> Breathed out proud vaunts, sounding to our reproach,
> Friendship and hardy valor, joined in one,
> Pricked forth Horatio, our knight marshal's son,
> To challenge forth that Prince in single fight.
> Not long between these twain the fight endured,
> But straight the Prince was beaten from his horse
> And forced to yield him prisoner to his foe.
>
> (1.2.65–80)

---

[1]   On why this is a "mystery," see Hunter 1965 89–93.

Nonetheless, despite the way aristocrats and gentlemen are singled out in this part of the narrative, and the way the fight is described as connected with their individual strengths, both Andrea and Balthazar are clearly leading groups of soldiers (the Spanish "brave lanciers" and, less explicitly, the "rescue" brought by Balthazar to "encourage" the Portuguese "multitude" to stay). Despite these acknowledgements of the complexity of battle, Horatio and Balthazar engage in a duel, "single fight," while surrounded by unnamed combatants.

The mingling of Homeric with Renaissance warfare in the account here accents the Homeric, but earlier in the General's long speech, the balance is different. We quote (again) at some length:

> GENERAL   Our battles both were pitched in squadron form
>   Each corner strongly fenced with wings of shot.
>   But ere we joined and came to push of pike,
>   I brought a squadron of our readiest shot
>   From out our rearward to begin the fight;
>   They brought another wing to encounter us.
>   Meanwhile our ordnance played on either side,
>   And captains strove to have their valors tried.
>   Don Pedro, their chief horsemen's colonel,
>   Did with his cornet bravely make attempt
>   To break the order of our battle ranks.
>   But Don Rogero, worthy man of war,
>   Marched forth against him with our musketeers,
>   And stopped the malice of his fell approach.
>   While they maintain hot skirmish to and fro,
>   Both battles join and fall to handy blows,
>   Their violent shot resembling th'ocean's rage,
>   When, roaring loud and with a swelling tide,
>   It beats upon the rampiers of huge rocks,
>   And gapes to swallow neighbor-bounding lands.
>   Now while Bellona rageth here and there,
>   Thick storms of bullets rain like winter's hail,
>   And shivered lances dark the troubled air.
>   *Pede pes et cuspide cuspis;*
>   *Arma sonant armis, vir petiturque viro.*
>   On every side drop captains to the ground,
>   And soldiers, some ill maimed, some slain outright.
>   (1.2.32–58)

One notices at once that this report emphasizes both the importance of firearms combined with "push of pike," the importance of the courage of individual aristocrats, and the overall ocean-in-storm-like impersonal chaos of battle.

We believe that Kyd intends the passage as a reflection on the transitional nature of Renaissance warfare – transitional from medieval warfare in which aristocrats strove individually to capture one another, largely protected by horses and armor from the common soldiers who fought each other on foot, to proto-modern battle with pikes and firearms in which aristocratic agency is largely confined to leading groups of armed soldiers (except in, say, WWI aerial dogfights). If so, Kyd's battle description also underlines another aspect of Renaissance warfare, in that this is a report by a general to a monarch on his successful defeat of a national attempt by Portugal to throw off Spanish hegemony. As Eugene Rice and Anthony Grafton remark of late-fifteenth- and sixteenth-century innovations in military technology and tactics,

> The new weapons and the new warfare benefited the ruler seeking to organize a large territory .... Gunpowder technology became normal in the West because it royalized warfare and helped the prince to establish a monopoly on the use of organized force within his territory.   (Rice and Grafton, 1994: 15)

They continue, however, by pointing out that gunpowder – or, more precisely, new infantry tactics involving the cooperation of musketeers and pikemen – not only made battle more royal but also more common:

> If in one perspective, the effect of firearms was to royalize warfare; in another perspective, the effect was to proletarianize it. Contemporaries seem to have been more struck by the second than the first ... Ariosto ... lamented the evil, devilish invention of the gun: 'O wretched and foul invention, how did you ever find place in a heart? Through you the soldier's glory is destroyed, through you the business of arms is without honor ... ' Here is the reverse of royal profit, the nostalgia for a past when only aristocrats had really fought, and did so – at least in theory – according to a code of honor. Now foot soldiers with pikes and arquebuses fought more decisively, if not better; and they attempted to win not by valorous clash of arms or acts of individual courage, but by disciplined industry and cunning ... (Rice and Grafton, 1994: 15–16, citing *Orlando Furioso* XI 26)

Kyd's battle-description emphasizes all these elements (note how it begins with "shot" and "pike"). Moreover, it makes the General a nameless royal servant and makes the two most important individualized participants on the Spanish side, Don Andrea and Horatio, gentleman rather than nobles, but gentlemen whose merit wins them both the honor-bestowing attention of the King and the erotic attention of his niece Bel-imperia. While we do not know much about the career path of Don Andrea, he appears like Horatio and Horatio's father Hieronymo to be an upwardly mobile servant of the crown. All three are valiant and clever meritocrats attempting to make their way among nobles of royal blood like Balthazar and Lorenzo who resent their aspirations. These aspirations are manifested in *The Spanish Tragedy* in Don Andrea's and Horatio's military valor, Hieronymo's courtly literature, Hieronymo's dispensations of justice, and Don Andrea and Horatio's thwarted liaisons with Bel-imperia: that is, they mix the arts of peace and love with those of war, but, in each case, violence, arising from aristocratic brutality, forces a tragic ending. This idea emerges as Horatio explains to Bel-imperia exactly how Balthazar defeated Don Andrea. The redescribed military struggle again mixes aristocratic individual agency with the realities of mass warfare: Don Andrea

> Was at the last by young Don Balthazar
> Encountered hand to hand. Their fight was long,
> Their hearts were great, their clamors menacing,
> Their strength alike, their strokes both dangerous.
>
> (1.4.12–15)

So far this sounds heroic, and indeed Homeric, and the well-educated Horatio knows he needs Greek terminology and Homeric allusion to describe it:

> But wrathful Nemesis, that wicked power,
> Envying at Andrea's praise and worth,
> Cut short his life to end his praise and worth.
> She, she herself, disguised in armor's mask
> (As Pallas was before proud Pergamus),
> Brought in a fresh supply of halberdiers,
> Which paunched his horsed and dinged him to the ground.
>
> (1.4.16–22)

But Homeric how? One of the most conspicuously unfair moments of combat in *The Iliad* is also the climax of combat in that poem. It comes in Book 22 where Athena impersonates Hector's brother Deiphobus to persuade Hector to stop running around Troy, turn around, and face Achilles. Athena not only stops Hector and deludes him into thinking he has an ally, she also surreptitiously returns to Achilles the spear with which Achilles missed Hector on his first cast, then disappears when Hector calls on Deiphobus to back him up in charging Achilles. It is the returned spear with which Achilles kills Hector (see *Iliad* 22:220–343, Homer, 1990: 548–53). This is the incident Horatio recalls economically by referring to Pallas "disguised in armor" "before proud Pergamus." This allusion glosses his account of the arrival of a set of nameless Portuguese halberdiers who gut Don Andrea's horse with their pikes and knock him to the ground. Their action seems even more out of the spirit of the duel than Athena's help for Achilles. Nor does Balthazar's completion of the struggle seem at all chivalrous:

> Then young Don Balthazar, with ruthless rage,
> Taking advantage of his foe's distress,
> Did finish what his halberdiers begun,
> And left not till Andrea's life was done.
>
> (1.4.23–26)

Note that Horatio does not explicitly call Balthazar's action dishonorable, but he does call it "ruthless." What is war, after all, but "taking advantage of [a] foe's distress"? Yet it is the manner of this killing that moves Belimperia to love Horatio; she comments in a soliloquy that she will embrace Don Andrea's friend "the more to spite the Prince that wrought his end" (1.4.68). For her, at least, "what was't else but murderous cowardice, / So many to oppress one valiant knight / Without respect of honor in the fight?" (1.4.73–75). Here we have the incompatibility of aristocratic individual agency and early modern warfare in a nutshell, brought in relation to love and favor.

Rice and Grafton could be glossing the passages we have cited from *The Spanish Tragedy* when they generalize about the ways Renaissance thinkers reacted to the transformation of warfare.

> Gradually, the increasing use of firearms modified even men's moral responses to war … . [In the inherited view] man was thought to possess a balanced capacity for both action and thought, arms and letters. The ideal man developed both. Venus and Mars were a favorite subject of Renaissance painting, their conjunction suggesting the necessary, indeed desirable coexistence of tenderness and violence … . But as the horror of firearms spread, men began to picture war in a more fearful image. In art, they revived the Roman war goddess Bellona, associated her with gunpowder, provided her with an arsenal of cannon, muskets, mines, and grenades, and lamented her ruinous brutality. The slow transformation of sensibility by a military technology that erases the poetry of war had begun. (Rice and Grafton, 1994: 17–18)

Remember that in the General's description of the battle between Spain and Portugal, "Bellona rageth here and there, / Thick storms of bullets rain like winter's hail, / And shivered lances dark the troubled air" (1.2.52–54). Moreover, in the rest of *The Spanish Tragedy*, the general treatment of vengeful violence, set loose by the unwillingness of the great nobles Lorenzo and Balthazar to see their martial and erotic preserves encroached on by the upright upwardly mobile Horatio, shows a crisis in which aristocratic inflexibility and family pride bring on a savage conflict in which even civilized and loving subjects like Hieronymo bend their literary creativity toward bloody-mindedness. A further factor is Machiavelli's "Raison d'etat," reason of state, the idea widely associated with Machiavelli's *The Prince* that the interests of the polity, often unavowable because secret or amoral, trump any other considerations in the task of ruling. "Raison d'etat" may partly justify

Lorenzo's elimination of Horatio because the royal plan to unite Spain and Portugal involves marrying Bel-imperia to Balthazar (see 2.3.1–28). Thus Renaissance revenge tragedy from its beginnings partly depicts individual crises of identity, allegiance, and love that are bound up with larger political crises of modernization. This combination is very evident in Marlowe's *Edward II.*

3.6   Two Bodies: State and Self in *Edward II*

This is a play often treated in discussions of erotic representation, as it offers the clearest treatment in English Renaissance drama of male–male love. But discussions of Edward's and Gaveston's love always merge with discussions of the play's presentation of politics. Marlowe's play offers one of the first and one of the greatest non-Shakespearean treatments of relations between politics and individual passion, operating like *The Spanish Tragedy* under an awareness that the institutions of political power are always changing, and that individual life paths will thrive or fail as they shape themselves in relation to general tendencies.

While there is no certain way of dating this play, it is usually put at the end of Marlowe's career, in 1592 or so, very possibly written in response to Shakespeare's account of a weak king's deposition in *Henry VI Part 3* (if Shakespeare indeed wrote all of that play). It draws on chronicle accounts of the 21-year reign of Edward II, son of a strong king who was a great war leader (Edward I) and father of another strong warrior-king (Edward III). The play's opening sets up the relations between the personal and the political with brilliant dramatic economy. Edward I has just died – the Bishop of Coventry is hurrying to perform a funeral service at 1.1.175 – and the new King Edward's first act has been to write a letter that is quoted in the opening lines of the play:

> 'My father is deceased. Come, Gaveston,
> And share the kingdom with thy dearest friend.'
> Ah, words that make me surfeit with delight!
> What greater bliss can hap to Gaveston
> Than live and be the favorite of a king?
> Sweet prince, I come. These, these thy amorous lines
> Might have enforced me to have swum from France,
> And, like Leander, gasped upon the sand,
> So thou wouldst smile and take me in thy arms.
>
> (1.1.1–9)

Gaveston has returned like Leander to Hero (although by a more prosaic mode of transport), seeking both the sociopolitical bliss of living as "the favorite of a king" and the sexual bliss of Edward's embrace.

We shortly learn that under Edward I his son's French lover Gaveston was banished to France on the advice of the Bishop of Coventry (1.1.177–184), and that the mighty peers who now oppose Gaveston's return "were sworn to your father at his death / That he should ne'er return into the realm" (1.1.82–3). Thus Gaveston's return creates an immediate crisis of authority for the new King, who has invited his minion back without consulting anyone, and in defiance of the wishes of a newly dead father. No coronation, no solemn pledging of allegiances, marks the transition in rule. Instead Edward's barons attempt to maintain over a new King the restrictions imposed on disapproved-of behavior by a domineering father. The new King immediately defies his dead father's representatives.

The major players in the first half of the play are, on one side, Edward himself, his beloved Gaveston, his brother Edmund (who wavers between anger at Edward for his feckless and politically disastrous favors to Gaveston and anger at the peers for their defiance of royal prerogative). They are to some extent joined by Edward's Queen Isabella, the King of France's sister, whom he neglects for Gaveston, but who seems in the early acts committed to Edward's well-being and hopeful of a partial reconstitution of relations with him, although she is accused early on of a liaison with Edward's chief enemy Mortimer, Jr., and this liaison later on is clearly a reality. Two upwardly mobile gentlemen, Spencer, Jr. and Baldock, members of the household of the Earl of Gloucester whose daughter and heir Edward marries to Gaveston, affiliate themselves with Gaveston and through him with the King. Like Gaveston, Spencer, Jr. and Baldock are "new men," hoping to ride the wave of Edward's favor to prominence and wealth. On the other side stand representatives of the Church (still at this point the universal Catholic church centered in Rome) and the old nobility, most importantly the Earls of Warwick and Lancaster and the two Mortimers, all peers of the realm outraged at the elevation of Gaveston and eager to rebanish or kill him. Through a series of vicissitudes the barons and the Archbishop of Canterbury use the threat of a papal excommunication to force Edward to sign an order banishing Gaveston. Then Edward tells Isabella that only if she can engineer Gaveston's return will she be readmitted to his love. Isabella speaks privately to Mortimer, Jr., and Mortimer then suggests to the other peers that they allow Gaveston's return and arrange for him to be assassinated. But when Gaveston does return, to a loving Edward and an openly sneering set of barons, there is an immediate brawl and Mortimer wounds Gaveston. Edward then takes up arms, is separated in a battle from Gaveston, and Gaveston is captured and then killed by Warwick. Edward, enraged and vengeful, sends Isabella and their young son Prince Edward to France, and returns to a full-fledged civil war against his barons. This time he wins, executing Warwick and Lancaster and imprisoning Mortimer, Jr. in the tower. Edward's brother Edmund, however, appalled at the elevation of Spencer, Jr.

to the favorite position vacated by the death of Gaveston, now connives with Mortimer to escape to France and take the side of Queen Isabella and Prince Edward against the King. (By this point in the play, the fiction that those opposing the King do so only in order to separate him from his corrupting favorites has worn quite thin, although lip service to it continues to be paid.) Finally Isabella, Prince Edward (protesting loyally that he wishes to speak to his father), and Mortimer, Jr. land in England and retake the country, defeating Edward and capturing him in an abbey where he has attempted to hide in disguise as a monk. Spencer and Baldock are immediately hanged, and a bishop and an earl persuade Edward to accept deposition and give them the crown to pass to his son (who is still under the control of Isabella and Mortimer, now open lovers). After an inept attempt at rescuing Edward by Edmund – who changes sides for the third time in the play – Mortimer sends a deniable Latin message to his two henchmen who have been keeping Edward imprisoned in a castle sewer, and as his messenger employs Lightborn, a stealth assassin who specializes in undetectable forms of murder:

> I learned in Naples how to poison flowers,
> To strangle with a lawn thrust through the throat,
> To pierce the windpipe with a needle's point,
> Or, whilst one is asleep, to take a quill
> And blow a little powder in his ears,
> Or open his mouth and pour quicksilver down.
>   (5.4.30–35)

Lightborn tantalizes Mortimer by claiming that, for Edward, he has "a braver way than these" that he will not tell. It turns out to be the spectacularly cruel parody of anal intercourse described in Holinshed's description of the murder:

> They came suddenly one night into the chamber where he lay in bed fast asleep, and with heavy featherbeds or a table (as some write) being cast upon him, they kept him down and withal put into his fundament an horn, and through the same they thrust up into his body an hot spit, or (as other have) through the pipe of a trumpet a plumber's instrument of iron made very hot, the which passing up into his entrails, and being rolled to and fro, burnt the same, but so as no appearance of any wound or hurt outwardly might be once perceived. His cry did move many within the castle and town. (Holinshed 1587 vol. 3 341, quoted in Wiggins, 1997: xxxi–xxxii)

Given that Lightborn's "braver way" of murdering Edward parodies a sex act in which Edward receives another's anal penetration, it may well be significant that Gaveston casts himself as the male Leander and Edward as the female Hero in his initial speech. Martin Wiggins suggests that this speech is a key to the reaction of Elizabethan audiences to the sexual representation:

> For audiences in 1592, then, Marlowe's tragedy of a royal sodomite must have been all very unlike the home life of their own dear Queen.... [When Gaveston] puts himself in the place of Leander, he leaves the woman's part to Edward.... it is he who buggers Edward, and not vice versa. Whereas Queen Elizabeth was celebrated for her inviolate body, King Edward's has been penetrated.   (Wiggins, 1997: xxiii)

This may be, although if so the barons (who unlike the audience have not heard Gaveston's opening soliloquy) misconstrue the situation when Mortimer Sr. compares Edward and Gaveston, respectively, to such classical pairs as Achilles and Patroclus, Alexander and Hephaestion, and Hercules and Hylas (1.4.390–93) – the assumption in such classical cases being, as Michel Foucault points out, that there is an "isomorphism between social and sexual relations" (Foucault, 1990: 215), so that the more socially powerful male penetrates the less powerful, also often younger and smaller, as clearly in the case of Hercules and Hylas. Of course, Mortimer, Sr. goes on to instance Cicero and Octavian (later the emperor Augustus), and Socrates and Alcibiades (1.4.94–6), so that his set of great men and their minions includes some minions who became great men themselves. Gaveston's likening himself to Leander has something to do with his having just crossed the English channel, but it may also echo the idea that he is the active rather than the passive partner. Issues of Edward's sexual behavior appear to have diminished in importance after Gaveston's death, but they come roaring back as he is murdered in this way.

Mortimer's henchmen immediately kill Lightborn in turn, but the burden of regicide (and perhaps the extremity of its method) is too much for their consciences, and one of them quickly confesses to the crime and makes Mortimer's role known. The newly crowned Edward III rushes to his council chamber, obtains the aid of unnamed peers, and instantly overthrows Mortimer, sending his mother to the Tower to await trial. He holds the funeral for his father that apparently never happened for his grandfather, adorning the royal bier with Mortimer's severed head.

The play thus personalizes a political struggle that was, very broadly speaking, part of the transition from the Middle Ages to the seventeenth century: a struggle between newer court-based monarchy, in which the royal favor of a semi-divine king was the chief road to wealth and political power, and an older feudal monarchy, where monarchs ruled through great regional nobles who commanded territories, held military strongholds of their own, and were in a position to impose their wills when kings got out of line. As noted earlier with respect to *The Spanish Tragedy*, changes in the technology of warfare had a great deal to do with this transition, although Marlowe does not in this play (set in the early fourteenth century, not the late sixteenth) discuss military processes. But his play traces the fragility of royal legitimacy amid the competing powers in the state, and shows the dangers of royal insistence on private happiness at the expense of an apparent commitment to public welfare.

With considerable dramatic economy, then, Marlowe brings not only these parties, but symbolic representatives of the common people, into his opening scene. Indeed, he has Gaveston, who, like Edward, is often rash, but, unlike Edward, is occasionally politic, comment on how unnecessary it is for a royal favorite to heed these powers:

> What need the Arctic people love starlight,
> To whom the sun shines both by day and night?
> Farewell, base stooping to the lordly peers!
> My knee shall bow to none but to the King.
> As for the multitude, that are but sparks
> Raked up in embers of their poverty,
> *Tanti*!
>
> (1.1.16–22)

Despite this dismissal (*"tanti"* is an Italian expression meaning "I couldn't care less about them"), Gaveston does conciliate three commoners who come to him seeking patronage at the outset: "You know that I came lately out of France, / And yet I have not viewed my lord the King; / If I speed well, I'll entertain you all" (1.1.43–45). Not that he actually plans to do this:

> These are not men for me.
> I must have wanton poets, pleasant wits,
> Musicians that with touching of a string
> May draw the pliant king which way I please.
> Music and poetry is his delight;
> Therefore I'll have Italian masques by night,
> Sweet speeches, comedies, and pleasing shows;
> And in the day, when he shall walk abroad,
> Like sylvan nymphs my pages shall be clad;
> My men, like satyrs grazing on the lawns,
> Shall with their goat-feet dance an antic hay.
>
> (1.1.49–59)

What Gaveston here announces is his intention to create a special aesthetic zone around the King and himself – a setting for their relationship and for Gaveston's power over Edward – that is explicitly erotic and implicitly antipolitical, at least in the terms in which Edward's peers understand politics. The homoerotic suggestions of having Gaveston's servants impersonating satyrs while his boy pages impersonate nymphs is expanded on in the rest of the speech:

> Sometime a lovely boy in Dian's shape,
> With hair that gilds the water as it glides,
> Crownets of pearl about his naked arms,
> And in his sportful hands an olive tree
> To hide those parts which men delight to see,
> Shall bathe him in a spring.
>
> (1.1.59–65)

Critics invariably assume that this description intends to evoke and arouse male–male erotic feeling, and surely they are on the whole right. Nonetheless, Marlowe also reflects on the ambiguous erotics of a cross-dressed theater where female characters are played by pretty boys. The olive tree in the playful hands of this imagined pretty boy hides his genitals, but also hides the (yet more imaginary) genitals, and perhaps breasts, of the goddess Diana. Which of these are "the parts that men delight to see," and must one choose?

Moreover, this scene of a male arousing a male turns out to point to a moral that has potential political aspects as well as erotic ones:

> … and there hard by
> One like Actaeon peeping through the grove
> Shall by the angry goddess be transformed,
> And running in the likeness of an hart
> By yelping hounds pulled down and seem to die.
> Such things as these best please His Majesty.
>
> (1.1.65–70)

Actaeon was killed by his own hounds after being unable to turn his eyes from a forbidden erotic object. In *Edward II*, the King, largely because he is unable to turn away from Gaveston, will be pursued, disempowered, and finally killed by his own barons: men feudally obliged, like loyal dogs, to hunt down the King's foes. Misdirected desire has the power to turn one from a master into a quarry. And given that Edward and Gaveston make their choices with full awareness of the risks involved, it seems right that Marlowe sets this emblematic warning in the mouth of Gaveston himself.

As a reflection on large-scale political structures, then, *Edward II* casts light not only on the contrasts between a court-centered monarchy and a feudal monarchy mentioned earlier, but also on the perils to monarchy posed by its dependence on the character of one individual. Edward II is a weak king. Distracted from the welfare of the realm by his all-consuming passion for his favorites, he experiences loss of territory abroad (to the French) and defeat at the northern borders (by the Scots), religious conflict with Rome, and then civil war. These are evils that Elizabethans thought a great deal about: their aging queen had no agreed-upon heir, she had toward the beginning of Marlowe's brief life as a playwright by luck or divine intervention escaped a formidable invasion attempt by Spain, and from the time Marlowe turned six she was under a papal excommunication that justified Catholics in assassinating her. Unlike Edward, Elizabeth never lost focus on political necessities, nor did she heedlessly alienate her nobles. But weak king plays like *Edward II* and Shakespeare's *Richard II* demonstrate how vulnerable social order and thus the lives of ordinary people are to the personality of the monarch – something that was a huge factor in the temporary destruction of the English monarchy in the middle of the next century.

Thus it makes some sense to see *Edward II* as a play about a monarch who mistakes the power of kingship and sees it as above the power of politics. At moments in the play, Edward invokes the absolute authority of an anointed monarch as part of the natural order of things on which he ought to be able to rely. (In this most realistic of Marlowe's plays, however, these invocations are usually desperate and almost hopeless – part of the histrionics of Edward's weakness rather than the metaphysics of his strength):

> How oft have I been baited by these peers,
> And dare not be revenged, for their power is great!
> Yet shall the crowing of these cockerels
> Affright a lion? Edward, unfold thy paws,
> And let their lives' blood slake thy fury's hunger
> (2.2.200–204)

In the next play we discuss, kingship has in everyone's mind the natural absolute authority that Edward here invokes in vain.

3.7   Resistance to Tyranny in *The Maid's Tragedy*

Between Marlowe, with Kyd one of the late Elizabethan inventors of English Renaissance tragedy, and the prolific and successful writing team of Francis Beaumont and John Fletcher, among the most important Jacobean stage poets, looms the gigantic presence of Shakespeare. Fletcher in fact succeeded Shakespeare as company playwright for the King's Men. Anyone reading *The Maid's Tragedy* of 1610–11 who has paid attention in a Shakespeare course will find numerous passages that sound a bit familiar, paraphrases of famous speeches from *A Midsummer Night's Dream* and *Hamlet* and *Othello*. There is also considerable evidence that Beaumont and Fletcher had paid close attention to Shakespeare's less familiar Roman tragedy *Coriolanus*.

Equally important in understanding differences in the way Beaumont and Fletcher portray monarchy in *The Maid's Tragedy* from the ways Kyd and Marlowe portray it is the transition in political rule from Elizabeth I to James I. Although both monarchs sought, with considerable success, to make the ambitions of important nobles run through the court, and both combined this with strategies for centralizing the administration of national affairs in the direction of a London-based bureaucracy, James was far more vocal than Elizabeth in formally asserting the philosophical and theological absoluteness of his rule. His court was also considerably more elaborate, festive, and expensive than that of the notoriously thrifty Elizabeth. One of the manifestations of James's interest in courtly celebrations of monarchical centrality was the court masque, an elaborate form of scripted entertainment in which ladies and gentlemen of the court took parts, with splendid sets, costumes, music, and dances created by professionals like Ben Jonson and Inigo Jones. Such entertainments existed under Elizabeth (although often they were provided for her during her royal progresses from one noble estate to another, so that they were paid for by others), but they were greatly elaborated under James. When Gaveston plans to bend the pliant Edward which way he pleases by having his men and pages enact the myth of Actaeon and Diana, he is describing the sort of scene that was frequently presented to Elizabeth, but he also plans for Edward "Italian masques by night"(1.1.54) of the kind that were more frequent under James.

Indeed, *The Maid's Tragedy* begins with preparations for a royal court masque to celebrate a court wedding. The King of Rhodes (he has no other name in the play, as if to accentuate that the play concerns his kingship) has commanded the important general Melantius to return from war to take part in a wedding ceremony, and it is clear from the opening scene that the play will not only make much of kingship, but will also focus on the distinction between a military aristocracy that finds its central identity on the battlefield and a court-based nobility that focuses obsessively on the attitudes and pleasure of a monarch and sees the purpose of aristocrats as pleasing a king. Strato critiques the masque as an art form that is tied to an absolutist court's appetite for praise:

> [Masques] must commend their king and speak
> In praise of the assembly, bless the bride
> And bridegroom in person of some god.
> They're tied to rules of flattery.
>
> (1.1.8–11)

While Strato's "some god" might point to the reliance of Christian masques on classical machinery, it should be noted too that the Rhodes of the play appears to be pre-Christian, in that characters consistently invoke "the gods" rather than God. By thus distancing the play from contemporary Christian kingship, Beaumont and Fletcher make their critique of royal absolutism and court culture safer, and they also affiliate their soldier protagonists with models of ancient republican valor like Coriolanus.

The King's brother, welcoming Melantius, draws an immediate distinction between military service and the King's desire for court participation:

> Noble Melantius, the land
> By me welcomes thy virtues home to Rhodes,
> Thou that with blood abroad buyest us our peace.
> The breath of kings is like the breath of gods;
> My brother wished thee here, and thou art here.
>
> (1.1.13–17)

And Melantius himself establishes immediately that he sees true virtue expressed in deeds, not words or ceremonies:

> My lord, my thanks; but these scratched limbs of mine
> Have spoke my love and truth unto my friends
> More than my tongue e'er could.
>
> (1.1.21–24)

Moreover, the exchange that follows between Melantius and his brother Diphilus demonstrates that at least sometimes the King's desire for courtly participation thwarts military virtue:

> MELANTIUS   I sent for thee to exercise thine arms
>   With me at Patria; thou cam'st not, Diphilus.
>   'Twas ill.
> DIPHILUS   My noble brother, my excuse
>   Is my king's strict command –   [*to Lysippus*] which you, my lord
>   Can witness with me.
> LYSIPPUS   'Tis most true, Melantius.
>   He might not come till the solemnities
>   Of this great match were past.
>
> (1.1.30–36)

Thus the opening scene of the play both stresses the deference owed to a king who is godlike and points up the tension between the self-regard of virtuous military aristocrats and the courtliness imposed by the royal will.

As the plot develops, the royal will emerges as a huge, arbitrary, selfish shaping force. The King, it turns out, has ordered Melantius's dear friend Amintor – a younger man who shows military promise – to break his troth-plight to Calianax's daughter Aspatia and marry Melantius's sister Evadne. Aspatia is suicidally miserable and echoes Ophelia and Desdemona in her pained incomprehension of male erotic unreliability. Calianax, an elderly courtier, is furious at everybody, especially Melantius and Amintor. And Amintor, who in obedience to royal command has transferred his affections from one beauty to another, but who expresses substantial but assuagable regret about wronging Aspatia on his way to Evadne's bed, experiences a huge shock when he gets there. Evadne refuses to consummate the marriage. When Amintor suggests that this may be a virgin's attachment to her maidenhead, Evadne is astonished at his naivete, and replies "A maidenhead, Amintor, / At my years?"(2.1.194–195). As David Bevington remarks, this "takes a little time to sink in" (Bevington *et al.*, 2002: 1165 n8); Amintor at first would rather think her insane than sexually experienced. Not only, he discovers in the ensuing intense conversation, is she not virginal, but she has "sworn ... by all things holy ... / Never to be acquainted with thy bed" (2.1.237-239). Poor Amintor exclaims, with some justice, "Was ever such a marriage night as this?" (2.1.242). He then, naturally, pleads with blonde Evadne to change her mind, and when she won't, he threatens her with marital rape or death (although of course he puts the first alternative in more honorable terms):

> AMINTOR   I sleep, and am too temperate. Come to bed
>   Or, by those hairs which, if thou hadst a soul
>   Like to thy locks, were threads for kings to wear
>   About their arms –
> EVADNE   Why, so perhaps they are.
> AMINTOR   I'll drag thee to my bed and make thy tongue
>   Undo this wicked oath, or on thy flesh
>   I'll print a thousand wounds to let out life!
>   (2.1.273–279)

Evadne has given the first hint to the real situation, although Amintor is too slow or too agitated to catch it. She then assures Amintor that she is as sexually desirous as anyone and bold in following her desires – she is not held back from his embraces by some antisexual sentiment:

>   No, in this heart
>   There dwells as much desire and as much will
>   To put that wished act in practice as ever yet
>   Was known to woman, and they have been shown
>   Both.
>   (2.1.289–293)

She follows up this Mae West- or John Donne-like assertion of successful sexual experience with an explanation that she's a woman who won't accept anything short of the most excellent man available: "I do enjoy the best, and in that height / Have sworn to stand or die" (2.1.296–297). At this point, she thinks she has said enough for Amintor to understand: "You guess the man" (2.1.297). But Amintor, realizing suddenly that he has a male rival, thinks he sees a manly way out of this demeaning situation: "No. Let me know the man that wrongs me so, / That I may cut his body into motes / And scatter it before the northern wind" (2.1.298–299). Mere dismemberment will not suffice: the rival must be atomized. Part of the interest in this scene, and in the play generally, is watching a novel moral situation cause cognitive dissonance in men with deeply conventional attitudes – Amintor especially shifts around like a weathercock throughout the play trying to find a morally satisfying position. The one he asserts here ("I have a rival who has dishonored my wife: my male obligation is to kill him") does not work well when Evadne reveals who the rival is:

> EVADNE   Why, 'tis the King.
> AMINTOR   The King!
> EVADNE   What will you do now?
> AMINTOR   'Tis not the King!
> EVADNE   What did he make this match for, dull Amintor?
> AMINTOR   Oh, thou hast named a word that wipes away
> All thoughts revengeful. In that sacred name,
> 'The King,' there lies a terror. What frail man
> Dares lift his hand against it?
>
> (2.1.303–310)

As a subject, Amintor cannot without sacrilege commit the father murder involved in regicide. As a man of honor, he cannot allow the corruption of his wife. And as a person of pride, he cannot put up with being made to act as a screen for his own cuckolding. (We are never told exactly why the King cannot marry Evadne, but he evidently does not choose to do so. Perhaps there is a queen somewhere, or perhaps some other reason of state precludes a match with the daughter of one of his councilors.)

At this point in the plot, it is clear that the play will turn on the question of how virtuous subjects respond to exploitative and personally degrading behavior in a monarch. An array of attitudes toward this matter was available in Renaissance political and moral thought – two areas that were not sharply distinguished. The one major author who contended that they should be distinguished – who felt that effective politics had to include the possibility of being immoral – was, of course, Machiavelli. And Machiavelli warned would-be princes specifically against doing the sort of thing that the King in *The Maid's Tragedy* has done. While Machiavelli feels that a prince should strive to be feared, he feels that it is very bad practice for him to be hated. Indeed, Chapter 19 of *The Prince* is titled "On avoiding being despised and hated," and in it Machiavelli comments "what makes a prince hated above all else is being rapacious and a usurper of the property and the women of his subjects; he must refrain from this; and in most cases, so long as you do not deprive them of either their property or their honor, the majority of men live happily; and you have only to deal with the ambition of a few, who can be restrained without difficulty and by many means"

(Machiavelli, 1979: 136). The King in *The Maid's Tragedy* has violated this sensible suggestion in two ways: he has usurped the woman of a subject, and in choosing Melantius's sister and then forcing Amintor to break faith with Aspatia and marry her, he has done so among the very most powerful of his subjects, the "few" whose prominence might well make them rivals in any case. Although for Machiavelli, significant subjects seem to be male, in *The Maid's Tragedy*, Evadne and Aspatia are political actors fully as important as the males associated with them, although as we have already seen and will see again, the men react to royal interference with Evadne as an abrogation of something like their property.

But as we remarked earlier, Renaissance thought in general applies moral as well as prudential categories to politics. Amintor, a boy scout type who takes all forms of honor with great seriousness, cannot initially imagine pursing violent revenge against his king. In this Amintor follows an official Renaissance line of thought, cherished by kings and queens and enunciated for the English in the Tudor homily *Against Disobedience and Willful Rebellion*. Noting that God allows bad kings as well as good ones, and that scripture enjoins obedience, the homily asks forthrightly,

> What shall Subiects doe then? shall they obey valiant, stout, wise, and good Princes, and contemne, disobey, and rebell against children being their Princes, or against vndiscreet and euill gouernours? God forbid!   (Lancashire, 1994)

Taking such judgments into their own hands usurps the prerogatives of God, and besides, as the homily also points out, one subject's tyrant is another's benevolent ruler, given the diversity of human experiences.

Nonetheless, a monarch endangers this hedge of divinity when he interferes directly in the marital lives of subjects. As the irascible Calianax (whose daughter's happiness has been destroyed by the King's interference) puts it: "The King may do this, and he may not do it. / My child is wronged, disgraced" (2.2.83–84). The reason that Machiavelli sees usurping the women of subjects as a bad idea for princes is that it brings the strongest moral justifications for violence up against the moral inhibitions that protect rulers from their subjects. It also, although Machiavelli does not point this out, makes it extremely difficult for the wronged subject to focus on the king's immortal, divinely sanctioned political body (one of the king's two bodies, the other being his mortal human one). Royal sexual interference with female subjects creates the strongest possible reminder of the prince's erring idiosyncratic embodied humanity by revealing him as driven by bodily desire and making him an object of sexual jealousy, an emotion that demeans and deidealizes everything it touches. It is partly to avoid these lowering consequences that codes of masculine honor enjoin immediate violence against male interlopers on the chastity of female family members. Both Melantius and Amintor, with almost comic alacrity, draw their swords to obliterate any man who brings sexual dishonor on Evadne. They do this even though, as we have seen, the Evadne of Acts 1 and 2 seems a woman very much in charge of her own sexual agenda, and one who scoffs at the idea that it might be incumbent on a grown unmarried woman to be a virgin. Melantius, indeed, initially considers it his duty to carve up Amintor for insulting his sister when he has forced Amintor to confess to him what makes Amintor such a miserable newlywed. After Amintor bares his breast to Melantius's blade, declaring that it would be a pleasure to be cut down and relieved from the misery of his existence, Melantius declares him dishonorable for not fighting. Then, when Amintor, angered, draws his sword, Amintor also says quite appropriately that "it was base in you / To urge a weighty secret from your friend / And then rage at it" (3.2.164–166). Melantius instantly realizes that "the name of friend is more than family" (3.2.169) and bares his own breast to Amintor's sword. All these sudden reversals bespeak the moral dissonance created by the King's behavior, while also bearing witness to the homosocial bonds that are paramount among military aristocrats, who show their love by fighting side by side but also by inviting one another to thrust weapons into their bared bodies. Melantius accepts Evadne's guilt and begins to plot the King's destruction.

Meanwhile, the King has become jealous of Amintor, assuming (partly on the basis of Amintor's heartbroken and fairly inept impersonation of a happy honeymooner) that Evadne and Amintor have had sexual relations. He quizzes Amintor on Evadne's sexual forthcomingness in front of a group of courtiers:

> KING   But, prithee, I should think, by her black eye
> And her red cheek, she should be quick and stirring
> In this same business, ha?
> AMINTOR   I cannot tell.
> I ne'er tried other, sir, but I perceive
> She is as quick as you delivered.
>
> (3.1.142–146)

In the double entendre mode so characteristic of this play, the unfortunate virgin Amintor thinks he's telling the King that Evadne, untouched by Amintor, is in the same state – possibly pregnant ("quick" means both "pregnant" and "sexually fast") – in which the King "delivered" her to him. But the King thinks Amintor is responding to his sexual nudge–nudge with a lascivious wink–wink, and immediately becomes suspicious:

> KING [*aside*]   I do not like this. –
> All forbear the room but you, Amintor,
> And your lady.
>
> (3.1.160–162)

The King then asks Amintor to step out of earshot and interviews Evadne in private, insulting her with his jealousy. He works himself into a state of mind in which he regards it as impossible that Amintor could (i) forbear to have sex with Evadne, given the semi-opportunity of a wedding night, however unwilling the bride; or (ii) if informed by Evadne that it was not to be, could forbear from immediately denouncing or killing her:

> What could he do,
> If such a sudden speech had met his blood,
> But ruin thee forever, if he had not killed thee?
>
> (3.1.210–12)

He then starts offstage, threatening Evadne with "what disgraces I can blot thee with" (3.1.216).

At this poor Evadne summons the even more pitiable Amintor back to bear witness to her good faith, or at least her consistent bad faith. She does so by accusing Amintor of dishonorable behavior:

> EVADNE   I do despise thee.
>   Why, nothing can be baser than to sow
>   Dissension amongst lovers.
> AMINTOR   Lovers! Who?
> EVADNE   The King and me –
> AMINTOR   Oh, God!
> EVADNE   Who should live long, and love without distaste
>   Were it not for such pickthanks as thyself!
>   Did you lie with me?
>
> (3.1.223–229)

This leads the baffled and miserable Amintor to hypothesize that he is being punished for breaking faith with Aspatia at the King's command. More importantly, it leads him to make a key moral–political assertion: that what the King is doing counts as tyranny and may thus, possibly, justify resistance:

> AMINTOR [*to the King*]   I will not loose a word
>   To this vile woman; but to you, my king,
>   The anguish of my soul thrusts out this truth:
>   You're a tyrant, and not so much to wrong
>   An honest man thus as to take a pride
>   In talking with him of it.
>
> (3.1.233–237)

Amintor's reproach underlines how the King's indelicate refusal (prompted by his own sexual jealousy of Amintor) to keep up appearances by at least not making Amintor talk about his travesty of a marriage has made Amintor feel that the King is glorying ("tak[ing] a pride") in making his subjects aware of his royal power to degrade them. Amintor threatens to draw his sword, and the King reminds him that "Thou know'st I cannot fear / A subject's hand" (3.1.245–246). Amintor, clearly in the process of trying to rid himself of this "knowledge," finds he has not shed it yet: "[T]here is / Divinity about you that strikes dead / My rising passions" (3.1.251–253). And as in this horrible situation, it is requisite that some male must kill some other male, Amintor decides that maybe the King should kill him: "As you are my king, / I fall before you and present my sword / To cut mine own flesh, if it be your will" (3.1.253–255). Clearly the King has not quite yet become purely a tyrant.

As we have seen in both Amintor's relation with Melantius and Amintor's relation with the King, *The Maid's Tragedy* shows military males as creatures of a discursive field of honorable masculine behavior that applies poorly to the complexity and corruption of an absolutist court centered on a king's pleasure. Honor gives them cues to violence and self-sacrifice that they cannot consistently follow. Evadne, who earlier seemed a forthright advocate of a court where female honor is the merest convention, sacrificed by sophisticated adult women to pleasure and ambition without second thoughts, turns out when confronted by her brother Melantius to be far less of a moral relativist than she seemed. Claiming that court rumor has branded her as a whore, he demands to know her lover, and confronts her with strong invocations of their father's honor.

> EVADNE   Let me consider.
> MELANTIUS   Do: whose child thou wert
> Whose honor thou hast murdered, whose grave opened,
> And so pulled on the gods that in their justice
> They must restore him flesh again and life,
> And raise his dry bones to revenge this scandal.
> (4.1.89–93)

Evadne manages a touch of her old cynicism in response to this rhetoric of family obligation, noting that such resurrections never happen: "The gods are not of my mind. They had better / Let 'em lie sweet still in the earth; they'll stink here" (4.1.94–95). This outrages Melantius, who draws his sword and threatens her with what sounds like vaginal impalement:

> Speak, you whore, speak truth,
> Or, by the dear soul of thy sleeping father,
> This sword shall be thy lover. Tell, or I'll kill thee;
> And, when thou hast told all, thou wilt deserve it.
> (4.1.98–102)

If she does not reveal her lover, he will leave her body naked with this shameful wound that will point to the nature of her crime:

> When I have killed thee – as I
> Have vowed to do if thou confess not – naked
> As thou hast left thine honor will I leave thee,
> That on thy branded flesh the world may read
> Thy black shame and my justice.
>
> (4.1.107–111)

Evadne confesses to Melantius what he already knows from Amintor: that the King is her lover. With her confession comes a surprisingly deep change of heart, occasioned perhaps by her discovery that the King's love cannot give her immunity from criticism or male violence or familial dishonor. She tells Melantius that she has lost all her sexual desire for the King: "I feel / Too many sad confusions here to let in / Any loose flame hereafter" (4.1.141–143). And Melantius then plays his trump card, invoking Evadne's "confusions" to set in motion the plot that will, as he plans it, protect him and Amintor from the consequences of regicide: "Dost thou not feel, amongst all those, one brave anger / That breaks out nobly and directs thine arm / To kill this base king?" (4.1.144–6). Evadne too knows about divine right, but Melantius sweeps aside her piety with references to the present and future degradation the King has forced upon her:

> EVADNE   All the gods forbid it!
> MELANTIUS   No, all the gods require it.
>   They are dishonored in him.
> EVADNE   'Tis too fearful.
> MELANTIUS   You're valiant in his bed, and bold enough
>   To be a stale whore and have your madam's name
>   Discourse for grooms and pages, and hereafter,
>   When his cool majesty hath laid you by,
>   To be at pension with some needy sir
>   For meat and coarser clothes; thus far you knew
>   No fear. Come, you shall kill him.
>
> (4.1.146–155)

He continues to threaten her with death should she not rescue Amintor and himself from disgrace by swearing to commit regicide:

> Canst thou live and know
> What noble minds shall make thee, see thyself
> Found out with every finger, made the shame
> Of all successions, and in this great ruin
> Thy brother and thy noble husband broken?
> Thou shalt not live thus. Kneel and swear to help me

When I shall call thee to it, or, by all
Holy in heaven and earth, thou shalt not live
To breathe a full hour longer, not a thought.
Come, 'tis a righteous oath.

(4.1.157–166)

Kneeling with her and raising their hands, he proposes the oath, harking back to Machiavelli in presenting the King's sexual misbehavior as a property crime against his subjects:

Give me thy hand,
And, both to heaven held up, swear that by that wealth
This lustful thief stole from thee, when I say it,
To let his foul soul out.

(4.1.166–169)

Evadne's response links her to a class of dead, wronged women, rather as her first speeches to Amintor linked her to a class of living, sexually liberated ones: "Here I swear it, / And, all you spirits of abusèd ladies, / Help me in this performance!" (4.1.169–171). Her soliloquy after Melantius's exit underlines the extent to which court culture bears blame for her corruption:

Gods, where have I been all this time? How friended,
That I should lose myself thus desperately,
And none for pity show me how I wandered?
There is not in the compass of the light
A more unhappy creature.

(4.1.178–183)

Having thus touched bottom, Evadne dedicates herself to recovery through redemption of her marriage, confessing herself to Amintor as a faithless woman, that worst of beings: "I do present myself the foulest creature, / Most poisonous, dangerous, and despised of men / Lerna e'er bred, or Nilus" (4.1.229–231). She promises to "redeem one minute of my age" (4.1.257) by an undefined act, receives Amintor's forgiveness, and exchanges a chaste kiss with her husband, announcing "never shall you see the foul Evadne / Till she have tried all honored means that may / Set her in rest and wash her stains away" (4.1.280–282).

The honored means turn out to arise when she keeps an assignation with the King, who has driven Amintor into regicidal rage by requesting the visit from him rather than his wife. Melantius, who has made great efforts to arrange for a survivable regicide by arming Evadne, gaining control of the fort from Calianax, and creating a small conspiracy of outraged family members, needs to persuade Amintor in the strongest terms not to rush toward the royal bedchamber with drawn sword in hand:

> MELANTIUS   'Twere a rash attempt
>   Not to be done with safety. Let your reason
>   Plot your revenge, and not your passion.
> AMINTOR   If thou refusest me in these extremes
>   Thou art no friend. He sent for her to me –
>   By heaven, to me, myself! ...
>   I'll do't myself alone
>   Though I be slain. Farewell.
>   [*He starts to go.*]
> MELANTIUS [*aside*]   He'll overthrow
>   My whole design with madness. – Amintor,
>   Think what thou dost. I dare as much as valor;
>   But 'tis the King, the King, the King, Amintor,
>   With whom thou fightest. (*Aside*) I know he's honest,
>   And this will work with him.
>
>   (4.2.299–313)

It does. Once again, the inhibition on regicide disarms honest Amintor: "thou hast charmed my sword / Out of my hand, and left me shaking here / Defenseless" (4.2.314–316).

It is not entirely clear whether Melantius has the preservation of Amintor as his highest priority amid these plots, but it is clearly a high one, and one for which he is happy to sacrifice the already-tainted Evadne. She, in compliance with her oath to her brother, and in hopes of reconciliation with her husband, goes smiling with a knife under her cloak to the meeting the King requested from Amintor.

> EVADNE   Sir, is the King abed?
> GENTLEMAN   Madam, an hour ago.
> EVADNE   Give me the key then, and let none be near
>   'Tis the King's pleasure.
> GENTLEMAN   I understand you, madam. Would 'twere mine!
>
>   (5.1.1–4)

She finds him sound asleep, ties his arms to his bed (something he, on waking, takes for foreplay), accuses him of tyranny, then stabs him repeatedly and wordily:

> EVADNE   Thou art a shameless villain
>   A thing out of the overcharge of nature
>   Sent like a thick cloud to disperse a plague
>   Upon weak, catching women – such a tyrant
>   That for his lust would sell away his subjects
>   Ay, all his heaven hereafter.

KING   Hear, Evadne
    Thou soul of sweetness, hear! I am thy king.
EVADNE   Thou art my shame. Lie still; there's none about you
    Within your cries; all promises of safety
    Are but deluding dreams. Thus, thus, thou foul man,
    Thus I begin my vengeance.
    Stabs him.
KING   Hold, Evadne!
    I do command thee, hold!
EVADNE   I do not mean, sir
    To part so fairly with you. We must change
    More of these love tricks yet.
KING   What bloody villain
    Provoked thee to this murder?
EVADNE   Thou, thou monster!
    [*Stabs him.*]
KING   Oh!
EVADNE   Thou kept'st me brave at court, and whored me, King
    Then married me to a young noble gentleman
    And whored me still.
KING   Evadne, pity me!
EVADNE   Hell take me, then! [*She stabs repeatedly.*] This for my lord
    Amintor
    This for my noble brother, and this stroke
    For the most wronged of women!
    Kills him.
KING   Oh, I die!
EVADNE   Die all our faults together! I forgive thee.
    Exit.

                       (5.2.91–113)

It may seem thus far that male violence toward women is largely threat-ened in the play, while female violence toward men is real. But while Evadne is killing the King and hoping thereby to save her marriage, the wronged and disconsolate Aspatia, dressed as a man and facially disguised with cosmetic scars, comes to Amintor's apartment, announces himself as Aspatia's brother back from the wars, draws his sword, and challenges Amintor to a duel for compromising Aspatia's honor and wrecking her happiness. Amintor demurs, thinking himself too much at fault *vis-à-vis* Aspatia already. Aspatia strikes him, then kicks him, and this he cannot endure. Enraged, he draws:

AMINTOR   A man can bear
    No more and keep his flesh. Forgive me, then;
    I would endure yet if I could ...
    They fight. [*She is wounded.*]
    What dost thou mean?

Thou canst not fight; the blows thou mak'st at me
Are quite besides, and those I offer at thee
Thou spread'st thine arms and tak'st upon thy breast
Alas, defenseless.

(5.3.95–103)

Frontispiece, *The Maydes Tragedie* (London, 1622)

At this point, when Aspatia has gained the mortal wound she was after, Evadne enters with the bloody regicidal knife. A tragicomic scene follows, in which Evadne expects Amintor's approval and marital reconciliation for having freed him from enforced cuckoldry and the moral impossibility of manly revenge against his king, while Amintor, appalled at Evadne's act of regicide, rejects her with horror. She demands on her knees that he either come to her bed or kill her. Amintor, refusing the second, feels drawn to the first: "In midst of all my anger and my grief, / Thou dost awake something that troubles me / And says I loved thee once" (5.3.163–166). Appalled at his own erotic impulse, he turns away to leave her, and she stabs herself with passive-aggressive nobility:

> Amintor, thou shalt love me now again.
> Go; I am calm. Farewell, and peace forever!
> Evadne, whom thou hat'st, will die for thee.
> *Kills herself.*   (5.3.167–169)

Amintor, now himself suicidal, decides that he must apologize to the wronged Aspatia before he meets "death…the boldest way" (5.3.186). When the bleeding youth on the floor groans to remind all of us that he's still there, then reveals herself as Aspatia in drag, Amintor catches a glimpse of a possible life path, but also realizes that he has personally wounded the woman he ought to have loved:

> ASPATIA   I am Aspatia yet.
> AMINTOR   Dare my soul ever look abroad again?
>
> (5.3.207–208)

Aspatia dies in his arms as he attempts a Rhodian version of the Heimlich maneuver:

>   Aspatia, speak! –
> I have heard, if there be any life, but bow
> The body thus, and it will show itself.
>   [*He tries to resuscitate her.*]
> Oh, she is gone!   (5.3.230–33)

He petitions the gods to "lend forth some few years / The blessèd soul to this fair seat again" (5.3.236–237), and when this fails, kills himself as a bereft lover:

> I wrong
> Myself, so long to lose her company.
> Must I talk now? Here's to be with thee, love!
> *Kills himself.*   (5.3.240–242)

But the play contrives yet another erotic death for Amintor. Melantius enters with the new king, Lysippus, having signed a treaty guaranteeing his own safety and Amintor's.

> MELANTIUS   Amintor, give a word
>   To call me to thee.
> AMINTOR   Oh!
> MELANTIUS   Melantius calls his friend Amintor. [*He embraces Amintor.*] Oh,
>   Thy arms are kinder to me than thy tongue.
>
> (5.3.255–258)

Diphilus discovers Evadne's corpse and points it out, and Melantius indignantly refuses to be distracted.

> DIPHILUS   Oh, brother
>   Here lies your sister slain! You lose yourself
>   In sorrow there.
> MELANTIUS   Why, Diphilus, it is
>   A thing to laugh at in respect of this.
>   Here was my sister, father, brother, son
>   All that I had. – Speak once again. What youth
>   Lies slain there by thee?
> AMINTOR   'Tis Aspatia.
>   My last is said. Let me give up my soul
>   Into thy bosom.
>   [*He dies in Melantius' arms*]
>
> (5.3.262–270)

So Amintor, the object of women's love, dies homosocially in a male embrace.

Melantius is forcibly prevented from immediate suicide, but vows to go without food, drink, and sleep until he can join Amintor. And in the play's last words, Lysippus points the moral for princes:

> May this a fair example be to me
> To rule with temper! For on lustful kings
> Unlooked-for sudden deaths from God are sent;
> But curst is he that is their instrument.
>
> (5.3.291–295)

The play may be regicidal in plot, but it closes on an orthodox note, doubtless with its own safety in mind. Suddenly, the gods have become God, we are back in a Christian dispensation, and the fate of bad kings is in inscrutable divine hands. God may use human revengers like Evadne or Melantius as His means but always does so in a way that reminds us that men cannot safely usurp His privileges. Just as the play gains much of its entertainment value from its flirtations with libertine attitudes toward sexual relations and gender flexibility, it gains much of its political interest from its flirtation with a Machiavellian analysis of natural conflict between the homosocial virtues of a military aristocracy and the epicurean attitudes fostered by an absolutist court. An absolutist regime, *The Maid's Tragedy* suggests, endangers itself through the attitudes it fosters in monarchs themselves as well as the conflicts it breeds in courts.

Whenever a character in *The Maid's Tragedy* resolves on violence against the King, he or she uses the word "tyrant" or "tyranny." As we have already seen, the level of resistance appropriate to tyranny was a problem in early modern culture, but at the same time, the word "tyrant" marks a boundary for rulers: the psychological boundary subjects must cross to even begin to think about resisting them. As Rebecca Bushnell puts it, writing of the political theorists of the period,

> Insofar as in sixteenth-century Britain almost all political writing responded to a particular situation or particular ruler, naming the tyrant was an essential strategy. No one was willing to go so far as to say that there should be no kings; the point was to be able to call your enemy a tyrant and on that ground to claim that he or she had forfeited a subject's respect due to a monarch in the natural order. Having named the tyrant, one must decide only, as John Ponet asks, "whether it be lawfull to kill suche a monster and cruell beast covered with the shape of a man." (Bushnell, 1990: 46)

Since the period of drama we are concerned with in this book is roughly bounded by on the one hand Elizabeth I's execution of Mary Queen of Scots in 1585, and on the other by the closing of the theaters in 1642 by a parliamentary government at war with King Charles I, whom a purged parliament would execute in 1649, questions of how a monarch loses the protective hedge of divinity and makes him or herself vulnerable either to private retribution or to formal arraignment were not purely theoretical. Charles I was named and ultimately arraigned as a tyrant, not on grounds of sexual impropriety (unlike his royal father James I and his royal son Charles II, Charles I was a model of marital probity), but on the constitutional ground that he had usurped to his person powers that rested with the king in parliament.

3.8 Tyranny as a Boundary Condition for a Subject's Violence: *The Duchess of Malfi* and *The Revenger's Tragedy*

Here it makes sense to look at two plays involving violence against rulers, one of which has been discussed earlier. In John Webster's *The Duchess of Malfi*, a play treated at length in Part 1, Duke Ferdinand, the Duchess's brother, suffers from lycanthropy: after the Duchess and her children are murdered at his command at the end of Act 4, he begins to think he is a wolf and act like one, and in Act 5, before he is killed by Bosola, we find him under medical care. A subtler but equally important transition takes place in Acts 3 and 4, as the words "tyrant" and "tyranny" begin to be used of Ferdinand and his brother the Cardinal, first by the Duchess and by Cariola, and then by Ferdinand's servant Bosola. The change begins as the Duchess and her husband Antonio are forced to part by Ferdinand. Antonio, characteristically, counsels stoic constancy: "Make patience a noble fortitude, / And think not how unkindly we are used. / Man, like to cassia, is proved best, being bruised" (*Duchess* 3.5.74–76). The Duchess replies with indignation, "Must I, like to a slave-born Russian, / Account it praise to suffer tyranny?" (3.5.77–78). Western Europeans in the Renaissance associated the unconditional obedience of subjects with Russia, partly because of the existence of slavery in Russia, and partly because the vast majority of Russians were bound in serfdom, an institution that grew more rigorous and widespread in the sixteenth century. So the Duchess's comment is a reminder of the different notions of the rights of subjects *vis-à-vis* arbitrary rule that existed in different cultures known to Renaissance Europeans. Western Europeans need not bear tyranny without resistance, or at least without free articulate complaint, she suggests. And her use of the word "tyranny" is taken up by Bosola repeatedly as he turns himself in the direction of vengeance against his ruler and master.

Roughly the same thing happens, in ways that suggest principled organized resistance to tyranny, in *The Revenger's Tragedy*. While Vindice pursues private revenge in ways that threaten to usurp God's prerogatives, a large group of noblemen, appalled above all by the rape of Antonio's chaste wife and the Duke's failure to punish it, bands together in a conspiracy that appears to involve something like an assembly of persons choosing revolt for the good of the state: semipublic and, by the end of the play, involving "five hundred gentlemen" (5.2.28) and nobles who band together to mount a coup against the wickedness of the Duke and that of his son Lussurioso who succeeds him. Although there are eighteen uses of the word "treason," the word "tyranny" does not appear in the play, perhaps to underline its focus on revenge rather than resistance theory.

3.9   Republic and Tyranny in *Sejanus*

So far all of our plays about the state have involved kings or princely rulers, courtiers, nobles, and occasional elevated gentlemen like Hieronymo in *The Spanish Tragedy*, Gaveston in *Edward II* or Antonio in *The Duchess of Malfi*. Common people are mentioned rarely, although occasionally brought in for choric commentary or as nameless participants in battle. Institutions that distribute power more widely through voting and debate in assemblies have hardly been discussed, although the conspiracy surrounding the virtuous Antonio in *The Revenger's Tragedy* may, as we have just suggested, gesture toward collective deliberation or, at any rate, organized upper-class solidarity.

This does not mean that republicanism – the idea that power should reside in some sort of deliberative institution, rather than be concentrated in or delegated by a single monarch – was unthinkable or not to be represented on the Renaissance stage. It was present partly in awareness that English and, in general, Western European kingship (unlike the oriental despotism experienced by the Duchess's "slave-born Russians" or by Turks) was mixed, qualified by laws, and involved representative institutions. As Sir Thomas Smith wrote in 1565 in *De republica Anglorum*, a book whose title suggests his interest in emphasizing English republican institutions,

The most high and absolute power of the realm of England is in the Parliament.

> … That which is done by this consent is called firme, stable, and *sanctum* and is taken for lawe. The Parliament abrogateth olde lawes, maketh newe, giveth orders for thinges past, and for thinges hereafter to be followed, changeth rights and possessions of private men, legittimateth bastards, establisheth forms of religion, altereth weights and measures, giveth formes of succession to the crowne … For everie Englishmen is entended to bee there present, either in person or by procuration and attornies, of what preheminence, state, dignitie, or qualitie soever he be, from the Prince (be he King or Queene) to the lowest person of Englande. And the consent of the Parliament is taken to be everie mans consent.   (Smith, 1982: 78, quoted in Loades, 2002: 207)

Few in Elizabethan England, and fewer under James, would be quite so categorical in asserting the parliament's centrality, at least outside the parliament itself, within which freedom of speech was a right. But all in England knew that, as the Magna Carta, the tax-imposing power of the crown, was limited by the necessity of parliamentary consent. And republican consciousness was also present, especially among intellectuals, in awareness that the most successful polity known, the Roman Empire, had risen to greatness as a republic, ruled by its senate after the expulsion of its early kings.

As we have noted earlier in discussing Machiavelli's influence on Renaissance drama, and the more general influence of humanist study of the pre-Christian classics, the example of Roman greatness was a source on the one hand for awareness of republican political alternatives to kingship, on the other, for a view of politics and morality as subject to an amoral logic of history. The latter view was especially associated with the Roman historian Tacitus (56–117 CE), whose *Annales* (or at least the books that have not been lost) documented the reign of Tiberius Caesar, the heir and successor of Augustus. As Blair Worden puts it,

> The influence and standing of Tacitus were at their peak around the early seventeenth century. In the new "civil" or "politic" history, which turned to past politics for an understanding of present ones, his influence was supreme, largely because of the parallels that were discerned between Tacitus's theme, the entrenchment of imperial rule at the expense of ancient senatorial liberties, and the rise of the Renaissance monarchies at the expense of the nobility and of conciliar and representative institutions.   (Worden, 1999: 152)

Both Augustus and Tiberius, although they were in effect ruling princes with near-tyrannical power, retained the fiction that they served the state at the will of Rome's Senate. Both in fact claimed to be preserving and even restoring republican institutions and freedoms after the damage the republic suffered in the civil wars, the topic of Shakespeare's tragedies *Julius Caesar* (1599) and *Antony and Cleopatra* (1606–7). Thus the Roman state as described by Tacitus features conflict between the real nature of politics and its formal institutions that is as radical as any in history before the twentieth century. Ben Jonson's *Sejanus His Fall*, first performed in a collaborative version in 1603 with a cast that included Shakespeare, and published in 1605 in a version solely by Jonson, treats politics and states of political consciousness toward the end of the long rule of Tiberius, at a point where much authority in the state has been delegated to an energetic and unscrupulous favorite, Sejanus. The play was not a success on stage, and Jonson published it with annotations in Latin, seemingly to exhibit not only his own scholarship but the play's seriousness as political commentary.

At the end of the "Argument," a brief prose summary of the plot, Jonson adds a paragraph of political moralization that sounds a great deal like the last lines of *The Maid's Tragedy* quoted earlier:

> This [play] do we advance as a mark of terror to all traitors, and treasons; to show how just the heavens are in pouring and thundering down a weighty vengeance on their unnatural intents, even to the worst princes; more to those, for guard of whose piety and virtue, the angels are in continual watch, and God himself mysteriously working.   ("The Argument" 45–52, in Jonson, 1989)

In a monarchy we know, or think we know, what treason is. It involves an attempt to harm the sacred body of the king or queen. But from the very beginning of English treason statutes in 1372, the crime is defined as "to compasse or imagine" the death of the monarch (along with other forms of damage to the state), and by the middle of Elizabeth's reign, the law had been substantially expanded. The Treason Act of 1571, passed in part to protect Queen Elizabeth from Catholic plots, reads as follows:

> if any person or persons whatsoever, at any time after the last day of June next coming during the natural life of our most gracious sovereign lady, Queen Elizabeth … , shall, within the realm or without, compass, imagine, invent, devise, or intend the death or destruction, or any bodily harm tending to death, destruction, maim, or wounding of the royal person of the same our sovereign lady, Queen Elizabeth; or to deprive or depose her of or from the style, honour, or kingly name of the imperial crown of this realm or of any other realm or dominion to her majesty belonging, or to levy war against her majesty within this realm or without, or to move or to stir any foreigners or strangers with force to invade this realm or the realm of Ireland or any other her

majesty's dominions being under her majesty's obeisance, and such compasses, imaginations, inventions, devices, or intentions, or any of them shall maliciously, advisedly, and expressly utter or declare by any printing, writing, ciphering, speech, words, or sayings; or if any person or persons whatsoever, after the said last day of June, shall maliciously, advisedly, and directly publish, declare, hold opinion, affirm or say by any speech, express words, or sayings that our said sovereign lady, Queen Elizabeth, during her life is not or ought not to be queen of this realm of England and also of the realms of France and Ireland, or that any other person or persons ought of right to be king or queen of the said realms ... , during her majesty's life, or shall by writing, printing, preaching, speech, express words, or sayings maliciously, advisedly, and directly publish, set forth, and affirm that ... our said sovereign lady, Queen Elizabeth, is an heretic, schismatic, tyrant, infidel, or an usurper of the crown of the said realms or any of them; that then all and every such said offence or offences shall be taken, deemed, and declared, by the authority of this act and parliament, to be high treason ...   (England 1571).

This catalog of possible forms of challenge to monarchy bespeaks the desire of the framers of the 1571 statute, who are following innovations in treason law passed in 1534 to buttress Henry VIII's authority over the church, to guard against complex challenges to the legitimacy of Elizabeth's rule, not merely against plots of violence against her person or against her offices or prerogatives. Her entitlement to rights she claims, such as the throne of France, cannot be disputed, nor can her behavior *vis-à-vis* religion be criticized in any very substantial way, without the words, spoken or published or possibly even thought, constituting high treason. One limit of this royal prerogative to impose loyalty, although a frail one, was parliamentary privilege. As Johann Sommerville points out of King James I,

> There were dangers in voicing voluble attacks on royal actions. It was safer to do so in the house of Commons than in most other places, since the commons enjoyed the privilege of free speech, at least in theory. (Sommerville, 2002: 476)

Given these contexts, one can see why a play about the corrupt subservience of the first-century Roman senate to a power-seeking imperial favorite who uses a network of informers and brings treason charges against his enemies might seem politically apt at the end of Elizabeth's reign and the beginning of James's. Jonson's play, probably at its production or at its publication around the time of the Gunpowder Plot of 1605, caused sufficient stir to have him called before the privy council to answer charges of treason and popery. Hence, perhaps, his defensive paragraph about the play's service as a "mark of terror to all traitors."

Although somewhat difficult to keep straight in reading because of its large cast of Latin-named characters, the plot of *Sejanus His Fall* is not supremely complicated. On the other hand, it presupposes some knowledge of early Roman imperial history, a history more prominent in Renaissance schooling than it is in our own – although if one has read Robert Graves' *I Claudius* or seen the BBC series that dramatized it, one has a vivid sense of the relevant events that on the whole accords with Jonson's, as both derive largely from Tacitus. In 31 BCE, Augustus defeated Antony and Cleopatra at Actium and became the sole ruler of the Roman world. He ruled it with a great deal of help from his wife, Livia Augusta, and on his death in CE 14 was deified. Augustus had no natural children, but adopted Livia's son by a previous marriage, Tiberius, who succeeded Augustus as emperor, although the most popular and charismatic of the descendants of the house of Julius Caesar in Tiberius's generation was Germanicus, a war hero who was wholeheartedly committed to the restoration of the Roman republic. Germanicus died, allegedly by poison, four years after Tiberius succeeded Augustus as emperor, and Germanicus's children with the virtuous Agrippina, Nero, Drusus Junior, and Caligula, represent the hopes for a republican future for those who cherish that ideal.

Sejanus begins with commentary by a set of "republican" or "Germanican" senators, Arruntius and Silius, on how the relatively lowborn Sejanus's apparently unbounded power has corrupted Rome. They dispense favor to an historian of the fall of the Republic, Cremutus Cordus, even as they watch Sejanus accept the approach of a would-be office buyer, the physician Eudemus. The Germanican senators, especially Arruntius, volubly recall the heroism of republican figures like Cato, who opposed the rise of Julius Caesar and then committed suicide when Caesar won:

> SABINUS　　But these our times
> 　　Are not the same, Arruntius.
> ARRUNTIUS　　Times? The men
> 　　The men are not the same: 'Tis we are base,
> 　　Poor, and degenerate from th'exalted strain
> 　　Of our great fathers. Where is now the soul
> 　　Of god-like Cato? he, that durst be good,
> 　　When Caesar durst be evil; and had power
> 　　As not to live his slave, to die his master.
> 　　　　　　　　　　　　　　　　(1.1.85–92)

So the theme of lost virtue – underwritten in Cato's case by stoic suicide – is introduced from the start. Meanwhile, on another part of the stage, Sejanus accepts Eudemus's bribe for a tribunate (a major office in the Roman state) and masterfully works on eroding Eudemus's loyalty to the Hippocratic Oath that enjoins physicians to keep the confidence of their patients. Sejanus wants access to Livia, the wife of Drusus, son of Tiberius and expected heir of empire. After quickly chatting about possible symptoms and habits of his other great patients with the very uncomfortable Eudemus, he asks,

> SEJANUS   Come, what's Livia?
> I know she's quick, and quaintly spirited
> And will have strange thoughts, when she's at leisure
> She tells 'em all to you?
> EUDEMUS   My noblest lord
> He breathes not in the Empire, or on earth,
> Whom I would be ambitious to serve
> (In any act, that may preserve mine honour)
> Before your lordship.
>
> (1.1.319–326)

That is, Eudemus tries to say, I am entirely at your service, Lord Sejanus, but I cannot honorably discuss my patients with you. With the frank, in some ways attractive cynicism that characterizes him whenever he is self-confident (which is most of the time), Sejanus responds,

> Sir, you can lose no honour,
> By trusting aught to me. The coarsest act
> Done to my service, I can so requite,
> As all the world shall style it honourable.
>
> (1.1.326–329)

And as is typical of the play, Sejanus supports this claim with a rhymed aphorism:

> Your idle, virtuous definitions
> Keep honour poor, and are as scorned, as vain:
> Those deeds breathe honour, that do suck in gain.
>
> (1.1.330–332)

The onstage juxtaposition of Cremutius Cordus, dedicated to writing histories that keep republican ideals of honorable self-sacrifice alive, with Sejanus's open cynicism about his own power to take any coarse deed and make it honorable by rewarding it with money and success, lays out a central idea of the play. A commitment to virtue, and some form of public speech celebrating virtue, can be of importance in keeping a model of healthy human behavior alive in bad times. We have every reason to believe that this goal was central to Jonson's understanding of his own activity as poet and dramatist. But at the same time, in bad times the powerful can, and usually will, do their best to stamp out or corrupt such forms of speech. Cremutius Cordus is noticed talking with Germanicans by one of Sejanus's informers at 1.1.75, and Sejanus then denounces him to Tiberius at 2.2.303, as an afterthought to a series of other denunciations. Again, after a main event in the senate – the accusation of Silius for treason, followed by Silius's suicide – Cordus is in turn accused for having written (or perhaps quoted) the comment that "Cassius was the last of all the Romans" (3.1.392). (This, interestingly, comes from Shakespeare's *Julius Caesar*, where, on the field of defeat at Philippi, Brutus says over Cassius's body, "The last of all the Romans, fare thee well!" (5.4.99) – it may be there to mark how Shakespeare shares Jonson's own interest in republicanism.) Cordus gives an extensive speech, translated directly from Tacitus, in his own defense, and Tiberius defers judgment: "Take him hence, / We shall determine of him at next sitting" (3.1.463–464). Without further commentary from Tiberius, Sejanus and his agents order the destruction of Cordus's writings:

> COTTA   Meantime, give order that his books be burnt
>   To the aediles.
> SEJANUS   You have well advised.
> AFER   It fits not such licentious things should live
>   T'upbraid the age.
>
> (3.1.465–468)

This occasions the following commentary from Arruntius and Sabinus – two of the Germanican senators who still survive at this point:

> ARRUNTIUS   Let 'em be burnt! Oh, how ridiculous
>   Appears the Senate's brainless diligence
>   Who think they can with present power, extinguish
>   The memory of all succeeding times!
> SABINUS   'Tis true, when (contrary) the punishment
>   Of wit doth make th'authority increase.
>
> (3.1.471–476)

One of the remarkable characteristics of *Sejanus* as a reading text is the number of political statements in it than can be read in opposite ways. Tiberius specializes in such statements, and the Germanicans, on the whole, do not. But Sabinus's comment is on its face ambiguous. Given his general position, we must take it to mean "punishing writers confers more authority upon their writings," but it could equally mean "punishing writers increases the authority of the authorities who do the punishing," a possible truth. Certainly, the first is suggested by the rest of Sabinus's speech suggests:

> Nor do they aught, that use this cruelty
> Of interdiction, and this rage of burning;
> But purchase to themselves rebuke, and shame,
> And to the writers an eternal name.
>
> (3.1.477–480)

Cremutius Cordus is a minor character in the play, only mentioned after this point in a self-congratulatory speech by Sejanus (who calls Cordus a "shrub" he has "grubbed up" (5.3.246–8)), but he exists in part to attest to Jonson's faith in the power of the written word, a power given extremely strong witness by the play's ending.

This brings us to the central plot, a plot on which the virtuous Germanicans are commentators and of which they are victims. Its principals are Sejanus and Tiberius, and its stake is the rule of the empire. Tacitus treats the episodes dramatized by Jonson as central parts of a transition to tyranny. By CE 23, Tacitus comments,

> Tiberius … began his ninth year of national stability and domestic prosperity …. But suddenly Fortune turned disruptive. The emperor himself became tyrannical – or gave tyrannical men power. The cause and beginning of the change lay with Lucius Aelius Sejanus, commander of the Guard.   (Tacitus, 1989: 157)

Note that Tacitus temporizes on whether Tiberius himself is the tyrant. Suetonius, whose lively treatment of Tiberius in *Twelve Caesars* Jonson also cites, spends the first half of his portrait praising Tiberius's wisdom and industry in his early years as emperor, and then (with little emphasis on Sejanus) in the second half describes with fascination the horrors of his later years. Tacitus, however, sees Sejanus as the possible culprit in Tiberius's transformation into tyranny, and he sketches Sejanus's character and history in terms that Jonson makes use of:

> Sejanus was born at Vulsinii. His father Lucius Seius Strabo, was a Roman knight. After increasing his income – it was alleged – by a liason with a rich debauchee named Marcus Gavius Apicius, the boy joined, while still young, the suite of Augustus's grandson Gaius Caesar. Next by various devices he obtained a complete ascendancy over Tiberius. To Sejanus alone the otherwise cryptic emperor spoke freely and unguardedly. This was hardly due to Sejanus' cunning; in that he was outclassed by Tiberius. The cause was rather heaven's anger against Rome – to which the triumph of Sejanus, and his downfall too, were catastrophic. Of audacious character and untiring physique, secretive about himself and ever ready to incriminate others, a blend of arrogance and servility, he concealed behind a carefully modest exterior an unbounded lust for power. Sometimes this impelled him to lavish excesses, but more often to incessant work. And that is as damaging as excess when the throne is its aim.   (Tacitus, 1989: 157)

In Jonson's play, all of Sejanus's actions (as opposed to some of his reactions to initiatives taken by Tiberius late in the play) serve a consistent and quite brilliant plan, a plan that he confides to the audience in an early soliloquy and appears first to formulate after a grave physical affront. Tiberius's

son and heir, the impulsive Drusus, walks with a group of Germanican senators on the street, seething over Sejanus's advancement in the state. He asks
them, "Is my father mad ... thus to heave / An idol up with praise! Make him
his mate! / His rival in the Empire!" (1.1.548–551). Sejanus, with a group of
clients, enters talking, and evidently bumps into Drusus or seems to crowd
his group into a less desirable part of the way:

> *Sejanus enters, followed with clients*
> SEJANUS   There is your bill, and yours; bring you your man:
>   I have moved for you too, Latiarus.
> DRUSUS   What?
>   Is your vast greatness grown so blindly bold,
>   That you will over us?
>
> (1.1.560–563)

Sejanus, either in spontaneous masculine response, or out of policy,
meets the aggressive challenge in kind: "Why, then give way" (1.1.564).
Giving way would be an acknowledgement of social inferiority, and Drusus
explodes in anger. His lines suggest that Sejanus not only continues to
crowd him, but prepares for a fight, although they also offer indignant
commentary on Sejanus's continued rise in the state:

> DRUSUS   Give way, Colossus? Do you lift? Advance you?
>   Take that.
> *Drusus strikes him.*
> ARRUNTIUS   Good! brave! excellent brave prince!
> DRUSUS   Nay, come, approach. What? stand you off? at gaze?
>   It looks too full of death, for thy cold spirits.
>   Avoid mine eye, dull camel, or my sword
>   Shall make thy bravery fitter for a grave,
>   Than for a triumph.
>
> (1.1.564–570)

Drusus exits being cheered by the onlookers, and Sejanus, alone, comments
on the solidification of his purposes the incident has caused.

> He that, with such wrong moved, can bear it through
> With patience, and an even mind, knows how
> To turn it back. Wrath, covered, carries fate:
> Revenge is lost, if I profess my hate.
> What was my practice late, I'll now pursue
> As my fell justice. This hath styled it new.
>
> (1.1.576–581)

Having successfully used the physician Eudemus to gain access to Livia,
and having successfully seduced Livia, he uses the two of them to kill Drusus

with a slow-acting poison that imitates illness. He also sends an agent to urge Livia Augusta, Tiberius's mother, to warn Tiberius of dangers from the Germanicans. As he reflects on these acts, he communicates his overall plan to the audience:

> This second (from his mother) will well urge
> Our late design, and spur on Caesar's rage:
> Which else might grow remiss. The way to put
> A prince in blood, is to present the shapes
> Of dangers, greater than they are (like late,
> Or early shadows) and sometimes, to feign
> Where there are none, only to make him fear;
> His fear will make him cruel: and once entered
> He doth not easily learn to stop, or spare
> Where he may doubt.
>
> (2.2.381–390)

By constantly reminding Tiberius of the dangers of conspiracy, and by sometimes making up dangers, Sejanus aims to drive Tiberius into a state of fearful cruelty and excessive punishment. Moreover, he aims to do through Tiberius what he could not easily do himself, despite the large political resources at his disposal: that is, to eliminate all the probable heirs of Tiberius.

> This have I made my rule,
> To thrust Tiberius into tyranny,
> And make him toil, to turn aside those blocks,
> Which I alone, could not remove with safety.
> Drusus once gone, Germanicus' three sons
> Would clog my way; whose guards have too much faith
> To be corrupted: and their mother known
> Of too too unreproved a chastity,
> To be attempted, as light Livia was.
> Work then, my art, on Caesar's fears, as they
> On those they fear, till all my lets be cleared.
>
> (2.2.390–400)

"Lets" here are "obstacles"; Sejanus intends to guide Tiberius into doing his killing for him. After Tiberius has destroyed his own family, Sejanus will finally turn on him, but not until

> ... he in ruins of his house, and hate
> Of all his subjects, bury his own state:
> When, with my peace, and safety, I will rise,
> By making him the public sacrifice.
>
> (2.2.401–404)

When Tiberius has fully disgusted the public by destroying popular members of his family, Sejanus will at last supplant him.

Obviously, this plan can only work if Tiberius has strong tendencies toward paranoid tyranny to start with. At the same time, note that, like Tiberius, Sejanus intends to make his ascent to empire accord with apparent republican aims, as he will make Tiberius "the public sacrifice" and appear to serve the common good in so doing.

Sejanus thus incarnates a political danger considerably more substantial and far-reaching than the reckless opportunism and distraction of the monarch from matters of state exemplified by favorites like Gaveston in *Edward II*. Sejanus has a coherent plan to take over the state, and given that he is a public exponent of cynicism with respect to Roman traditions of public virtue, and of flagrant venality with respect to the distribution of offices, we can expect him to be a very dangerous emperor indeed (although perhaps no more dangerous than the insane Caligula who in fact succeeded Tiberius).

The counterforce to Sejanus turns out to be not the ineffectual virtue of the Germanicans – although Jonson does take seriously their claim that virtue will have the last word – but Tiberius himself. Both Tacitus and Jonson are unspecific about the nature of Sejanus's hold on Tiberius's affections. It clearly is partly an erotic closeness, and Jonson has Arruntius repeat the rumor cited by Tacitus above to the effect that Sejanus gained wealth early by selling himself sexually to a rich Roman: "for hire, / He prostituted his abusèd body / To that great gourmand, fat Apicius / And was the noted pathic of the time" (1.1.213–16). Arruntius, in whom Roman moral indignation clearly combines with a libidinous imagination, depicts Tiberius after he leaves Rome in Sejanus's apparent control to live on the island of Capri as cultivating nameless forms of bisexual voyeurism and lust:

> Thither, too,
> He hath his boys, and beauteous girls ta'en up,
> Out of our noblest houses, the best formed
> Best nurtured, and most modest: what's their good
> Serves to provoke his bad. Some are allured,
> Some threatened; others (by their friends detained)
> Are ravished hence, like captives, and in sight
> Of their most grievèd parents, dealt away
> Unto his spintries, sellaries, and slaves,
> Masters of strange, and new-commènted lusts,
> For which wise nature hath not left a name.
> (4.4.391–401)

Tiberius has, for these pleasures, made both Rome and himself dependent upon Sejanus, so that Tiberius has in Arruntius's pungent formulation

> become the ward
> To his own vassal, a stale catamite:
> Whom he (upon our low, and suffering necks)
> Hath raised from excrement, to side the gods,
> And have his proper sacrifice in Rome.
>
> (4.4.403–407)

"Spintries" and "sellaries" are male prostitutes, and "catamites" are boys whom men have sex with. Thus while the play offers no clear claim that Tiberius and Sejanus have been sexual partners, it suggests that they may have been, or that Arruntius at any rate thinks they may. Sejanus's preservation of Tiberius during the collapse of a grotto in which they are dining, as Jonson has Nero describe it, also reminds us of this possibility:

> Only Sejanus, with his knees, hands, face,
> O'erhanging Caesar, did oppose himself
> To the remaining ruins, and was found
> In that so labouring posture, by the soldiers
> That came to succour him. With which adventure,
> He hath so fixed himself in Caesar's trust,
> As thunder cannot move him.
>
> (4.2.53–59)

But Nero is wrong that Sejanus's physical services to Tiberius have "fixed [Sejanus] in Caesar's trust," and so, in his way, is Arruntius. Tiberius, although far less open than Sejanus with the audience about his thoughts, and offstage entirely after Act 3, has already set in place a counterplot – not in the name of Roman virtue, or his own future reputation, but following a proverb that Jonson has Tiberius utter in Greek, "While I can live, I will prevent earth's fury: / *Emou thanontos gaia michthaeto pyri*" (2.2.329–330): "when I am dead let fire consume the earth." This may seem like recklessness, but it underlines Tiberius's primary commitment to his own survival, whatever happens after it.

So we have basically two lines of plot, one brazenly open, the other partly concealed: Sejanus seeks the empire by playing on Tiberius's fears and driving Tiberius into tyranny; Tiberius seeks security from any present threat, and seems for the first part of the play to be finding that security in Sejanus. Moreover, Tiberius pays consistent, careful attention to Roman republican traditions, even as he permits terrible things to be done in their name; Sejanus makes his cynical impatience with these traditions evident, and unlike Tiberius, is eager to court deification by accepting "sacrifices" to his statue, which has displaced the great Pompey's.

We have, we hope, illustrated the subtlety of political developments in Jonson's play. Reading it for the first time is a bit like reading the later novels of Henry James: one can read along and then suddenly realize that something very important happened some time ago that one did not notice. Such a subtle turning point occurs when, after destroying Silius at the senate and scheduling future denunciations of Germanicans, Sejanus attempts to cash in Tiberius's gratitude and marry Tiberius's niece Livia, now widowed by the poisoning of Drusus.

> SEJANUS   The only gain, and which I count most fair
> Of all my fortunes, is that mighty Caesar
> Hath thought me worthy his alliance. Hence
> Begin my hopes.
> TIBERIUS   H'mh?
> SEJANUS   I have heard, Augustus
> In the bestowing of his daughter, thought
> But even of gentlemen of Rome: if so
> (I know not how to hope so great a favour)
> But if a husband should be sought for Livia,
> And I be had in mind, as Caesar's friend,
> I would but use the glory of the kindred.
> It should not make me slothful ...
>
>   (3.2.512–522)

That Jonsonian interjection "H'mh?" marks the turn. Tiberius suddenly recognizes a potential rival where before, it seems, he saw a degraded love object and a supremely useful tool. Instantly, his speech takes on the hesitant, pause-laden, formal quality we see in his public performances: "We cannot but commend thy piety, / Most loved Sejanus, in acknowledging / Those, bounties; which we, faintly, such remember" (3.2.530–532). (As it may have been noticed, the edition of *Sejanus* we quote has chosen not to modernize Jonson's punctuation, on the theory that it offers guidance as speech rhythms in performance: the effect is particularly marked in this passage, as Tiberius pauses before "bounties," marking his own mental labor over acknowledging dependence on another.) Moreover, the reply is deeply ambiguous, responding perhaps to the unusually blatant hypocrisy of Sejanus's claim at the end of his request that he seeks marriage with Livia "for dear regard / Unto my children, this I wish: myself / Have no ambition farther, than to end / My days in service of so dear a master" (3.2.526–529). Is Tiberius saying that it is very good for Sejanus to be so grateful for the little Tiberius has done for him? Or is he saying that it is very good for Sejanus to be pious, and that this piety should be reckoned among the good things that Sejanus does for Tiberius, things Tiberius does his best to keep in mind, but succeeds only partly in remembering? The sentence seems designed not to be easily understood: while it may express devotion to Sejanus, it may also encode a threat of withdrawal of attention. But Tiberius proceeds to suggest that he himself cannot marry Sejanus to Livia even if he wishes to:

But to thy suit. The rest of mortal men,
In all their drifts, and counsels, pursue profit:
Princes, alone, are of a different sort,
Directing their main actions still to fame.

(3.2.533–536)

This waffling prologue, preparing the idea that many weighty long-range considerations may intervene between Tiberius's natural desire to grant any suit from his beloved Sejanus, and the fulfillment of that desire, of course, contrasts markedly with Tiberius's earlier comment that as long as he survives, the earth may be consumed with fire after his death. Here it leads into timid, slowly articulated worries about how the marriage might "divide th'imperial house" (3.2.546). Thinking of the likely anger of Agrippina, he continues, "What if it cause some present difference? / Thou art not safe, Sejanus, if thou prove [i.e. 'attempt'] it" (3.2.549–550). After a lengthy passage of worry about opposition to Sejanus in the senate, Tiberius concludes with a large but vague reassurance:

Only, thus much
Believe, our loved Sejanus, we not know
That height in blood, or honour, which thy virtue,
And mind to us, may not aspire with merit.
And this we'll publish, on all watched occasion
The Senate, and the people shall present.

(3.2.571–576)

What, again, does Tiberius mean? One could assume (as Sejanus appears to), that Tiberius is saying, please be assured that I am aware of what extremely high office and family alliance your merit deserves, – indeed, I do not know of any high office or honor you *don't* deserve – and I intend to make a public announcement about this soon when the moment is right. But what he says could also mean, believe me, Sejanus, after this request of yours I don't know exactly what your behavior and your intentions toward me might or might not deserve, but when I do know, I'll present my judgment on the matter to the Senate and the people. Sejanus comes away from this conversation sure that he has Tiberius just where he wants him, but also eager to get Tiberius away from Rome before Tiberius can change his mind, as Caesar has begun – with apparent ponderous uncertainty – to reflect on what trouble his favorite is causing:

SEJANUS   Caesar hath taught me better to refuse
Than I knew how to ask. How pleaseth Caesar
T'embrace my late advice, for leaving Rome?
TIBERIUS   We are resolved.

(3.2.579–582)

When Tiberius exits, reading a memorandum of further suggestions for a life of pleasure-filled retirement that Sejanus has composed, Sejanus exults at his own mental superiority to his master: "Dull, heavy Caesar!" (3.2.586)

>   Sleep,
>   Voluptuous Caesar, and security
>   Seize on thy stupid powers, and leave them dead
>   To public cares, awake but to thy lusts.
>   The strength of which makes thy libidinous soul
>   Itch to leave Rome; and I have thrust it on.
>   (3.2.598–603)

Tiberius does so itch, and he will not abandon his desires. As he says to the servant he summons, "To leave our journey off, / Were sin 'gainst our decreed delights" (3.2.630–631). But before this, he has reflected in soliloquy on what he has just learned about Sejanus.

>   To marry Livia? will no less, Sejanus,
>   Content thy aims? no lower object? well!
>   Thou know'st how thou art wrought into our trust;
>   Woven in our design; and think'st, we must
>   Now use thee, whatsoe'er thy projects are:
>   'Tis true. But yet with caution, and fit care.
>   (3.2.623–628)

Tiberius takes "fit care" by employing Macro, a man as unscrupulous as Sejanus, to spy on Sejanus (as well as the Germanicans) and report to him in his retreat on Capri on what he learns. Sejanus believes that he controls access to Tiberius, and thus in effect rules for him, and Sejanus quickly works to destroy the surviving sons of Germanicus, making the Senate his tool, and using formerly honorable men to tempt their relatives into speaking treason. But Macro helps Caligula escape to Capri, and Tiberius sends a series of letters to Rome that bafflingly both confirm and undermine his advocacy of Sejanus. Lepidus, the quiet Germanican who has survived Sejanus's purges thus far, analyzes Tiberius's letter-writing strategy:

>   His subtlety hath chose this doubling line,
>   To hold him even in: not so to fear him
>   As wholly put him out, and yet give check
>   Unto his farther boldness. In meantime,
>   By his employments, makes him odious
>   Unto the staggering rout, whose aid (in fine)
>   He hopes to use.
>   (4.4.465–471)

Thus, Lepidus suggests, Tiberius now follows the plan Sejanus developed in Act 2: to make him do his dirty work, thus allowing him to become publically despised, then to offer him as a "sacrifice."

The play gathers momentum throughout Act 5, as Tiberius nominates a consul hostile to Sejanus alongside one devoted to him, then (after a series of ominous omens involving the statues of Sejanus) summons the Senate to an emergency session without telling Sejanus. This naturally terrifies Sejanus, but Macro appears to invite Sejanus to the Senate, assuring him that, although it is meant to be a surprise, Tiberius intends to invest Sejanus with "tribunicial dignity, and power"(5.4.363) – that is, that he will in effect become emperor. Sejanus, delighted, utters a hubristic soliloquy on the folly of fear: "When I do fear again, let me be struck / With forkèd fire and unpitied die: / Who fears, is worthy of calamity" (5.4.397–399).

The final scene of the play – one of the great scenes of political theater – is dominated by the reading aloud of Tiberius's letter. After some praise for freedom of speech, the letter turns to Sejanus (Jonson uses parentheses to indicate audience interjections):

> PRAECO [*Reading letter*]   'True it is, conscript fathers, that we have raised
> Sejanus, from obscure, and almost unknown gentry,'
> (SENATORS How! How!)
> 'to the highest, and most conspicuous point of greatness, and (we hope)
> deservingly; yet not without danger: it being a most bold hazard in that
> sovereign, who, by his particular love to one, dares adventure the hatred
> of all his other subjects.'
>
> $\hspace{8cm}$ (5.7.573–581)

As the letter unfolds, Tiberius presents himself as uncertain how to interpret Sejanus's actions:

> Some there be, that would interpret this his public severity to be particular ambition; and that, under a pretext of service to us, he doth but remove his own lets ... What we should say, or rather what we should not say, lords of the Senate, if this be true, our gods and goddesses confound us if we know! Only, we must think, we have placed our benefits ill: and conclude, that, in our choice, either we were wanting to the gods, or the gods to us.
> *The senators shift their places.* $\hspace{4cm}$ (5.7.644 ... 656)

The stage direction indicates a shuffling movement away from Sejanus, as the Senate begins to parse Tiberius's intentions. As soon as Tiberius's letter requests that Sejanus be suspended from office, Sejanus attempts to stop the reading, but as prearranged with Macro, Laco enters with armed men. The letter continues, and himself suspended from all exercise of place, or power, but till due and mature trial be made of his innocency, which yet we can faintly apprehend the necessity to doubt.... In the meantime, it shall not be fit for us to importune so judicious a Senate, who know how much they hurt the innocent, that spare the guilty: and how grateful a sacrifice, to the gods, is the life of an ingrateful person.   (5.7.656 ... 664)

The Senate rushes to expel him, Macro abuses him, he is executed, and his body is torn to pieces by the crowd. Since Roman law forbids the execution of a virgin, Macro orders the hangman to rape Sejanus's daughter before strangling her – a deference to republican tradition worthy of Tiberius himself.

In *Sejanus*, as in *Edward II*, the public theater attempts to represent the interaction of principle, personality, and contingency in power politics. Shortly before his death, Sejanus sacrifices to the goddess Fortuna, and her statue rejects his sacrifice. But, as Tiberius's letter says, Sejanus himself is the grateful/ingrateful sacrifice. Jonson here offers a slightly twisted version of Tacitus's deadpan comment that the whole business must be attributed to "heaven's anger against Rome – to which the triumph of Sejanus, and his downfall too, were catastrophic" (Tacitus, 1989: 157). That is, for Tacitus, Sejanus's destruction does not seem an instance of divine mercy, but a further indication of divine displeasure. Jonson hopes that bringing the horror and folly of tyranny to the stage, and surrounding it with morally intelligent commentary that remembers better times, will evoke the kind of morally responsible political community that is absent from the Rome he depicts. Andrew Marvell, writing during the English Civil War, has the ghost of Jonson speak of the responsibility of the writer in bad times:

> When the Sword glitters ore the Judges head,
> And fear has Coward Churchmen silenced,
> Then is the Poets time, 'tis then he drawes,
> And single fights forsaken Vertues cause.
> He, when the wheel of Empire, whirleth back,
> And though the World disjointed Axel crack,
> Sings still of ancient Rights and better Times,
> Seeks wretched good, arraigns successful Crimes
> (Marvell, 1681: 37)

Marvell clearly has *Sejanus* in mind, and he sees a theater poet who unmasks political error and puts it in historical perspective as heroic.

Part 4

Not Shakespeare – Lives of the Theater Poets

4.1 "Non-Shakespearean": The Dire Privative

An adjective constructed by negating a categorical description is called a "privative," meaning that it constructs a second category by depriving the field of reference of whatever was named by the first one. "Non-Shakespearean," then, is a privative, and this book has set out to show that it is a somewhat dangerous or dire one in the study of Early Modern drama. Colin Burrow aptly called "nondramatic," as in "Shakespeare's nondramatic works," "the dire privative prefix" in his edition of Shakespeare's Poems and Sonnets, but "non-Shakespearean" is even direr (Burrow, 2002: 2). As understood by most readers, "Shakespearean" and "non-Shakespearean" divide English Renaissance drama between the Best and the Rest. While we yield to few in bardolatry – the Shakespeare-worship that has been an enormous force in literary studies and in the cultural politics of the English-speaking world since the mid-eighteenth century – we hope that our book will help readers see how worthy both of comparison with Shakespeare and of admiration in their own right his contemporaries are.

One way to divide Shakespeare's contemporaries is broadly to put them into two camps: the ones who were in a position to approach their own plays and those of their cohort in the way we do, as an enterprise to be discussed in comparison to Shakespeare, and those who were not. The difference is mostly a generational one. The playwrights who started writing for the theater from the mid-1590s through 1610 or so worked in response to Shakespeare's greatness. This was because Shakespeare was the dominant London playwright when they began working on plays. That generation includes many of the playwrights in this book, certainly John Fletcher, Francis Beaumont, Thomas Middleton, John Marston, and John Webster, and arguably Ben Jonson; in

Studying Shakespeare's Contemporaries, First Edition. Lars Engle and Eric Rasmussen.
© 2014 Lars Engle and Eric Rasmussen. Published 2014 by John Wiley & Sons, Ltd.

a different way, Shakespeare's tragedies seem to be in Elizabeth Cary's mind as she writes *Mariam*. We will return to Jonson because he is an interesting special case. The other group of playwrights would be those whom Shakespeare regarded as known masters when he began working in the theater, and to whom Shakespeare reacted in his own writing. Christopher Marlowe is preeminent here and Thomas Kyd is also important.

This said, it should be pointed out that no one at the time would have seen any individual theater poet, including Shakespeare, as having the degree of preeminence that we attribute to Shakespeare. In comparison, both to our views of playwrights contemporary with us, and to our general attitude now toward English Renaissance writing, Elizabethan and Jacobean theater poets were in their time not as important a component in the theatrical enterprise, and the theatrical enterprise was not as high in cultural status, as it is when we think of going to see a play by Tom Stoppard, August Wilson, or Caryl Churchill. It is hard to see in very many of Shakespeare's followers any sort of intellectual struggle to surpass him or find new paths to explore. This approach does however yield rewards when brought to Jonson, whom we know from other writings to have felt competitive with Shakespeare as well as affectionate toward him, and it will also help us in discussing Middleton.

To elaborate on this qualification, we should point out that companies commissioned and adapted plays in constant competition with one another; companies also to some degree developed competing styles of drama. So scripts that might seem to a modern reader to betoken a poetic struggle for artistic preeminence between writers might really give evidence for market competition in the theater world. The Early Modern theater was not on the whole an enterprise that encouraged most theater poets to think of themselves as individual artists. Some, such as Marlowe and Jonson, may have been prone to do this, not only by temperament but also because they were pursuing careers as poets in other ways.

Playwriting even more than other forms of writing was a mode for the middling sort. Upward social mobility (at best) or survival in a cold-hearted city (at least) seems to have been the motive in the lives of most playwrights at least as important as the possibility of literary immortality. The generation of writers dominant in theatrical writing and pamphleteering when Shakespeare got his start around 1590, the so-called "University Wits" represented in this book by Marlowe and Kyd, on the whole led lives of noisy desperation. Shakespeare, by contrast, provided a model for civic engagement and upward mobility through the theater that nobody else followed with quite Shakespeare's degree of quiet success. But several of the notable members of the next theatrical generation – Middleton, Jonson, Fletcher, and Dekker – had successful lives that like Shakespeare's were sustained in large part by writing in some form for the stage, whether the court stage or the public theater.

It is clear that for the diligent, reliable, and inventive theater poet, writing plays, collaborating on plays, and updating plays for a company was quite profitable. G. E. Bentley's conclusion long ago that "the professional playwrights made more money than other literary men of their time, and more than could have made as schoolmasters or curates" has on the whole stood up amid a general recontextualization of the theatrical enterprise (Bentley, 1971: 108). That recontextualization has emphasized the way play publication seems to imply more literary ambition than Bentley accorded to most dramatists (Erne, 2003) without disputing that working in close association with a company could yield a substantial income.

Three careers stand out, both in terms of the number of plays we have discussed in detail above, and as providing an example that can be juxtaposed with Shakespeare's without evident imbalance: those of Christopher Marlowe, Ben Jonson, and Thomas Middleton. Accordingly, we treat their lives in greater length and detail below.

4.2 Christopher Marlowe

Christopher Marlowe is one of the towering presences in English drama, spectacularly gifted, radically innovative, and marked out for trouble. The son of a Canterbury cobbler, born, like Shakespeare, in 1564, he went on a scholarship to the Cathedral School and thence on further scholarship to Corpus Christi College, Cambridge, where he proceeded to a B.A. and an M.A., probably beginning work as a government secret agent during absences from Corpus in his M.A. years. Marlowe seems to have begun writing plays and poems while still a student: *Dido, Queen of Carthage* and his translations of Ovid's *Amores* and Lucan's *Pharsalia* perhaps date from that time. He appears on the London stage with the Admiral's Men's production of *Tamburlaine the Great* (likely in summer 1587), one of the greatest debuts ever, and over the next five years wrote a series of powerful and varied plays in a range of genres (although he does not seem to have been drawn to comedy). His biographers have also documented a series of clashes with the law, including arraignment in a killing and arrest for counterfeiting. Various comments from literary rivals (notably his fellow University Wits Robert Greene and Thomas Nashe) suggest that he became as famous for articulating outrageous positions on religious and social topics as he was for literary excellence.

Rumors of Marlowe's personal willingness to flout the religious, sexual, and political order of the time gain credence from his writing. Marlowe's literary excellence is hard to separate from a daring willingness to challenge authority. Much of *Tamburlaine*'s appeal was its protagonist's successful self-assertion at the expense not only of existing monarchs and states, but also existing gods and religions: Greene comments in a 1588 pamphlet that Greene's own plays are now "in derision" because his verses could not "dar[e] God out of heaven with that atheist Tamburlan" (Nicholl, 2004). Machiavel's Prologue to *The Jew of Malta*, with its description of religion as a "childish toy," its assertion that "there is no sin but ignorance," and its claim that "might first made kings" (Prologue 14, 15, 20), sets out a program for the demystification of the Tudor social order; even though the play depicts Mediterranean Catholics, Jews, and Muslim Turks betraying one another for power and money and, at times, justifying their actions by references to their faiths, it is easy to see that the same motives and same mystifications applied to Protestant England. *The Massacre at Paris* touches on similar issues closer to home. Faustus's eagerness to sell his soul to obtain power and knowledge, as we have discussed above, cast him as an Epicurean intellectual willing to articulate his view of the stifling of human possibility entailed by Calvinism. And *Edward II*, with its representation of an English king undone by homosexual preoccupation with a minion and by the ambition of over-mighty subjects, boldly stages issues about sexuality and power that were, in general, associated with sodomy, designated *peccatum horribile inter Christianos non nominandam* – the horrible sin not to be named by Christians. Marlowe's play comes close to naming it, as do passages describing pederastic desire among Greek deities in *Dido* and in Marlowe's poem *Hero and Leander*.

So when the informer Richard Baines, and then Marlowe's friend and roommate Thomas Kyd when put under torture, alleged that Marlowe sought to convert others to atheism, asserted that Jesus and St. John were lovers, or claimed that all who loved not tobacco and boys were fools, they were attributing to him views that can seem consonant with his plays. Marlowe's violent death may partly have been an official reaction to the challenge he presented as person and author. He was stabbed in 1593, when he was 29, in what the inquest describes as a quarrel over the bill after a day in Deptford with acquaintances who, like Marlowe, were involved in the Elizabethan spy system run by Sir Francis Walsingham.

In any case, Marlowe's life and works mark him as a playwright who shows readers and audiences how to cast off superstitious reverence and inherited inhibitions. His death doubtless reinforced what his contemporaries already knew about the dangers of openly defying authority. But among Shakespeare's contemporaries, Marlowe was the prime example of how plays could test the limits of the doable and the thinkable for their audiences. This commitment to radical self-remaking, and to the casting-off of the constraints one is born into, has given him a special place as a brilliant martyr to art's defiance of conventionality and the state, anticipating Byron and Wilde, and echoing Ovid.

Thus it is helpful and interesting to frame the three contemporaries of Shakespeare to whom we give most attention in this book, Marlowe, Jonson, and Middleton, according to what readers and theatergoers seek and find in their works. In Marlowe, they find a playwright who, while cynical about the established order, cherishes the possibilities of self-remaking by casting it off.

4.3   Ben Jonson

Born around 1573, and coming into the London theater world when Shakespeare's career was at its height in the late 1590s, Ben Jonson is probably the Shakespearean contemporary who would have felt most keenly the direness of being categorized as "non-Shakespearean," although he may also have been the dramatist who most intelligently distinguished himself from Shakespeare, establishing dramatic and poetic patterns in conscious difference from his older friend and competitor. Jonson seems to have been rivalrous by nature, killing fellow-actor Gabriel Spencer in a duel in 1597, and engaging as a vigorous combatant in the so-called War of the Theaters during 1599–1603 in which Marston satirized Jonson in *Histriomastix*, Jonson satirized Marston and Dekker in *Poetaster*, and Dekker in turn resatirized him in *Satiromastix*. His rivalrous interest in Shakespeare is variously attested. In the *Informations* recorded by William Drummond of Hawthornden from a visit Jonson paid him in Scotland two-and-a-half years after Shakespeare's death, Jonson is quoted as declaring that "Shakespeare wanted art" (Donaldson, 2011: 47). There are small touches of mockery in lines within plays, which seem to take up Shakespearean lines Jonson thought absurd – in Jonson's 1609 *Epicene*, for instance, Truewit registers Dauphine's success in deceiving not only his uncle but his best friends in the line "Well, Dauphine, you have lurched your friends of the better half of the garland by concealing this part of the plot!" (5.4.221–223). In Shakespeare's *Coriolanus* (1606–1608), Cominius praises Caius Martius's battlefield supremacy with the remark "and in the brunt of seventeen battles since / He lurched all swords of the garland" (2.2.98–99). Jonson comments to Drummond on the geographical absurdity of the Bohemian sea coast in *The Winter's Tale*, and in *Timber* Jonson cites rhetorically "ridiculous" lines in *Julius Caesar* (Drummond, 1842: 16; Jonson, 2004 "De Shakespeare nostrat"). At the same time, in "To the memory of my beloved, The Author, Mr. William Shakespeare," his prefatory poem to the 1623 Folio edition of Shakespeare's works, Jonson offers the clearest recognition of Shakespeare's exceptionality that is recorded among Shakespeare's contemporaries. *Timber*, moreover, records Jonson's personal feelings alongside his criticisms:

> I remember the players have often mentioned it as an honour to Shakspeare, that in his writing (whatsoever he penned) he never blotted out a line. My answer hath been, "Would he had blotted a thousand," which they thought a malevolent speech. I had not told posterity this but for their ignorance who chose that circumstance to commend their friend by wherein he most faulted; and to justify mine own candour, for I loved the man, and do honour his memory on this side idolatry as much as any. He was, indeed, honest, and of an open and free nature, had an excellent phantasy, brave notions, and gentle expressions, wherein he flowed with that facility that sometimes it was necessary he should be stopped.
> (Jonson, 2004 "De Shakespeare nostrat")

Jonson's involvement with the Shakespeare folio came naturally, as Jonson pioneered folio publication of stage plays in his own folio *Works* of 1616. Of all the dramatists of the period, he was the most concerned with being a literary dramatist. He seems to have attended closely to the quarto publication of some of his early works, notably *Every Man In His Humour* in 1598 and *Cynthia's Revels* in 1601, where the very high incidence of press variants suggests a keen-eyed author proofing pages as they came off the press. He then substantially revises some of these works for folio publication – for instance reworking *Every Man in His Humour* to give it a London rather than Italian setting, and rewriting an unnamed collaborator's contributions to *Sejanus* to make the published version entirely his own. He also omits a number of coauthored plays in which he had a major hand from his *Works*: he places a high value on what we would call "authorship."

High value was placed not only on authorship, but on authority. For a hugely independent person, Jonson spent a great deal of time and energy establishing a place in the court culture of James and his son Charles, and, in doing so, maintained that a poet's just praise was an important aspect of a virtuous hierarchical state. Thus Jonson claims independence within a deferential relation to virtuous excellence, while vigorously and often obscenely derogating corruption. Jonson wrote masques for Jacobean court performance featuring the juxtaposition of virtuous order with chaotic disruption. As a masque author, he worked in often vexed collaboration with the architect and artist Inigo Jones, who constructed the sets. He also wrote lyrics and epigrams, many addressed to noble or royal patrons, and he is the father of the English country-house poem in "To Penshurst," which celebrates the authority and generosity of a noble household.

Jonson took pride in his own scholarship, having studied with William Camden at the Westminster School, and, although he was not a graduate of either university, receiving honorary degrees from both Oxford and

Cambridge. He is often thought to have slighted Shakespeare's education, but if we put the apparently derogatory line in its context Jonson's generosity, the flip side of his competitiveness, shines through. "Buskins" were the high boots worn by Greek tragic actors, "socks" the footwear of the comic stage.

> And though thou hadst small Latine, and lesse Greeke,
> From thence to honour thee, I would not seeke
> For names; but call forth thund'ring AEschilus,
> Euripides, and Sophocles to us
> Paccavius, Accius, him of Cordova dead,
> To life again, to heare thy Buskin tread,
> And shake a stage: Or, when the Sockes were on,
> Leave thee alone, for the comparison
> Of all, that insolent Greece, or haughtie Rome
> Sent forth, or since did from their ashes come.
> Triumph, my Britaine, thou hast one to showe,
> To whom all Scenes of Europe homage owe.
> He was not of an age, but for all time!
> (Jonson, 1968: 286, 31–43)

In other words, Shakespeare has nothing to fear from Greek or Latin literature, equaling the ancients in tragedy and outdoing them in comedy.

Jonson's own relation to public theater audiences was stormy, and he often suggests that he is, in Hamlet's phrase, offering caviar to the general. After the failure of *The New Inn* in 1629, he renounced the stage, writing an "Ode to Himselfe" to mark his resolution:

> Come leave the loathed Stage,
> And the more loathsome Age,
> Where pride and impudence in faction knit,
> Usurpe the Chaire of wit:
> Inditing and arraigning every day,
> Something they call a Play.
> Let their fastidious vaine
> Commission of the braine,
> Runne on, and rage, sweat, censure, and condemn:
> They were not made for thee, lesse thou for them.
> (Jonson, 1968: 298, 1–10)

His anger here aims as much at bad playwrights who nourish the public's poor taste while condemning true excellence (both "inditing" pseudo-plays in the sense of writing them, and "indicting" proper plays like Jonson's), as at the public that prefers "Akornes" to "pure bread," "their pallat's with the swine" (12, 15, 20). Jonson's sense of his own importance as a model playwright shows in his prefatory poem to a 1632 play by Richard Brome:

> I had you for a Servant, once, Dick Brome;
> And you performed a Servants faithfull parts:
> Now, you are got into a nearer roome,
> Of Fellowship, professing my old Arts.
> And you doe doe them well, with good applause,
> Which you have justly gained from the Stage,
> By observation of those Comick Lawes
> Which I, your Master, first did teach the Age.
> (Jonson, 1968, 308: 1–8)

Jonson believed, and believed rightly, that his example would form posterity, both in poetry and stagecraft. His admiration for Shakespeare notwithstanding, he knew he had created a model for satiric comedy that others would imitate.

Jonson held the vague title of "Poet Laureate" and in his later years and for several generations after his death was looked up to by younger lyric poets who called themselves "Sons of Ben." As his recent biographer Ian Donaldson puts it, "numerous writers throughout the seventeenth century did indeed set out to be Ben Jonson's students, modelling their work directly or indirectly on his practice" (Donaldson, 2011: 435). As a dramatist, his plays are consistently satirical and contestatory, with many scenes of "gulling" or elaborately deceiving foolish gullible characters. Partly as a result of this, and of their careful construction, Jonson's best plays, like *The Alchemist* or *Volpone*, have kept their theatrical effectiveness. Coleridge commented that three perfect plots were those of *Oedipus Rex*, *The Alchemist*, and *Tom Jones*. Jonson's political tragedies, *Sejanus* and *Catiline*, dramatize episodes in Roman history when a corrupt political culture threatens to extinguish the possibility of virtuous public life. In both plays writers serve – not necessarily effectively – as the last voice of an almost-extinguished public conscience, and Jonson certainly thought of himself, and in many ways deserves to be thought of, as such a voice in his own writing. In discussing *Sejanus* above, we quoted one of the greatest and last of the Sons of Ben, Andrew Marvell, borrowing the voice of Ben Jonson's ghost to characterize the true poet as one who, in times of public weakness and degradation, "single fights forsaken virtue's cause." In a volume mourning Jonson's death in 1637, Sidney Godolphin calls him

> The wonder of a learned age, the line
> Which none can pass, the most proportioned wit
> To nature, the best judge of what was fit;
> The deepest, plainest, highest, clearest pen;
> The voice most echoed by consenting men,
> The soul which answered best to all well said
> By others, and which most requital made.
> (Donaldson, 2011: 431–432)

One would not think, from such tributes, that Jonson's plays would be as full of dirt, error, and energetic malice as they are. Nonetheless, it is clear that Jonson believed that the role of art is to contain and control such chaotic and degrading elements within a structure of just authority.

4.4 Thomas Middleton

Thomas Middleton, born in London in 1580, is with Ben Jonson the most important of the dramatists whose work developed in a theatrical milieu dominated by the successes of Shakespeare in roughly the way Shakespeare's work developed in a milieu dominated by the successes of Christopher Marlowe. Middleton was born both a citizen and a gentleman. His father William Middleton, a successful member of the Bricklayers and Tilers guild, obtained a coat of arms in 1568, and Middleton's first years were spent in moderate prosperity. His father died, however, in 1586 when Middleton was five or six, and his mother then married a difficult, unlucky, improvident, litigious, and probably violent man, William Harvey, whose attempts to remain solvent by using William Middleton's estate plunged the family into lawsuits and debt. Although Middleton entered Queens College, Oxford, in 1598, he seems to have moved back to London in 1600 without a degree and from then on to have lived by his pen while watching his family's prosperity disappear into the pockets of lawyers. His early publications were poems, satires, almanacs and prose pamphlets, but his major works were as a playwright and an author of civic pageants.

As a designer of civic celebrations, he participated in the massive ceremonial welcome designed to receive the new King James into London in 1603, writing speeches for the allegorical characters on various elaborate temporary arches erected on the King's route (collaborating with Jonson and Thomas Dekker, among others). Middleton continued this sort of work throughout his career, and he was appointed the first City Chronologer in 1620.

1603 also saw Middleton's first surviving play, *The Phoenix*: the previous year he had collaborated on a lost play about Julius Caesar for the Admiral's Men, and been paid by Henslowe for an apparently single-authored *Chester Tragedy*. *The Phoenix* was acted at court by Paul's Boys, a children's company for whom Middleton wrote a series of comedies over the next five years, notably *Michaelmas Term* (1604), *A Mad World, My Masters* (1605), and *A Trick to Catch the Old One* (1606). For the King's Men, Shakespeare's company, Middleton wrote *The Yorkshire Tragedy* (a short brilliant play about family violence) apparently staged with other short plays in a mixed bill, collaborated with Shakespeare on *Timon of Athens* (1605), and wrote *The Revenger's Tragedy* (1607). He also wrote for Blackfriars' Boys, Prince Henry's Men, and Lady Elizabeth's Men, spreading his work around among competing companies and collaborating often with fellow theater poets. Particularly important later plays in his very substantial oeuvre – 29 surviving plays, not counting possible retrospective contributions to *Macbeth* (likely), *Measure for Measure* (plausible), and *All's Well That Ends Well* (under debate) – are *The Roaring Girl* (with Thomas Dekker, 1611), *A Chaste Maid in Cheapside* (1613), *Women Beware Women* (1621), *The Changeling* (with William Rowley, 1622), and his last play, the brilliant political allegory *A Game at Chess*, which enjoyed the longest continuous run of any English Renaissance play when the King's Men staged it at the Globe in 1624. It was closed by the government at the request of the Spanish Ambassador, who was memorably satirized in it, and Middleton went into hiding and was by his own account imprisoned. Gary Taylor speculates that he was released on condition that he no longer write for the stage. Middleton died in 1527, having written only pamphlets and civic entertainments in his last several years.

Attempts to provide a general characterization of what in particular we should go to Middleton to find have varied. Some time ago, Margot Heinemann and others, modifying Irving Ribner's view of Middleton as a Calvinist playwright, sought to portray Middleton as a fairly consistent politically engaged playwright taking the side of the City and the middling sort in a nascent opposition to the Stuart court (Heinemann, 1980, Ribner, 1962, Tricomi, 1989). Heinemann sought to see Middleton as part of a political movement, in effect, that had its telos and thus demonstrated its importance in the English Civil War. More recently, Middleton has been presented by Swapan Chakravorty as a demystifier of the operations of power, someone whose plays trace "the encounter of ideological formation and historical experience" (Chakravorty, 1996: 195), and by Paul Yachnin as a parodist highly conscious of the work of peers like Shakespeare and Jonson in the public theater, whose awareness of the lability of his own social role leads him to represent human behavior and choice as the adoption of available circulating discourses: for instance, "[l]ove [in Middleton] is a discursive formation that operates automatically *through* a would-be inward subject who is in fact only a shimmering composite of discursive surfaces" (Yachnin, 1997: 63). The more general claim that Middleton should be embraced as "our second Shakespeare" (Taylor, 2007: 25) does not (perhaps strategically) tie Middleton to any particular mythic form of excellence. Gary Taylor, in the General Introduction to the Oxford Middleton, asserts Middleton's high value on a wide variety of fronts: commercial success in his lifetime (the uniqueness in this regard of *A Game at Chess*), capacity to write great works in a variety of genres (in which Middleton resembles Shakespeare and is a contrast gainer over Jonson, Marlowe, and Webster), and realism in portraying human life (in which Middleton resembles Hogarth, Hals, and Caravaggio) (Taylor, 2007: 25–58). Elsewhere,

Taylor commends Middleton's portrayal of varieties of human sexual expression (in which Middleton is a contrast gainer over Shakespeare) (Taylor, 2000: 54–58).

We ourselves see Middleton's distinctiveness in terms of three attributes: (i) Middleton shows how people catch new desires and new aims from each other; (ii) Middleton shows us how to refer the general or transcendent to the local and social; (iii) Middleton cares about how one might be moral without being transcendent.

(i) and (ii) mark something in Middleton that differs, in its emphasis on local surfaces and repudiation of deep causes, from what is sometimes called Shakespearean pragmatism, the tendency to enact or redescribe social structures which present themselves ideologically as fixed and natural in plays which show them to be mutable economies that are subject to evolution (Engle, 1993, 2012b). Thus the mythic Middleton we propose remains mimetic, skeptical, and pragmatic: a playwright who highlights the primacy of the immediate and local over anything that presents itself as settled and fundamental. (iii) marks Middleton as different from Marlowe and Jonson, as both Marlowe and Jonson insist on the connection between the moral and the transcendent, Jonson in order to assert both and Marlowe to refute both (Engle, 2008, 2012a). Emphasizing these particular qualities of social apprehension in Middleton allows us to place him as a playwright, in the way pervasive opposition to moralizing places Marlowe, or the way a preoccupation with the relation between idealizing order and chaotic filth places Jonson.

4.5 Thomas Kyd

Thomas Kyd was born in 1558. He attended the Merchant Taylors grammar school but there is no record that he went on to university. In 1589, Thomas Nashe criticized those who "imitate the Kidde at *Aesop*," suggesting that Kyd may have worked as a translator. Nashe also implies, provocatively, that Kyd may have written an early version of *Hamlet*: "if you intreate him faire in a frostie morning, hee will afford you whole *Hamlets*, I should say handfuls of Tragicall speeches." Whether or not Kyd was the author of an "Ur-*Hamlet*," he certainly laid the groundwork for Shakespeare's tragedy with his popular revenge play, *The Spanish Tragedy*, which was one of the most frequently performed plays during the 1590s in the repertory of the Admiral's Men. Kyd was something of a "one-hit wonder" whose only other known dramatic work was *Cornelia*, a translation into English of Robert Garnier's French tragedy *Cornélie*.

In his commendatory verse in the Shakespeare First Folio, Ben Jonson cited "sporting Kyd" and Christopher Marlowe as two of the early dramatists that

Shakespeare eclipsed. Kyd himself links the two as well, attesting that he and Marlowe would write "in one chamber." In 1593, Kyd was arrested and papers that were considered to be "atheistic" (actually, a Unitarian sermon) were discovered in his rooms. Although Kyd told the authorities that the papers in question belonged to Marlowe, Kyd was nevertheless tortured by strappado. Shortly thereafter, he died intestate, having been broken both physically and financially, in 1594.

4.6   Thomas Dekker

Thomas Dekker was born around 1572, probably in London where he lived and wrote throughout his life. Although not educated at a university, he seems to have had a grammar school education and shows familiarity with the Latin classics. As a playwright, he emerges around 1594, and is one of the most-mentioned theater poets in Philip Henslowe's *Diary*: G. E. Bentley uses Henslowe's entries on Dekker as a measure of what an energetic dramatist could earn, and concludes that in the years covered by the *Diary*, late 1597 to 1603, Dekker "had a hand in 45 plays prepared for these companies [i.e., those associated with Henslowe] and was paid a total of £110 9s 6d in six years" (Bentley, 1971: 101), which is in contemporary terms about £20,000. Dekker's most famous individual play is *The Shoemaker's Holiday*, discussed Part 3; he was a notable collaborator, and seems to have specialized in compassionate accounts of working Londoners – a major feature of his collaboration with Middleton, *The Roaring Girl*. He became involved in the so-called War of the Theaters in 1599–1602, in which he and John Marston satirized Ben Jonson and were satirized in turn. He was also a prolific pamphleteer and translator, producing among many other works *The Gull's Hornbook*. Dekker was not as lucky as his and Middleton's character Jack Dapper, who is rescued from arrest for debt by Moll, the Roaring Girl. He spent seven years in the King's Bench Prison after his 1613 arrest for a £40 debt to John Webster's father, and seems to have struggled to stay afloat thereafter, while continuing to write prolifically. He died in 1632, evidently still in debt.

4.7   Francis Beaumont

Francis Beaumont was born circa 1585, briefly attended Broadgates College, Oxford from 1596–1597, and was admitted to the Inner Temple in 1600. He began writing under the influence of Ben Jonson to whom (according to John Dryden) Beaumont "submitted all of his writings to his censure." (For his part, Jonson averred that "Francis Beaumont loved too much himself and his own verses.") Beaumont met John Fletcher in 1608 and they began a four- or five-year collaboration that ranks among the most famous in the history of world literature. Remarkably, the two actually collaborated on only half a dozen plays; the extent of their collaboration was greatly magnified by the actors and publishers who issued the 1647 folio collection of fifty-three plays, all described as "by Francis Beaumont and John Fletcher." The supposed closeness of their collaboration has become legendary, with John Aubrey recording in his *Brief Lives* that they "lived together on the Bankside, not far from the playhouse, both bachelors, lay together, had one wench in the house between them, which they did so admire, the same clothes and cloak between them."

In 1613, Beaumont married an heiress from Kent named Ursula Isley. Many scholars assume that, as none of Beaumont's writings can be confidently dated later than 1613, he readily abandoned his career after his marriage and retired to gentlemanly inactivity in the country for the last years of his life. However, a contemporary poem relates that the figure of Death sent "an apoplex, to shend his brain," implying that Beaumont may have suffered a debilitating stroke in 1613 and was thus unable to write thereafter. At his death in 1616, Beaumont was accorded the high honor of being the third writer, after Chaucer and Spenser, to be interred in what has come to be known as "Poets' Corner" in Westminster Abbey.

4.8 John Fletcher

John Fletcher was born in 1579, the son of Richard Fletcher, who became Bishop of London in 1594. Although some scholars believe that he was the "John Fletcher of London" who entered Corpus Christi, Cambridge in 1591, others maintain that his youth – he would have been 12 years old – argues against this identification. By 1608, Fletcher was writing plays not only with Francis Beaumont but also with Shakespeare, with whom he collaborated on *Henry VIII*, *The Two Noble Kinsmen*, and the lost play *Cardenio*. It would appear that as the chief dramatist of the King's Men approached retirement, he chose to collaborate with his presumed successor as a way of passing the baton.

Following Shakespeare's death in 1616, Fletcher wrote exclusively for the King's Men for the remaining nine years of his career. Of the fifty-three plays published in the 1647 Beaumont and Fletcher folio, all had been performed by the King's Men and Fletcher had a hand in all of them, whereas Beaumont had only collaborated on six. A contemporary poem noted the injustice done to Fletcher in ascribing the folio's works to "Beaumont and Fletcher," as

"Beaumont (of those many) writ in few," whereas "the main / Being sole issues of sweet Fletcher's brain."

The outbreak of plague of 1625 was one of the worst in London's history, with over 4000 deaths per week. Fletcher was one of the victims. John Aubrey's *Brief Lives* relates that Fletcher planned to escape from London to the country but "stayed but to make himself a suit of clothes, and whilst it was making, fell sick of the plague and died."

4.9   John Ford

The only documentary records of John Ford's life indicate that he was baptized on 12 April 1586 at Islington in Devon, that he matriculated on 26 March 1601 at Exeter College, Oxford, and that he joined the Middle Temple on 16 November 1602. The Inns of Court in this period functioned as residential inns as well as centers of legal learning (of the 66 students admitted with Ford in 1602, only 12 were called to the bar); it is possible that Ford lived in Middle Temple for his entire life. Unfortunately, there were two "John Fords" in the Middle Temple, so it is impossible to know whether the dramatist was the "John Ford" who was expelled from his inn for several years for failure to pay his buttery bill in 1605, or whether he was the "John Ford" who was among a group who were disciplined for an organized protest in 1617 against the requirement for lawyers to wear caps in hall. Still, some scholars have argued that his plays' focus on transgressive behaviors such as incest and adultery can be linked to "his childish rebellion against the necessary discipline of the Temple, not only in youth but in full maturity" (Ewing, 1969: 114–115).

In 1606, Ford published a pamphlet, *Honour Triumphant*, celebrating the King of Denmark's visit to England that year, and a long verse eulogy on Charles Blount, *Fames Memoriall*. It appears that *A Funeral Elegy for William Peter* (1612), once thought to be by Shakespeare, was, in fact, written by Ford. In 1613, John Heminges received a payment for six plays that Shakespeare's company had performed before the King, one of which was titled *A Bad Beginning Makes a Good Ending*; later in the century, a bookseller listed a play attributed to Ford called "*An Ill Beginning has a Good End & A Bad Beginning May Have a Good End*, which may provide evidence that Ford was writing for the King's Men early in his career. In the 1620s, Ford began collaborating with established playwrights (Middleton, Rowley, Webster, and Dekker) on plays such as *The Witch of Edmonton* and *The Fair Maid of the Inn*, before moving on to solo-authored works in the 1630s such as '*Tis Pity She's a Whore*, *The Broken Heart*, and *Perkin Warbeck*.

4.10 John Marston

John Marston graduated from Brasenose College, Oxford in February 1594, at the precocious age of eighteen. He entered the Middle Temple in the late 1590s but seems to have had little interest in law (his father wrote hopefully of his son in the law books that he gave to him, "whom I hoped would have profited by them in the study of the law but man proposeth and God disposeth"). In 1598, Marston published several satires under the pseudonym "W. Kinsayder.". In the following year, he received a payment from the theater owner Philip Henslowe, probably for his share of a collaborative play, *The King of Scots*. He then began writing satirical dramas for the newly formed boys' company, the Children of Paul's. In several of these plays, the object of Marston's satire was Ben Jonson, with *Jack Drum's Entertainment* and *What You Will* serving as salvos in the so-called "War of Theatres." Jonson wrote that "he had many quarrels with Marston, beat him, and took his pistol from him, wrote his *Poetaster* on him; the beginning of them were that Marston represented him in the stage."

By 1604, Marston appears to have patched things up with Jonson (with whom he collaborated on *Eastward Ho!*), left Paul's Boys, and became a sharer in the Queen's Revels. Marston is unique among the theater poets of the period in that every one of his plays was published in quarto within a year or two of its composition. In 1608, however, Marston was committed to Newgate prison, possibly for writing a play that openly criticized King James, and abruptly gave up playwriting, leaving *The Insatiate Countess* unfinished. In 1616, he took holy orders and lived out his days as parish priest in Christchurch, Hampshire. (Even after his former adversary had left the profession, Jonson couldn't resist taking one final dig: he gossiped that "Marston wrote his father-in-law's preachings, and his father-in-law [wrote] his comedies.") When the publisher William Sheares brought out *The Works of Mr. John Marston, Being Tragedies and Comedies, Collected into one Volume* in 1633, Marston apparently insisted that his name be removed and the volume was reissued as simply *Tragedies and Comedies*.

4.11 Philip Massinger

Philip Massinger was born in 1583 and entered St Alban Hall, Oxford in 1602 but apparently never graduated. It would seem that sometime during the following decade he began writing for Philip Henslowe, the owner of the Rose Theatre; in 1613, he wrote to Henslowe from debtors' prison asking for an advance in order to bail himself out. Massinger had a hand in fifty-five plays during his career, about twenty of which are now lost. Up to 1620, he wrote exclusively in collaboration, usually with John Fletcher for the King's Men. Massinger's share in fifteen of these collaborative plays that appeared in the 1647 Beaumont and Fletcher folio was never acknowledged in his lifetime, and was not fully appreciated until it was revealed by stylometric analyses in the twentieth century.

In the early 1620s, Massinger began writing single-authored works for Christopher Beeston's companies at the Phoenix (Cockpit) Theatre in Drury Lane. When Fletcher died in 1625, Massinger took over Fletcher's position as chief dramatist for the King's Men, for whom he wrote exclusively until his death in 1640. A collection of eight early quarto editions of Massinger's plays now in the Folger Shakespeare Library contains extensive manuscript corrections in Massinger's hand, providing a unique record of a playwright from the period checking his own printed work, and may be evidence that he was preparing a collection for publication (which in the event never appeared).

4.12   Elizabeth Cary

Elizabeth Cary, Lady Falkland, born Elizabeth Tanfield in 1585, is unique among the playwrights considered in this book not only in being a woman but also in being an aristocrat and in writing for posterity or private edification rather than for money. Her play *Mariam*, probably written between 1604 and 1608 and published in 1613, was never staged in professional theaters, although some think it may have had private amateur performances. If so, they would have taken place in one or another of the aristocratic literary circles Cary frequented, perhaps that of Mary Herbert, Countess of Pembroke.

Elizabeth Cary was the daughter and heir of Lawrence Tanfield, a prominent lawyer who was knighted and became chief baron of the exchequer under King James and was already a very wealthy man when Elizabeth married Sir Henry Cary in 1602, at the very end of the reign of Queen Elizabeth. The marriage seems to have been a fairly typical exchange of Sir Henry's gentility for the Tanfield's money: the marriage settlement guaranteed Henry Cary £2000 on the spot, a further £2000 after two years, and Tanfield's estate on Tanfield's death should Tanfield not produce another heir. £2000 in 1602 was roughly equivalent to half a million 2012 dollars. The couple did not set up house together until well after the second payment had been made, but once they began cohabiting they had eleven children, the first in 1609 and the last two in 1624. When James made Henry Cary Viscount Falkland in 1620, Cary became Lady Falkland. Her father's disinheritance of her in favor of her eldest son in 1622 when she tried to mortgage her jointure to pay Viscount Falkland's debts, and her conversion to Roman Catholicism in

1626, estranged her from her husband, and she spent much of the rest of her life in poverty, while attempting to guarantee that her younger children were raised as Catholics, much against the wills of her husband and her eldest son. At one point, she had her younger children kidnapped in order to educate them as Catholics in France, and she succeeded with her daughters, four of whom became nuns. *Mariam*, composed in the earliest years of her marriage, demonstrates that she was thinking hard about marital estrangement before her own most severe experiences of it.

As a writer, Cary was precocious, translating a geographical treatise from French at 13 and composing a lost tragedy before she was twenty. *Mariam* was her next work, written at a time when she appears to have been close to a number of prominent authors, including John Davies of Hereford and Michael Drayton. *Mariam*'s stageworthiness, as well as her composition of a lost verse life of Tamburlaine, and a prose history of Edward II published after her death, suggests that she may have been a theatergoer who took plays seriously as vehicles for thought.

Appendix

Performance History

Sarah Stewart

Francis Beaumont

The Knight of the Burning Pestle

The play was first performed between June 1607 and April 1608 by the Children of the Queen's Revels at the Blackfriars Theatre. It was revived in 1904 in London. F.R. Benson directed a production at the Shakespeare Memorial Theatre in 1910. The play was revived in 1920 by the Birmingham Repertory Theatre and featured a young Noel Coward as Rafe. The Old Vic production of 1932 featured Ralph Richardson as Rafe and Sybil Thorndike as the Citizen's Wife. The Old Globe Theatre in San Diego mounted a production of the play in 1957. Ellen Pollock directed an open-air production in 1960 in Stratford-upon-Avon in conjunction with the Shakespeare Memorial Theatre using actors from the Royal Academy of Dramatic Arts. There was a production in 1975 at the Greenwich Theatre. The 1981 RSC production was directed by Michael Bogdanov and featured Timothy Spall as Rafe. The Stratford Festival, Ontario, Canada staged a production in 1990. The 2005 Barbican Theatre production featured Rafe Spall, named after the character from the play and the son of Timothy Spall, as Rafe. The American Shakespeare Center has staged the play three times in 1999, 2003, and 2010.

Elizabeth Cary

Mariam

This is a closet drama composed sometime between 1603 and 1612. I was unable to find any information on earlier productions. Portions of the play

Studying Shakespeare's Contemporaries, First Edition. Lars Engle and Eric Rasmussen.
© 2014 Lars Engle and Eric Rasmussen. Published 2014 by John Wiley & Sons, Ltd.

were included in a compilation performance script put together by Sharon Ammen and Catherine Schuler called *Attending to Renaissance Women* in 1990. A full production of the play was directed by Stephanie Hodgson-Wright in 1994 and performed by the Tinderbox Theatre Company at the Alhambra Studio in Bradford, England. In 1995, Elizabeth Schafer directed a production at Royal Holloway. A staged reading of the play was directed by Paul Stephen Lim at the English Alternative Theatre in 1996 at the University of Kansas.

Thomas Dekker

The Shoemaker's Holiday

The play was first performed in 1599 by the Admiral's Men. It was performed at court in early 1600. There was a performance in 1913 by the Oxford University Dramatic Society at the Shakespeare Memorial Theatre. There was a Mercury Theatre production in 1938 directed by Orson Welles. The Stratford Festival, Ontario, Canada, featured a production in 1989. In 1994, the Utah Shakespeare Festival staged a production. Peter Dobbins directed the 2005 New York production by the Storm Theatre. The Rose Theatre staged a production in 2008 directed by David Pearce and Pepe Pryke. Jemma Gross directed the open-air production by the Black Sun Theatre in Stratford-upon-Avon in 2010. Also in 2010, the American Shakespeare Center staged a production in the Blackfriars Theatre, Staunton, Virginia. The Red Bull Theater, New York featured a production in 2011.

John Fletcher

The Woman's Prize

The play was first performed between December 1609 and April 1610 at the Whitefriars Theatre by the Children of the Queen's Revels. It was revived in 1633 and performed again on 23 June 1660. There were performances again at the Cockpit in Drury Lane on 30 October 1660 and the Theatre Royal on 31 July 1661. Another performance took place at some point at the Red Bull in 1660. Another performance at an unknown theater was staged on 23 December 1661. The play was performed for Charles II at court in 1668 and at a public theater in 1674. David Garrick's adaptation of the play was performed twice in 1757 and once in 1760. There were no other recorded performances until 1979 when the play was revived in Baltimore, Maryland. After this production, there were apparently three others in Queensland, Australia, New York, and Seattle. In 2001, the play was performed at the Arcola Theatre in London. The RSC then staged a production in 2003 directed by Gregory Doran featuring Rory Kinnear as Tranio. Shakespeare Santa Cruz staged a production in 2004 directed by Danny Scheie. The 2005 Shakespeare and Company production at the Rose Footprint Playhouse, Lenox, Massachusetts was directed by Michael Burnet.

The Maid's Tragedy

The first officially recorded performance of this play was 20 May 1613 when John Heminges was paid for performances by the King's Men at the court celebrations of the marriage of the Princess Elizabeth. The first and second quartos indicate that the play was performed at the Blackfriars theater by the King's Men. It is likely that the play was performed at either the Blackfriars sometime after the King's Men took up winter residence there in 1609 or their summer home, the Globe, prior to the court performance in 1613. Owing to the outbreaks of plague during 1609 and 1610, the first performance of the play was probably in 1611. A pared-down version of the play that consisted of the Calianax scenes appeared during the closure of the theaters and was called *The Testy Lord*. The play was next performed in 1660 as part of the repertory being performed by the acting company of the Red Bull. The play was seen by Charles II in 1667 and by James II in 1687. The role of Melantius became a staple role for Thomas Betterton and his last performance of the role was on 13 April 1710, just weeks before his death. There are additional performances recorded in 1744 and 1745. A nineteenth century adaptation called *The Bridal* was written by W.C. Macready and was performed in Dublin in 1834 and the Haymarket Theatre, London in 1837. It was also performed on the American stage between 1843 and 1844. The original play was revived in the twentieth century by the Phoenix Society at the Lyric Theatre, London on 15 November 1921 and featured Sybil Thorndike as Evadne. It was performed again by the Renaissance Theatre acting company at the Scala Theatre, London on 17 May 1925 with Edith Evans as Evadne. Bernard Miles directed a production for the Mermaid Theatre on 2 June 1964. There was a production in 1972 at the Equity Library Theatre in New York. On 16 November 1979, the Philip Prowse-directed production premiered at the Citizen's Theatre, Glasgow and featured a young Pierce Brosnan as the King. Barry Kyle's production for the RSC premiered at The Other Place on 30 April 1980. This production featured Tom Wilkinson as Melantius and Sinead Cusack as Evadne. A nonprofessional production appeared at the Guildhall School of Music and Drama in November 1985. The Immediate Theatre Company, New York staged a production directed by Jose Zayas in 2003. Claire Lovett directed the 2005 production at the White Bear, London.

John Ford

'Tis Pity She's a Whore

The play was first performed sometime between 1629 and 1633 by Queen Henrietta's Men at the Cockpit Theatre. It was revived after the Restoration and was seen in 1661 by Samuel Pepys at the Salisbury Court Theatre. Maurice Maeterlinck translated the play into French and it was produced at the Théâtre de l'Œuvre in 1894. In 1961, Luchino Visconti directed a French adaptation at the Théâtre de Paris. An Italian film version directed by Giuseppi Patroni Griffi was made in 1971. In 1972, David Giles directed Ian McKellan in the role of Giovanni for The Actors' Company. Ron Daniels directed the 1977 RSC production that opened at The Other Place, Stratford-upon-Avon and then transferred to the Gulbenkian Studio, Newcastle-upon-Tyne, and the Warehouse, London. The 1978 Belgian television version of the play was directed by Dré Poppe and Jaak Van de Velde. Declan Donnellan directed the 1980 production at the Theatre Space and the Half Moon Theatre, London. A 1980 BBC television version of the play was directed by Roland Joffé. In 1988, Alan Ayckbourn directed a production that was featured on the National Theatre's Olivier Theatre stage. The RSC staged another production in 1991 directed by David Leveaux, which opened at the Swan Theatre, Stratford-upon-Avon and then transferred to the Newcastle Playhouse, Newcastle-upon-Tyne and finally The Pit, London. The 2005 production by The Actors' Company was directed by Tom Hunsinger. Edward Dick directed the 2005 Southwark Playhouse production. Carey Perloff directed the 2008 production for the American Conservatory Theatre, San Francisco. Chris Meads directed the 2010 Liverpool Everyman production of the play. Donnellan directed another production for Cheek by Jowl in 2011 that toured through 2012 and appeared at locations such as the Barbican, Les Gémeaux/Sceaux/Scène Nationale, the Sydney Festival, the Brooklyn Academy of Music, and the Freud Playhouse, Los Angeles. The 2011 West Yorkshire Playhouse production was directed by Jonathan Munby. In 2012, the American Shakespeare Center featured a production of the play at the Blackfriars Playhouse, Staunton, Virginia.

Ben Jonson

Sejanus

First performed in 1603, the play was staged at the Globe Theatre by the King's Men. There is little evidence regarding actual performances after this either before the closing of the theaters in 1642 or after the Restoration. In the 1708 work *Roscius Anglicanus*, John Downes mentions it as part of the repertory of Killigrew's company, but there is no evidence that it was performed. William Poel directed a production of the play in 1928 at the Holborn Empire Theatre. Seb Perry directed a production in 2000 that was staged at Merton College Chapel, Oxford. The play featured as part of the RSC's Gunpowder Season in 2005–2006 and was directed by Gregory Doran.

Epicene

The play was first performed at the Whitefriars Theatre by the Children of the Queen's Revels in late 1609 or early 1610. It seems likely there were two court performances in the 1630s but other than this there is little evidence of additional performances prior to the closure of the theaters in 1642. Upon the Restoration, the play was likely one of the first plays to be performed. Pepys records having seen a performance in the early summer of 1660. Between 1660 and 1752, there was at least one performance of the play almost every year. It then seems to drop off after David Garrick's 1752 production featuring Sarah Siddons flopped and does not appear again until Garrick attempted a revival in 1776. It reappears in 1895 at Harvard University and then again in 1909 at Cambridge University. The Phoenix Company staged a production in 1924. In 1948, the Oxford University Dramatic Society staged a production directed by Frank Hauser. In 1960, George Brandt directed an open-air production in Stratford-upon-Avon in conjunction with the Shakespeare Memorial Theatre, featuring students from Bristol University. There was a production in the 1970s by Jean Cocteau Repertory in New York. Danny Boyle directed the 1989 RSC production that featured John Hannah as Epicene on the Swan Theatre stage. In 2003, there was a production by the Shakespeare Theatre Company, Washington, D.C. The 2010 (re:) Directions production in New York was directed by Tom Berger and was heavily adapted.

Every Man in His Humor

The play was first performed in 1598 by the Lord Chamberlain's Men at the Curtain Theatre. It was performed at court in 1605. It appears the play continued to be acted, but there are no other confirmed performances prior to the closure of the theaters in 1642. It appears to have been performed by the King's Men in 1675. There is also evidence of a performance at Lincoln's Inn Fields in 1725. David Garrick's revival, and adaptation, of the play in 1751 gave it a new lease on life and between 1751 and 1776, there are performances of the play every single year. George Frederick Cooke revived the play in the early nineteenth century with mixed success. Edmund Kean starred in a production in 1816. The Haymarket Theatre production of 1838 featured William Charles Macready. An 1845 benefit performance featured Charles Dickens as Bobadill, George Cruikshank as Cob, and John Forster as Kitely. It proved to be so popular that they performed it several more times over the next few years. F.R. Benson directed the 1903 production for the Shakespeare Memorial Theatre in Stratford-upon-Avon. The Manchester Repertory Company production in 1909 was directed by Ben Iden Payne. The 1937 production for the Shakespeare Memorial Theatre was also directed by Payne. The RSC staged a production in 1986 that was directed by John Caird that featured Simon Russell Beale, Joely Richardson, Tony Church, and Pete Postlethwaite. This production ultimately transferred to The People's Theatre, Newcastle-upon-Tyne and the Mermaid Theatre, London.

Thomas Kyd

The Spanish Tragedy

This play was a huge success from the start. According to the records kept by Philip Henslowe, the play was performed at least 29 times between 1592 and 1597. After 1597, the play was performed by at least three different acting companies including the Admiral's Men, Pembroke's Men, and maybe even the Lord Chamberlain's Men (later the King's Men). It is likely the play was performed right up until the theaters were closed in 1642. There is little evidence of the play being performed after the Restoration. 1973 saw a production at the Mercury Theatre, London. Robert David MacDonald directed a production in 1978 at the Citizens' Theatre, Glasgow. The National Theatre staged a production in 1982 directed by Michael Bogdanov. In 1997, the RSC staged a production in the Swan Theatre directed by Michael Boyd. Mitchell Moreno directed the play in 2009 at the Arcola Theatre, London. In June 2009, students at Oxford University staged an outdoor performance at Oriel College. The Hyperion Shakespeare Company, in conjunction with students from Harvard University, performed the play in October 2010 in the New College Theatre. Another joint production was staged in autumn 2012 by the Perchance Theatre group and Cambridge's Marlowe Society in King's College Chapel.

Christopher Marlowe

The Jew of Malta

The first recorded performance of the play is in 1592 by Lord Strange's Men. It remained popular up until the closing of the theaters in 1642 and was performed at various times by the Queen's Men, the Admiral's Men, and Queen Henrietta's Men. In 1818, the play was revived in a production starring Edmund Kean. The Phoenix Society staged a production in 1922. The Marlowe Theatre Company staged a production in 1964 directed by Donals Bain. Clifford Williams directed the 1964 London and subsequent 1965 Stratford transfer production for the RSC. Another 1964 production was directed by Peter Cheeseman at the Victoria Theatre in Stoke-on-Trent. In 1971, the Mobile Theatre staged a production. Bernard Sobel directed a production in 1976 for Gennevilliers and the Théâtre de la Renaissance in Paris. Oracle Productions staged the play in 1984 at the Donmar Warehouse. Andy Johnson directed and adapted the play in 1984 for the Nervous Theatre. In 1987, the RSC once again staged a production, this time directed by Barry Kyle. In 1993, BBC Radio presented a production of the play that starred Ian McDiarmid. King Alfred's Performing Arts Company staged a production in Winchester in 1997 that was directed by Stevie Simkin. In 1998, The Globe staged a reading of the play. 1999 saw Michael Grandage direct Ian McDiarmid in a production at the Almeida Theatre. Jeff Bailey also directed a production in 1999 for the Marlowe Project, New York. Teatro della Contraddizione and the Hit & Run Theatre Company staged a production in 2005 at the Southside Theatre, Edinburgh. F. Murray Abraham starred in a production for the Theatre for a New Audience, New York in 2007. An independent film version of the play, adapted and directed by Douglas Morse, was released in February 2013.

Doctor Faustus

The play was first performed by the Lord Admiral's Men on 30 September 1594. There were an additional 13 performances between this first performance and the end of 1595. There were additional performances in 1596. There were documented revivals in 1662 and 1675 that shifted the scene at the Pope's court to Babylon. The productions in 1896 and 1904 were directed by William Poel. The play featured in the 1929 Canterbury Festival and was directed by Nugent Monck. The 1934 Birmingham Repertory production was directed by H.M. Prentice. The 1937 production in New York starring Orson Welles was codirected by Welles and John Houseman. There was a production in 1940 at the Rudolf Steiner Hall. In 1944, the Old Vic staged a production. John Moody directed a production at the Playhouse Theatre, Liverpool in 1944. During the period 1946–1947, Walter Hudd directed a production at the Shakespeare Memorial Theatre, Stratford-upon-Avon. The Old Vic production at the New Theatre, London was directed by John Burrell. John Crockett directed the Compass Players in a touring production in 1950. Michael Benthall directed the Old Vic production that opened at the Edinburgh Festival in 1961. Richard Burton played Faustus in a 1965 production directed by Nevill Coghill that also starred Elizabeth Taylor. This production was then adapted into a film in 1967. The 1968 production by the Glasgow Citizens was directed by Charles Marowitz. Gareth Morgan directed a production for the RSC in 1970. The 1974 RSC production was directed by John Barton and starred Ian McKellen. The Perth Repertory Theatre staged a production in 1976, directed by Andrew McKinnon. In 1977, Alan Drury directed a production with the York Theatre Royal Company. David Thacker directed the Chestergateway Theatre Company production in 1977. A production titled *Faustus' Last Supper* was staged in 1978 at the Belgrade Theatre, Coventry and in 1982 at the Wolsey Theatre, Ipswich. The Sherman Arena Company staged a production directed by Duncan Miller and Frances Brookes at the Sherman Theatre, Cardiff. 1978 saw a production staged at the Nuffield Theatre, Southampton. Nicholas Young directed a production at the Connaught Theatre, Worthing in 1979. In 1980, the Lyric Studio, Hammersmith featured a production directed by Christopher Fettes. Adrian Noble directed the 1981 production at the Royal Exchange, Manchester. There was a production in 1984 at one of the Oxford colleges. The 1982 Swan Theatre, Worcester production was directed by Ian Granville Bell. Directed by Michael Winter and Jeremy Howe the Nottingham-based 1983 production was a joint effort by the Nottingham Playhouse Company and the York Theatre Royal Company. Andy Johnson adapted and directed the 1984 production by the Nervous Theatre at the Bridge House, London. The 1984 Royal Lyceum Theatre, Edinburgh production was directed by Ian Woolridge. The 1984 Edinburgh Festival featured a 30-min street theater version of the play by the Wooden O Company. In 1986, the Park Bench Theatre Company staged a production at the Cambridge Festival Fringe. In 1989, Barry Kyle directed Gerard Murphy in a Royal Shakespeare Theatre production. The Nottingham Playhouse staged a production in 1993 directed by Phelim McDermott. Philip Franks directed a production at the Greenwich Theatre in 1993. In 1994, Patrick Sandford directed a production at the Nuffield Theatre, Southampton. The Kaos Theatre Company staged a production directed by Xavier Leret in 1994. Another film version was directed by Jan Svankmajer and appeared in 1994. In 1996, the Compass Theatre Company staged a production directed by Neil Sissons. Jonathan Best directed the 1997 production at The Other Place. The Brute Farce Theatre Company staged a production in 1997 directed by Philip Graham and Rob Crouch. In 1997, Andrew Potter directed a production at the Wycombe Swan Town Hall Theatre. The Galleon Theatre Company staged a production directed by Simon Bell at The Prince Theatre, Greenwich in 1998. The Shifting Sands Theatre Company staged a production in 2002 at Hoxton Hall, London. 2002 also saw a production at the Young Vic starring Jude Law directed by David Lan and another at the Royal and Derngate Theatres in Northampton directed by Rupert Goold, with additions written by Goold and Ben Power. Paul Garnault directed the 2004 production by the Wales Actors Company. A musical adaptation was directed by Marchus Eyre at Barons Court Theatre, London in 2004. Also in 2004, Martin Duncan, Edward Kemp, Stephen Pimlott, and Dale Rooks directed a production at the Chichester Festival Theatre in association with Chichester Cathedral. In 2004, a series of selected scenes was directed by Rupert Goold and adapted by Ben Power at the Theatre Royal, Northampton. Philip Wilson directed the 2005 production for the Everyman and Playhouse, Liverpool. In 2005, the Etcetera Theatre featured a production directed by Chris Jamba. Another musical adaptation, written and directed by Adrian Schiller, was staged in 2005 at the Menier Theatre, London. The Utah Shakespeare Festival also staged a production in 2005. In 2006, the Third Party Productions staged a touring production directed by John Wright. The Headlong Theatre staged the Rupert Goold-directed and Rupert Goold and Ben Power-adapted production at the Hampstead Theatre in 2006. Elizabeth Freestone directed a production at the Greenwich Theatre, London in 2009. In 2012, the Globe Theatre, London staged a production of the play starring Arthur Darvill as Mephistopheles. This stage production was broadcast on movie screens across the United States that same year.

Tamburlaine 1/Tamburlaine 2

Internal evidence suggests that the plays were first performed in the 1580s but the first performances we have record of are found in Henslowe's diary in 1594 and 1595. It is likely the play was performed on and off during the seventeenth century. The next record we have of a performance was the one in June 1919 at Yale University directed by Edger Montillion Woolley. The 1933 production in Oxford by the Buskins dramatic group at Worcester College was directed by Nevill Coghill. The 1951 Old Vic production was directed by Tyrone Guthrie. The same production was revived in 1956 in Toronto and New York. In 1960, there was an Oxford University Dramatic Society production at St. John's College Garden, directed by John Duncan. In 1964, Robert Pennant Jones directed the Tavistock Repertory Company production at the Tower Theatre. There was also a BBC Radio production in 1964 that was directed by Charles Lefeaux. There was a staged reading at Harvard University directed by David Seltzer the same year and a production at The Everyman Theatre in Cheltenham. In 1966, The Canterbury Theatre Trust produced the play directed by R.D. Smith. There was another production at the 1972 Edinburgh Festival from the Glasgow Citizens, directed by Keith Hack. In 1976, there was a production at the National Theatre directed by Peter Hall and starring Albert Finney. There was a French production in 1989 directed by Antonio Diaz-Florian. In 1993, there was an

RSC production directed by Terry Hands starring Antony Sher. Jeff Dailey directed Part 1 of the play in 1997 and Part 2 in 2003 for the American Theatre of Actors, New York. Sam Shammas directed the 1999 production at the Cochrane Theatre, London. Ben Naylor directed and Ben Power adapted the 2003 production at the Rose Theatre. In 2004, The Globe Education Centre Theatre, as part of their Read Not Dead season at The Globe, staged a reading. David Farr directed and adapted the collaborative effort of the Bristol Old Vic and the Young Vic in 2005. Michael Kahn directed a production of the play in 2007 for the Shakespeare Theatre Company, Washington, D.C. The 2012 season of the American Shakespeare Center featured a production at the Blackfriars Playhouse, Staunton, Virginia.

Edward II

The play was first performed by the Earl of Pembroke's Men sometime prior to the publication of the first quarto in 1594. As stated by the 1622 quarto, it was later performed by Queen Anne's Men at the Red Bull Theatre. The 1903 London production was directed by William Poel. The 1905 production was directed by Frank Benson at the Stratford-upon-Avon Festival. There was a 1923 production in London at the Regent Theatre by the Phoenix Society. There were also productions in Prague in 1922 and in Berlin in 1923. The play was then adapted by Bertolt Brecht in 1924 for the Munich Chamber Theatre. The BBC produced a version of the play for television in 1947. In 1951, John Barton directed Toby Robertson in a production of the play. The play was then produced by Joan Littlewood at the Theatre Royal in May 1956. Toby Robertson then went on to direct Derek Jacobi in a 1958 production for the Cambridge University Marlowe Society. In 1959, Richard Eyre directed an abbreviated version of the play for the BBC. The BBC produced another version of the play in 1961, this time in two parts. 1964 saw multiple productions of the play including that of the Leicester Phoenix Theatre Company directed by Clive Perry and featuring Anthony Hopkins in several of the smaller roles. The other productions that year were by the Marlowe Society Drama Company, the Bristol Old Vic Theatre School directed by Glynne Wickham, the Theatre Royal in Bristol, and a staged reading at Harvard University. The Brecht adaptation was revived at the National Theatre in 1968. Toby Robertson also directed Ian McKellen, although McKellen was not the original lead, in a production of the play that was part of a double bill with *Richard II* in 1969 for the Prospect Theatre Company as part of the Edinburgh Festival. This version, featuring Ian McKellen, was eventually filmed and broadcast by the BBC in 1970. Ellis Rabb directed a production for John Houseman's The Acting Company in 1975. The 1978 Edinburgh Festival featured a production by the Royal Lyceum Theatre Company. The Bristol Old Vic produced the play in 1980. A French film version of the play directed by Bernard Sobel was released in 1982. In 1984, the Compass Theatre Company staged the play. Nicholas Hytner directed a production for the Manchester Royal Exchange in 1986 starring Ian McDiarmid and featuring Michael Grandage. Gerard Murphy directed a production of the play for the RSC in 1989, starring Simon Russell Beale. In 1991, a film version of the play appeared that was adapted and directed by Derek Jarman and featured Tilda Swinton as Isabella. Jim Stone directed a production for the Washington Stage Company in 1993. A 1995 production in Budapest was directed by Jozsef Ruszt. There was another production in Vienna in 1998 at the Burgtheater. Michael Grandage directed Joseph Fiennes in 2001 at the Sheffield Crucible. The 2003 season at Shakespeare's Globe featured a production directed by Timothy Walker. It should be noted that a ballet adaptation of the play was commissioned by the Stuttgart Ballett. With choreography by David Bintley and music by John McCabe, it premiered in 1995 in Stuttgart and was subsequently performed at the Birmingham Hippodrome in 1997. Don Stewart directed a production in 2000 for the ARK Theatre Company in Los Angeles. The 2005 Stratford Festival, Ontario, Canada featured a production. In 2007, the Shakespeare Theatre Company of Washington, D.C. staged a production. The 2011 Rose Theatre, Bankside, London production was directed by Peter Darney.

John Marston

The Malcontent

The play was first performed circa 1603 by the Children of the Queen's Revels at the Blackfriars Theatre. It was subsequently acquired by the King's Men and revised for performance at the Globe Theatre. There is some evidence that the play was performed in 1635. The next documented production is when it was revived by George Bolton in 1850 at the Olympia Theatre, London. There were several university productions in the 1960s, one at Southampton by the Southampton University Theatre Workshop in 1964 and another at Oxford by the Oxford University Dramatic Society in 1968. In 1973, Jonathan Miller directed a production at the Nottingham Playhouse. In 1983, the ADC Theatre in Cambridge staged a production. Boston University staged a production in 1998 with Michael Walker directing. The RSC production in 2002 was directed by Dominic Cooke and featured Antony Sher as Giovanni Altofronto/Malevole. It opened at the Swan Theatre, Stratford-upon-Avon, transferred to the Newcastle Playhouse, Newcastle-upon-Tyne, and ultimately closed at the Gielgud Theatre, London. Christopher Grabowski directed the 2010 production by the Shakespeare Theatre Company, Washington, D.C. 2011 saw the American Shakespeare

Center stage a production at the Blackfriars Playhouse, Staunton, Virginia. Rae McKen directed the Custom/Practice and Graffiti Productions staging of the play at the White Bear Theatre, London in 2011. The Antaeus Company production at the West Deaf Theatre, Los Angeles also appeared in 2011 and was directed by Elizabeth Swain.

Philip Massinger

A New Way to Pay Old Debts

This play was first performed in 1626 by Queen Henrietta's Men at the Cockpit Theatre. It continued in regular performance at the Red Bull Theatre until the closure of the theaters in 1642. It was revived by David Garrick in 1748. It was regularly performed through the rest of the eighteenth and the nineteenth centuries. It appears to have first been staged in the United States in 1794 or 1795 in Philadelphia. Edmund Kean debuted his legendary Sir Giles Overreach in 1816. In 1836, there was production at the National Theatre of the United States that starred Junius Brutus Booth as Sir Giles. There was another production of the play at the US National Theatre in 1870. Edwin Booth starred as Sir Giles in the 1867 production at the Boston Theatre. There was a production in 1869 at Daly's Fifth Avenue Theatre, New York. There was another New York production in 1870 at Booth's Theatre. A production was staged in Princeton, New Jersey in 1908 at Alexander Hall. Adrian Noble directed the 1983 RSC production that opened at The Other Place, Statford-upon-Avon. The production later transferred to the Gulbenkian Studio, Newcastle-upon-Tyne before finally closing at The Pit, London. The Classic Theatre, New York production of 1983 was directed by Maurice Edwards. Michael Kahn directed the 1985 New York production for the Acting Company at the Marymount Manhattan Theatre. In 2009, a production was presented by the University of Tampa and directed and adapted by Bob Gonzalez. In 2011, Highly Strung Productions, in partnership with Terra Incognita Theatre, staged a production at the Rose Theatre, London as directed by Liz Bagley.

Thomas Middleton

The Revenger's Tragedy

The play was entered in the Stationer's Register on 7 October 1607 and the title page states it was performed by the King's Men. This evidence indicates that the play was performed at the Globe Theatre sometime prior to October 1607. Brian Shelton directed a production at the Pitlochry Festival, Scotland in July 1965. There were also amateur productions at Oxford in 1964 and

Cambridge in 1965. Trevor Nunn directed a production for the RSC in 1966, featuring Ian Richardson as Vindice. In 1978, David Schalkwyk directed a production at the Libertas Theatre in Stellenbosch, South Africa. In 1987, Di Trevis directed another RSC production in the Swan Theatre with Antony Sher as Vindice. Antony Sher directed a production at the Protean Theatre, New York in 1996. In 2000, there was a student production at Cornell University directed by Jeremy Lopez and Margaret Collins. There was another student production in 2000 at The Studio at Stratford College. The American Shakespeare Center staged a production in 2000 at the Blackfriars Playhouse, Staunton, Virginia. Alex Cox directed a feature film version of the play in 2002 using a screenplay by Frank Boyce. The film starred Christopher Eccleston as Vindice, Derek Jacobi as the Duke, and Eddie Izzard as Lussurioso. LAMDA staged a production in July 2004 directed by Rodney Cottier and Jamie Harper. 2008 saw a production directed by Melly Still at the National Theatre starring Rory Kinnear as Vindice and another at the Royal Exchange, Manchester directed by Jonathan Moore. The American Shakespeare Center staged another production in 2009 at the Blackfriars Playhouse, Staunton, Virginia. The Old Red Lion Theatre, Islington staged a production in the summer of 2012. That same summer saw a joint production by the Immersion Theatre and the Theatre of the Broken Dolls directed by James Tobias. In late 2012, Sub Das directed a production at Hoxton Hall, London.

The Roaring Girl

The first performance of this play was probably in late April or early May 1611 at the Fortune Theatre by Prince Henry's Men. There was a revival in 1951 at the Brattle Theatre in Cambridge, Massachusetts. The Dundee Repertory Company production in 1970 was directed by Keith Darvill. The 1983 RSC production of the play was directed by Barry Kyle and featured Helen Mirren as Moll. In 1989, Sonia Fraser directed a production for the Bristol Old Vic at the Bristol Theatre Royal. Craig Bradshaw directed the 1997 production for A Theatre Under the Influence in Seattle, Washington. An adaptation of the play was presented in 1999 by the Chicago-based company Shakespeare's Motley Crew. An acting company called *The Steam Industry* staged a production of the play in 2000 at the Finborough Theatre, London. In 2011, Toi Whakaari directed a production for the National Dance and Drama Center in Wellington, New Zealand.

Women Beware Women

We have no record of the play in performance prior to the closure of the theaters in 1642. There are no recorded performances between 1642 and 1962, although the first printed edition appeared in 1657. Anthony Page directed a production for the RSC in 1962. In 1965, Gordon Flyming directed a production for the ITV Play of the Week series, which featured Diana Rigg as Bianca. Traverse Theatre Limited staged a production in 1968 directed by Gordon McDougall at the Traverse Theatre, Edinburgh. In 1968, Anthony Carrick directed a production at the Queen's Theatre, Hornchurch. Terry Hands' 1969 RSC production was presented on the Royal Shakespeare Theatre stage in Stratford-upon-Avon. The Avon Touring Company staged a production in 1980 directed by Tim Albery both at the Church Museum, Bristol and on tour. In 1981, Nick Levinson produced a television adaptation of the play for the BBC. Gordon McDougall directed another production for the Oxford Playhouse Company in 1982 at the Oxford Playhouse. In 1985, the Wayward Players staged a production at the Bear Gardens, Blackfriars, London that was directed by Diane West. Contact Theatre Company's production opened in late 1985 at the University Theatre, Manchester and was directed by Brigid Larmour. A production directed by William Gaskill and adapted by Howard Barker was staged at the Royal Court in 1986. In 1988, the National Theatre staged a production starring Miranda Richardson as Beatrice-Joanna. Birmingham Repertory Theatre staged the play in 1989. Valerie Ellis directed a production for the American Repertory Theatre in Cambridge, Massachusetts in 1991. The 1994 production at the Duke of Cambridge Theatre, Kentish Town, London was directed by Christopher Geelan and was a production of the Buttonhole Theatre Company. Howard Barker's adaptation was staged again in 1994, this time at the Lilian Baylis Theatre by the GBH Theatre Company. Philip Prowse directed the 1995 Glasgow Citizens' Company production at the Glasgow Citizens' Theatre. The 1999 Sarah Harding directed film *Compulsion* is an adaptation of the play. The RSC staged another production in 2006 at the Swan Theatre, Stratford-upon-Avon that was directed by Laurence Boswell. Jesse Berger directed a production for the Red Bull Theatre, New York in 2008. The Constellation Theatre staged a production in 2010. The 2010 National Theatre production was directed by Marianne Elliot. In 2012, Joe Hill-Gibbons directed a production for the Young Vic, London.

A Trick to Catch the Old One

The first performance of this play was most likely sometime in 1605 and was certainly prior to the disbanding of the Children of Paul's in 1606. There was a court performance for James I sometime in 1607 or 1608. There are recorded productions in 1662 and 1665. There was a production at the Mermaid Theatre, London 1952. In 1964, there was a staging in Dorset using an all-male cast. An all-female cast was used in the 1976 Toronto production. Theatr Clwyd, Wales staged a production in 1978. In 1985, there was a staging at the Bear Gardens Museum. Instant Classics acting company staged a production that cut the Dampit scenes at the White Bear Pub in 1994. In 2011, the American Shakespeare Center staged a production at the Blackfriars Playhouse in Staunton, Virginia. As part of their Read Not Dead series, the Globe staged a reading of the play directed by James Wallace.

William Rowley and Thomas Middleton

The Changeling

The play was first licensed for performance at the Phoenix Theatre by the Queen of Bohemia's Company on 7 May 1622. It was then performed at court in 1624. In 1661, Samuel Pepys records having seen a performance at the Whitefriars. Another court performance is recorded by Joost Daalder in 1668. The first modern performance was in 1924 by a group of Yale University Students. The next recorded professional production is that of 1961 directed by Tony Richardson for the English Stage Company at the Royal Court Theatre, London. The Oxford Stage Company staged a production directed by Frank Evans in 1966 at the Jeannetta Cochrane Theatre, London. The 1970 Edinburgh International Festival featured a production by the Royal Lyceum Theatre Company that was directed by Richard Eyre. A University of Sussex production was directed by Gordon McDougall, designed by John Halle, and featured original music by Francis Shaw. It was staged in 1971 at the Gardner Arts Centre, University of Sussex, Brighton and starred Alfred Lynch, Sinead Cusack, and Jane Seymour. Michael Simpson directed the 1973 Birmingham Theatre Company production at the Birmingham Repertory Theatre. There was a production in 1974 at the South London Theatre Centre. Philip Prowse directed a production in 1976 for the Glasgow Citizens' Company at the Glasgow Citizens' Theatre. Peter Gill's 1978 production was presented at the Riverside Studios, Hammersmith, London. 1978 also saw an RSC production directed by Terry Hands. The Bristol Old Vic staged a production in 1978 directed by Adrian Noble at the Theatre Royal, Bristol. Richard Williams also directed a production in 1978 for the Contact Theatre Company at the University Theatre, Manchester. In 1979, Kate Crutchley directed a production at the Victoria Theatre, Stoke-on-Trent. Match Theatre staged a production in 1979 at the Midland Arts Centre, Birmingham. The New Classical Theatre Company staged a production in 1981 at the Northumberland Park School, London that was directed by Lindsay Parker. Howard Curtis directed an adapted production, in which the subplot was cut, for the Voices Theatre Company in 1984 at the Hollywood Arms public house, London. The Crucible Company also staged a production in 1984 that was directed by Jane Collins at the Crucible Studio Theatre, Sheffield. Another 1984 production was directed by Nigel Harrison for the Albion Artists at the Cockpit Theatre, London. Jonathan Petherbridge directed a production at the Duke's Playhouse, Lancaster in 1985. The Pelican Theatre Company staged a production in 1985 at the Bear Gardens Theatre, London. Michael Batz directed a 1986 production for the Yorick Theatre Company that was performed at both the Buxton Festival and at Saint Cuthbert's Hall, Edinburgh. The Arts Theatre, Cambridge staged a production in 1986 directed by Bill Pryde at the Arts Centre, Cambridge. The National Theatre featured a production in 1988 in the Lyttelton Theatre as directed by Richard Eyre. The 1989 Stratford Festival, Ontario, Canada featured a production. In 1990, the Newcastle Playhouse featured a rather informal fringe production with RSC actors. Andrew Manley directed a 1992 production at the Harrogate Theatre. The 1992 RSC production was directed by Michael Attenborough and was presented at the Swan Theatre, Stratford-upon-Avon. This production also transferred to the Newcastle Playhouse and The Pit, London. Tassos Stevens directed the 1998 Battersea Arts Centre production. In 1999, the Kneehigh Theatre Company presented an adaptation titled *The Itch* that was directed by Emma Rice. The Salsberg Studio, Salisbury staged a production in 1999 that was directed by Guy Retallack. John Wright directed a production in 2001 for Third Party Productions at the Battersea Arts Centre, London. An adaptation by Claire McIntyre, directed by Jenny Sealey, and presented by the Graeae Theatre Company at the Phoenix Theatre, Exeter appeared in 2001. The Mamamissi Production Theatre Company staged the play at the Southwark Playhouse in 2002 as directed by Dawn Walton. A production adapted by Dominic Power and directed by Andrew Hilton was presented by the Tobacco Factory, Bristol in 2004. KDC Theatre staged a production directed by Sarah Drinkwater in 2005 at the Courtyard Theatre, London. Declan Donnellan directed a 2006 production for Cheek by Jowl and BITE:06 that appeared at the Barbican, Les Gémeaux/Sceaux/Scène Nationale, and the Grand Théâtre de Luxembourg. There was a 2007 production by the English Touring Theatre. The American Shakespeare Center staged a production in 2009 at the Blackfriars Playhouse, Staunton, Virginia. Michael Oakley directed a production at the Southwark playhouse in 2011. Several film versions of the play have also been made. ITV aired a version of the play directed by Derek Bennet in 1965. Antony Page directed Helen Mirren as Beatrice-Joanna and Brian Cox as Alsemero in the play for the BBC in 1974. In 1993, Simon Curtis directed a version of the play adapted by Michael Hastings for the BBC. This version completely cut the subplot and featured Elizabeth McGovern as Beatrice, Hugh Grant as Alsemero, and Bob Hoskins as De Flores. Marcus Thompson directed a feature film version of the play in 1998, which starred Ian Dury as De Flores. In 2006, Jay Stern directed a film version of the play.

John Webster

The Duchess of Malfi

The first performance of the play occurred prior to 16 December 1614, when William Ostler, the man who originally played Antonio, died, and after the autumn of 1609, when the King's Men took up residence at the Blackfriars Theatre. It is likely that *The Duchess* referred to by a Spanish chaplain in his report from 7 February 1618 was a revival of Webster's play. There was probably another revival sometime after 13 March 1619 when Burbage died and Joseph Taylor, who is referenced in the printed text, joined the company. This revival is also supported by the fact that the quarto also references John Thompson as Julia and Thompson did not join the company until 1621. Another performance is recorded as being seen by King Charles I at the new Cockpit Theatre in Whitehall on 26 December 1630. At the Restoration, the play was given to Davenant and there are recorded performances in 1662, 1668, and at the court of King James II in 1686. On 22 July 1707, there was a revival under the title *The Unfortunate Duchess of Malfy, or The Unnatural Brothers: a tragedy* that appeared at the Haymarket Theatre. 1735 saw the performance of Lewis Theobald's adaptation of the play called *The Fatal Secret* performed at the Theatre Royal. A version by R.H. Horne was performed multiple times throughout the nineteenth century. In 1850, Isabella Glynn appeared in the play at Sadler's Wells and she directed and starred in another production at the Standard Theatre, Shoreditch in 1868. Emma Waller performed the title role at the Broadway Theatre in New York in 1858. Alice Marriott appeared in a production at Sadler's Wells in 1864. A new version directed by William Poel was performed in October 1892 at the Opéra Comique by the Independent Theatre Society. A 1919 production at the Lyric, Hammersmith was directed by Allan Wade. John Fernald directed a production at the Embassy Theatre in 1933. 1937 saw a production at the Gate, Dublin that was directed by Peter Powell. In 1938, a film version of the play came out starring Esme Percy and John Laurie. Peggy Ashcroft and John Gielgud starred in a production at the Haymarket, London in 1945 and were directed by George Rylands. An adaptation by W.H. Auden was directed by George Rylands with music by Benjamin Britten at the Ethel Barrymore Theatre, New York in 1946. This production featured Canada Lee as Bosola. Lee was the first African American actor to achieve true success in mainstream Broadway productions and, in this production, was one of the first black actors to play a white character in whiteface. Jack Landau directed a production at the Phoenix Theatre, New York in 1957. In 1960, Donald McWhinnie directed a production for the RSC at the Shakespeare Memorial Theatre and the Aldwych Theatre, London that featured Peggy

Ashcroft as the Duchess. Brain Shelton directed a production at the Pitlochry Festival, Scotland in 1967. In 1970, there was a production by the Freehold Company at the Young Vic, London. Peter Gill directed a production at the Royal Court Theatre in 1971. Clifford Williams also directed a production in 1971 for the RSC starring Judi Dench as the Duchess. The Stratford Festival in Ontario, Canada featured a production in 1971 directed by Jean Gascon. The 1972 BBC television production of the play was directed by James MacTaggart and featured Eileen Atkins as the Duchess. Philip Prowse directed productions at the Glasgow Citizen's Theatre in 1975 and 1978. Eileen Atkins starred in a production at the Mark Taper Forum in Los Angeles in 1976. Adrian Noble directed a production at the Royal Exchange, Manchester in 1980 that featured Bob Hoskins as Bosola and Helen Mirren as the Duchess. In 1985, the National Theatre featured a production directed by Philip Prowse with Ian McKellan as Bosola and Eleanor Bron as the Duchess. There was another RSC production in 1989 that was directed by Bill Alexander and starred Harriet Walter as the Duchess. The 1995–1996 season saw two productions of the play at the Wyndhams Theatre, London. The first was directed by Philip Franks and featured Juliet Stevenson as the Duchess and Simon Russell Beale as Ferdinand. The second was by the Cheek by Jowl company and directed by Declan Donnellan. In 2000, Gale Edwards directed a production for the RSC. On 23 January 2003, the Phyllida Lloyd-directed production premiered on the Lyttelton stage at the National Theatre starring Janet McTeer as the Duchess. There was a production by the Apricot Theatre Company in 2004. Colin McColl directed a production in 2005 for the Auckland Theatre Company. The Chicago's Writers' Theatre featured a production in 2006 directed by Michael Halberstam. Also in 2006, Philip Franks directed a production for the West Yorkshire Playhouse featuring Imogen Stubbs as the Duchess. The Stratford Festival, Ontario, Canada featured another production in 2006 directed by Peter Hinton. Elizabeth Freestone directed the 2009 production at the Greenwich Theatre, London. On a side note, this play features within the 2001 film *Hotel* directed by Mike Figgis. The movie stars Selma Hayek, Saffron Burrows, Danny Huston, and Rhys Ifans and the plot revolves around a documentary being made about the filming of a movie version of *The Duchess of Malfi*.

Uncertain Authorship

Arden of Faversham

None of the early printed editions indicate a playing company or playhouse that was associated with the play. George Lillo adapted the play circa 1759 and this adapted version was the common stage text until the twentieth century. The play was also adapted into a ballet in 1799 and an opera titled *Arden Must Die* in 1967. In 1955, Joan Littlewood's Theatre Workshop performed the play at the Paris International Festival of Theatre. Buzz Goodbody directed the 1970 RSC production at the Roundhouse, London. The 1982 RSC production that opened at The Other Place, Stratford-upon-Avon was directed by Terry Hands and featured Mark Rylance as Michael. This production subsequently transferred to the Gulbenkian Studio, Newcastle-upon-Tyne and finally closed at The Pit, London. The Empty Space Theatre of Seattle, Washington staged a production in 1991 as directed by John Russell Brown. During the summer of 2001, the play was directed by Ian Garner in an open-air staging by the What You Will Theatre Company in the garden of the original home in Faversham, Kent. The Metropolitan Playhouse of New York's 2004 production was directed by Alex Roe. The Skin and Bone Theatre production at the White Bear Theatre, London in 2006 was directed by Samantha Potter. Peter Darney directed the 2010 Em-Lou Productions staging at the Rose Theatre, London. Terry Hands directed the play for a second time in 2010 for the Theatr Clwyd at Emlyn Williams Theatre, Wales. University of Northern Alabama staged a production in 2011.

Bibliography

Allen, Michael J. B. and Kenneth Muir 1981. *Shakespeare's Plays in Quarto: A Facsimile Edition of Copies Primarily from the Henry E. Huntington Library*. Berkeley and Los Angeles: University of California Press.

Auden, Wystan Hugh 1966. *Collected Shorter Poems 1927–1967*. New York: Random House.

Bakhtin, Mikhail Mikhailovich 1981. *The Dialogic Imagination*. Trans. Caryl Emerson and Michael Holquist, ed. Michael Holquist. Austin, TX: University of Texas Press.

Bakhtin, Mikhail Mikhailovich 1986. *Speech Genres and Other Late Essays*. Trans. Vern William McGee, eds. Caryl Emerson and Michael Holquist. Austin, TX: University of Texas Press.

Barker, Simon and Hilary Hinds 2003. *The Routledge Anthology of Renaissance Drama*. London: Routledge.

Baro, Peter 1588. *"Two Theames or Questions, handled and disputed openly in the Schooles at Cambridge, in the Latin tung, by P. Baro, Doctor of Divinity, and Englished by I. L."* In Hyperius 1588 502–541.

Bartels, Emily C., ed. 1995. *Critical Essays on Christopher Marlowe*. New York: G. K. Hall.

Bartels, Emily 1993. *Spectacles of Strangeness: Imperialism, Alienation, and Marlowe*. Philadelphia: University of Pennsylvania Press.

Barton, Anne 1984. *Ben Jonson: Dramatist*. Cambridge: Cambridge University Press.

Bate, Jonathan and Eric Rasmussen, eds. 2007. *William Shakespeare Complete Works*. New York: Random House.

Bawcutt, Nigel W. 1973. "Introductory Note." In Middleton and Rowley 1653.

Bentley, Gerald Eades 1971. *The Profession of Dramatist in Shakespeare's Time, 1590–1642*. Princeton: Princeton University Press.

Bevington, David, ed. 1992. *The Complete Works of Shakespeare*, 4th edition. New York: HarperCollins.

Bevington, David, Lars Engle, Katharine Eisaman Maus, and Eric Rasmussen, eds. 2002. *English Renaissance Drama: A Norton Anthology*. New York: Norton.

Studying Shakespeare's Contemporaries, First Edition. Lars Engle and Eric Rasmussen.
© 2014 Lars Engle and Eric Rasmussen. Published 2014 by John Wiley & Sons, Ltd.

Bevington, David 1962. From *Mankind to Marlowe: Growth of Structure in the Popular Drama of Tudor England*. Cambridge, MA: Harvard University Press.

Belsey, Catharine 1985. *The Subject of Tragedy*. New York: Methuen.

Blayney, Peter 1997. "The Publication of Playbooks." In Cox and Kastan 1997 383–422.

Bloom, Harold 1998. *Shakespeare: The Invention of the Human*. New York: Riverhead Books.

Brigden, Susan 2000. *New Worlds, Lost Worlds: The Rule of the Tudors, 1485–1603*. London: Penguin.

Bunker, Nancy 2005. "Feminine and Fashionable: Regendering the Iconologies of Mary Frith's 'Notorious Reputation.'" *Explorations in Renaissance Culture* 31 2. 211–257. 2222

Burrow, Colin, ed. 2002. *The Oxford Shakespeare: The Complete Sonnets and Poems*. Oxford and New York: Oxford University Press.

Bushnell, Rebecca 1990. *Tragedies of Tyrants: Political Thought and Theater in the English Renaissance*. Ithaca: Cornell University Press.

Butler, Martin, ed. 1999. *Re-presenting Ben Jonson: Text, History, Performance*. Basingstoke: Macmillan and New York: St. Martins.

Chakravorty, Swapan 1996. *Society and Politics in the Plays of Thomas Middleton*. Oxford: Oxford University Press.

Church of England 1590. Articles whereupon it was agreed by the archbishops and byshops of both prouinces and the whole cleargie, in the conuocation holden at London in the yeere of our Lorde God 1562. according to the computation of the Church of England, for the auoyding of the diuersities of opinions, and for the stablishing of consent touching true religion. Put foorth by the Queenes authoritie. London: Christopher Barker.

Clark, Katerina and Michael Holquist, 1984. *Mikhail Bakhtin*. Cambridge, MA: Harvard University Press.

Cox, John and David Scott Kastan, eds. 1997. *A New History of Early English Drama*. New York: Columbia University Press.

Cunningham, Karen 1990. "Renaissance Execution and Marlovian Elocution: The Drama of Death." *PMLA* 105. 209–222. In Bartels 1995.

Dawson, Anthony and Paul Yachnin, 2001. *The Culture of Playgoing in Shakespeare's England: A Collaborative Debate*. Cambridge: Cambridge University Press.

Donaldson, Ian 2011. *Ben Jonson: A Life*. Oxford and New York: Oxford University Press.

Drummond, William of Hawthornden 1842. *Notes of Ben Jonson's Conversations*. London: Shakespeare Society.

Dutton, Richard, ed. 2009a. *The Oxford Handbook of Early Modern Theatre*. Oxford and New York: Oxford University Press.

Dutton, Richard, ed. 2009b. "*The Court and the Master of the Revels*." In Dutton 2009 362–379.

Eliot, Thomas Stearns 1932. In Leech 1964, 12–18.

Ellis-Fermor, Una 1927. In Marlowe 1974 133–162.

Empson, William 1974. *Some Versions of Pastoral* (corrected edition). New York: New Directions.

Engle, Lars 1993. *Shakespearean Pragmatism: Market of his Time*. Chicago and London: University of Chicago Press.

Engle, Lars 2008. "Oedipal Marlowe, Mimetic Middleton." *Modern Philology* 105 3. 417–436.

Engle, Lars 2012a. "*Middleton and Mimetic Desire.*" In Taylor and Henley 2012 437–451.

Engle, Lars 2012b. "*Pragmatism.*" In Kinney 2012 641–662.

Erne, Lukas 2003. *Shakespeare as a Literary Dramatist.* Cambridge: Cambridge University Press.

Ewing, S. Blaine 1969 *Burtonian Melancholy in the Plays of John Ford.* New York: Octagon Books.

Fineman, Joel 1986. *Shakespeare's Perjured Eye: The Invention of Poetic Subjectivity in the Sonnets.* Berkeley: University of California Press.

Foakes, Reginald A., ed. 2002. *Henslowe's Diary*, 2nd edition. Cambridge: Cambridge University Press.

Foucault, Michel 1990. *The Use of Pleasure: The History of Sexuality, Vol. II.* Trans. Robert Hurley. New York: Vintage Books.

Fowler, Alastair 1998. *Milton: Paradise Lost*, 2nd edition. New York: Addison Wesley Longman.

Fraser, Russell and Norman Rabkin 1976a. *Drama of the English Renaissance I: The Tudor Period.* New York: Macmillan.

Frye, Northrop 1949. "The Argument of Comedy." *English Institute Essays.* New York: Columbia University Press. Reprinted in McDonald 2004.

Gibbons, Brian 1980. *Jacobean City Comedy.* New York: Methuen.

Gibbons, Brian 1976b. *Drama of the English Renaissance II: The Stuart Period.* New York: Macmillan.

Girard, René 1977. *Violence and the Sacred.* Trans. Patrick Gregory.Baltimore: Johns Hopkins University Press.

Gomme, Andor Harvey 1969. *Jacobean Tragedies.* Oxford: Oxford University Press.

Grafton, Anthony and Eugene F. Rice, 1994. *The Foundations of Early Modern Europe, 1460–1559*, 2nd edition. New York: W. W. Norton.

Gurr, Andrew 1996. *The Shakespearian Playing Companies.* Oxford: Clarendon Press.

Gurr, Andrew 2009. "*Why the Globe Is Famous.*" In Dutton 2009 186–208.

Heinemann, Margot 1980. *Puritanism and Theatre: Thomas Middleton and Opposition Drama under the Early Stuarts.* Cambridge: Cambridge University Press.

Homer 1990. *The Iliad.* Trans. Robert Fagles. New York: Penguin.

Homer 2000. *The Odyssey.* Trans. Stanley Lombardo. Indianapolis: Hackett.

Howard, Jean 2007. *Theater of a City: The Places of London Comedy, 1598–1642.* Philadelphia: University of Pennsylvania Press.

Hunter, George Kirkpatrick 1997. *English Drama 1586–1642, The Age of Shakespeare.* Oxford: Clarendon Press.

Hyperius, Andreas 1588. A speciall treatise of Gods prouidence and of comforts against all kinde of crosses and calamities to be drawne from the same. With an exposition of the 107. Psalme. Heerunto is added an appendix of certaine sermons & questions, (conteining sweet & comfortable doctrine) as they were vttered and disputed ad clerum in Cambridge. By P. Baro D. in Diui. Englished by I.L. vicar of Wethers-fielde. London: John Wolfe.

Jackson, Gabriele Bernhard 1969. "*Introduction and Notes.*" In Jonson 1969 1–34.

Jonson, Ben 1969. *Every Man In His Humor*, ed.Gabriele Bernhard Jackson. The Yale Ben Jonson. New Haven, CT: Yale University Press.

Jonson, Ben 1971. *Every Man in His Humour: A Parallel-Text Edition of the 1601 Quarto and the 1616 Folio*, ed. Julius Walter Lever. Regents Renaissance Drama Series. Lincoln, NE: University of Nebraska Press.

Jonson, Ben 1989. *The Selected Plays of Ben Jonson, Vol. I*, ed. Joanna Proctor. Cambridge: Cambridge University Press.

Jonson, Ben 1968. *Poems of Ben Jonson*, ed. George Burke Johnston. Cambridge, MA: Harvard University Press.

Jonson, Ben 2004. *Timber, or Discoveries*. Boston: Gutenberg.

Kahn, Coppélia 2007a. "*The Roaring Girl* or *Moll Cutpurse*." In Taylor and Lavagnino 2007a 721–726.

Kinney, Arthur, ed. 1999. *Renaissance Drama: An Anthology of Plays and Entertainments*. Oxford: Blackwell.

Kinney, Arthur, ed. 2012. *The Oxford Handbook of Shakespeare*. Oxford and New York: Oxford University Press.

Lancashire, Ian 1994. *Against Disobedience and Wilful Rebellion*. Renaissance Electronic Texts 1.1. http://www.anglicanlibrary.org/homilies/bk2hom21.htm. University of Toronto.

Leech, Clifford 1964. *Marlowe: A Collection of Critical Essays. Twentieth Century Views*. Englewood Cliffs, NJ: Prentice-Hall.

Lever, Julius Walter 1971, "*Introduction*." In Jonson 1971 xi–xxviii.

Loades, David 2002. "Literature and National Identity." In Loewenstein and Mueller 2002 201–228.

Loewenstein, David and Janel Mueller, eds. 2002. *The Cambridge History of Early Modern English Literature*. Cambridge: Cambridge University Press.

Machiavelli, Niccolò 1979. *The Portable Machiavelli*. Ed. and Trans. Peter Bondanella and Mark Musa. New York: Penguin.

Marlowe, Christopher 1973. *The Complete Works of Christopher Marlowe, Vol. I*, ed. Fredson Bowers. Cambridge and New York: Cambridge University Press.

Marlowe, Christopher 1974. *Christopher Marlowe's Tamburlaine, Parts I and II: Text and Major Criticism*, ed. Irving Ribner. Indianapolis and New York: Odyssey Press.

Marlowe, Christopher 1993. *Doctor Faustus: A- and B- Texts*, ed. David Bevington and Eric Rasmussen. Revels. Manchester: Manchester University Press.

Marlowe, Christopher 1997a. *Edward the Second*, eds. Martin Wiggins and Robert Lindsey. New Mermaids. London: A&C Black; New York: W. W. Norton.

Marlowe, Christopher 1997b. *Tamburlaine*, ed. Anthony Dawson. New Mermaids. London: A&C Black; New York: Norton.

Marvell, Andrew 1681. *Miscellaneous Poems by Andrew Marvell, Esq*. London: Robert Boulter.

Maus, Katharine Eisaman 2002. "Introductions." In Bevington, Engle, Maus, and Rasmussen 2002.

Maus, Katharine Eisaman 1995. *Inwardness and Theater in the English Renaissance*. Chicago: University of Chicago Press.

McDonald, Russ 2001. *The Bedford Companion to Shakespeare: An Introduction with Documents*. 2nd edition. New York: Bedford/St. Martins.

McDonald, Russ 1979. "Othello, Thorello, and the Problem of the Foolish Hero." *Shakespeare Quarterly* 30 1. 51–67.

McDonald, Russ, ed. 2004. *Shakespeare: An Anthology of Criticism and Theory, 1945–2000*. Oxford: Wiley-Blackwell.

Middleton, Thomas 1988. *Five Plays*, eds. Bryan Loughrey and Neil Taylor. London: Penguin.

Middleton, Thomas 1999. *Women Beware Women and Other Plays*, ed. Richard Dutton. Oxford: Oxford University Press.

Middleton, Thomas and William Rowley, 1961. *The Changeling*, ed. N. W. Bawcutt. The Revels Plays. Cambridge, MA: Harvard University Press.

Middleton, Thomas and William Rowley, 1998. *The Changeling*, ed. N. W. Bawcutt. Revels Student Editions. Manchester: Manchester University Press.

Middleton, Thomas and William Rowley, 1990. *The Changeling*, ed. Joost Daalder. New Mermaids. New York: Norton.

Middleton, Thomas and William Rowley, 1653. *The Changeling: As it was Acted (with great Applause) at the Private house in Drury Lane, and Salisbury Court*. London: Humphrey Moseley.

Milton, John 1998. *Paradise Lost*, 2nd edition. Alastair Fowler. London: Longman.

Muldrew, Craig 1998. *The Economy of Obligation: The Culture of Credit and Social Relations in Early Modern England*. Houndsmills, UK: Palgrave MacMillan.

Neill, Michael 2000. *Putting History to the Question: Power, Politics, and Society in English Renaissance Drama*. New York: Columbia University Press.

Nicholl, Charles 2004. "Christopher Marlowe." *Oxford Dictionary of National Biography Online*. Oxford and New York: Oxford University Press.

Orgel, Stephen 1996. *Impersonations: The Performance of Gender in Shakespeare's England*. Cambridge and New York: Cambridge University Press.

Paster, Gail Kern 1993. *The Body Embarrassed: Drama and the Disciplines of Shame in Early Modern England*. Ithaca, NY: Cornell University Press.

Ribner, Irving 1962. *Jacobean Tragedy: The Quest for Moral Order*. London: Methuen.

Riggs, David 1989. *Ben Jonson: A Life*. Cambridge, MA: Harvard University Press.

Riggs, David 2004. *The World of Christopher Marlowe*. London: Faber and Faber.

Rowe, Katherine 1999. *Dead Hands: Fictions of Agency, Renaissance to Modern*. Stanford, CA: Stanford University Press.

Schalkwyk, David 2004. *Literature and the Touch of the Real*. Newark, DE: University of Delaware Press.

Shakespeare, William 1600. *"The Cronicle Hitorie of Henry the fift: With his battell fought at Agin Court in France. Together with Auntient Pistoll."* In Allen and Muir 1981.

Shakespeare, William 1623. *The Norton Facsimile: The First Folio of Shakespeare*. In Charlton Hinman 1968. New York: W. W. Norton.

Shapiro, James 1996. *Shakespeare and the Jews*. New York: Columbia University Press.

Shepard, Alan 1998. *"'Thou art no soldier; Thou art a merchant': The Mentalité of War in Malta."* In White 1998 109–129.

Shepard, Alexandra 2000. "Manhood, Credit, and Patriarchy in Early Modern England c. 1580–1640." *Past and Present* 167 1. 75–106.

Smith, Sir Thomas 1978. *De republica Anglorum*, ed. Mary Dewar. Cambridge: Cambridge University Press.

Sommerville, Johan P. 2002. "Literature and National Identity." In Loewenstein and Mueller 2002 459–486.

Tacitus, Publius Cornelius 1989. *The Annals of Imperial Rome*. Trans. Michael Grant. Harmondsworth: Penguin Classics.

Taylor, Gary 2000. *Castration: An Abbreviated History of Western Manhood*. London: Routledge.

Taylor, Gary 2007. "Thomas Middleton: Lives and Afterlives." In Taylor and Lavagnino 2007 25–58.

Taylor, Gary and Trish Henley, eds. 2012. *The Oxford Handbook of Middleton*. Oxford and New York: Oxford University Press.

Taylor, Gary and John Lavagnino, eds. 2007a. *Thomas Middleton: The Collected Works*. Oxford: Clarendon Press.

Taylor, Gary and John Lavagnino, eds. 2007b. *Thomas Middleton and Early Modern Textual Culture*. Oxford: Clarendon Press.

Taylor, Gary and Andrew Sabol, 2007. "Middleton, Music, and Dance." In Taylor and Lavagnino 2007b 119–181.

Tricomi, Albert 1989. *Anticourt Drama in England, 1603–1642*. Charlottesville: University Press of Virginia.

Watson, Robert N. 1987. *Ben Jonson's Parodic Strategy*. Cambridge, MA: Harvard University Press.

Wayne, Valerie 2007. *Introduction to A Trick to Catch the Old One* in Taylor and Lavagnino 2007. 373–376.

Whigham, Frank 1996. *Seizures of the Will in Early Modern English Drama*. Cambridge: Cambridge University Press.

White, Paul Whitfield 1998. *Marlowe, History, and Sexuality*. New York: AMS Press.

White Peter 1992. *Predestination, Policy, and Polemic: Conflict and Consensus in the English Church from the Reformation to the Civil War*. Cambridge: Cambridge University Press.

Wiggins, Martin 1997. "Introduction." In Marlowe 1997 xi–xxxvii.

Wittgenstein, Ludwig 1974. *Philosophical Investigations*. Trans. Gertrude Elizabeth Margaret Anscombe. Oxford: Basil Blackwell.

Woolrych, Austin 2002. *Britain in Revolution: 1625–1660*. Oxford: Oxford University Press.

Worden, Blair 1999. *"Politics in Catiline: Jonson and his Sources."* In Butler 1999 152–173.

Wrightson, Keith 2000. *Earthly Necessities: Economic Lives in Early Modern Britain*. New Haven and London: Yale University Press.

Yachnin, Paul 1997. *Stage-wrights: Shakespeare, Jonson, Middleton and the Making of Theatrical Value*. Philadelphia: University of Pennsylvania Press.

Yeats, William Butler 1921. "A Prayer for my Daughter." *Michael Robartes and the Dancer*. Dundrum: Cuala Press.

Index

Note: Page numbers in **bold** refer to the main discussion of the play, to the main section on a topic, or to the entry on the playwright's life; page numbers in *italics* refer to a play's performance history in Sarah Stewart's appendix

Studying Shakespeare's Contemporaries, First Edition. Lars Engle and Eric Rasmussen.
© 2014 Lars Engle and Eric Rasmussen. Published 2014 by John Wiley & Sons, Ltd.